UNDERGROUND POLITICS

Gold Mining and State-Making in Colombia

Jesse Jonkman

T0281816

PENN

UNIVERSITY OF PENNSYLVANIA PRESS

PHILADELPHIA

Published by
University of Pennsylvania Press
Philadelphia, Pennsylvania 19104–4112
www.pennpress.org

Printed in the United States of America on acid-free paper

10 9 8 7 6 5 4 3 2 1

A catalogue record for this book is available from the
Library of Congress.

Hardcover ISBN: 978-1-5128-2458-2
Paperback ISBN: 978-1-5128-2457-5
Ebook ISBN: 978-1-5128-2459-9

To Rocío

CONTENTS

ABBREVIATIONS

AGC	Autodefensas Gaitanistas de Colombia / Gaitanista Self-Defense Forces of Colombia
ARE	Área de Reserva Especial para Comunidades Mineras / Special Reserve Area for Mining Communities
ASOBAMINARMEA	Asociación de Barequeros de Minería Artesanal del Medio Atrato / Medio Atrato Association of Artisanal Miners
AUC	Autodefensas Unidas de Colombia / United Self-Defense Forces of Colombia
CIRDI	Canadian International Resource and Development Institute
COCOMACIA	Consejo Comunitario Mayor de la Asociación Campesina Integral del Atrato / Upper Community Council of the Peasant Association of Atrato
COCOMOPOCA	Consejo Comunitario Mayor de la Organización Popular del Atrato / Upper Community Council of the Popular Organization of Atrato
CONALMINERCOL	Confederación Nacional de Mineros de Colombia / National Confederation of Colombian Miners
CODECHOCO	Corporación Autónoma Regional para el Desarrollo Sostenible del Chocó / Regional Autonomous Institute for Chocó's Sustainable Development
DANE	Departamento Administrativo Nacional de Estadística / National Administrative Department of Statistics

DIAN	Dirección de Impuestos y Aduanas Nacionales / National Directorate of Taxes and Customs
ELN	Ejército de Liberación Nacional / National Liberation Army
FARC	Fuerzas Armadas Revolucionarias de Colombia / Revolutionary Armed Forces of Colombia
FEDEMICHOCO	Federación Minera del Chocó / Mining Federation of Chocó
IIAP	Instituto de Investigaciones Ambientales del Pacífico / Institute for Pacific Environmental Research
IVA	Impuesto al Valor Agregado / Tax of Added Value
OHCHR	Office of the United Nations High Commissioner for Human Rights
PTO	Programa de Trabajo y Obras / Work and Construction Plan
RUT	Registro Único Tributario / Unique Tax Registry
UMATA	Unidad Municipal de Asistencia Técnica Agropecuaria / Municipal Unity for Technical Assistance in Agriculture and Livestock
UNIDO	United Nations Industrial Development Organization
UNIMIL	Unidad Nacional contra la Minería Ilegal y Antiterrorismo / National Police Unit Against Illegal Mining and for Anti-Terrorism
USAID	United States Agency for International Development

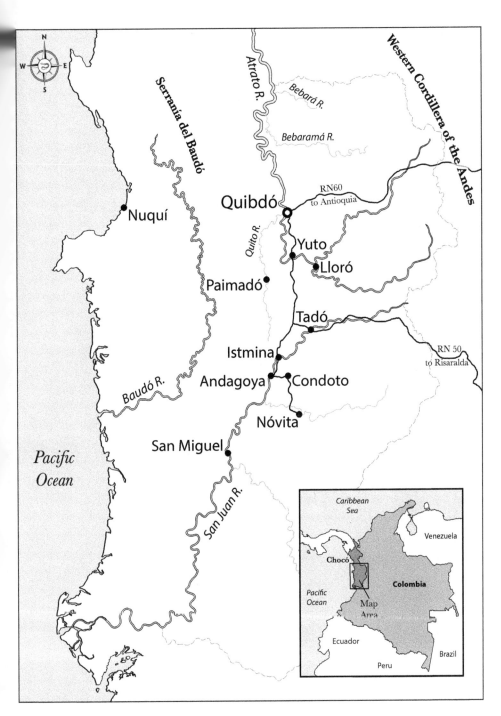

Map 1. Department of Chocó, Colombia

Introduction

Gold, Governance, and the Politics
of the Underground

Soon, we'll start killing each other.
                                        —*Miner from Tadó*

The drizzling rain dripping on us did not deter us from crowding in the streets. The rain did, however, spur the better-prepared spectators to draw out their umbrellas, and the unprepared, including me, to draw ourselves toward some cramped but dry spots beneath the corrugated-metal roofs of nearby buildings. Under the umbrellas and roofs, we continued our waiting. And with us waited the football pitch around which we had assembled on these outskirts of the town of Tadó. The pitch was cordoned off with yellow plastic ribbon, keeping its worn-out grass vacant for the helicopter that would soon land in our midst and drop off the person we were waiting for: Juan Manuel Santos, president of Colombia.

While I had been in Colombia's northwestern department (*departamento*)[1] of Chocó for only a month, I had already heard on various occasions the story of another presidential helicopter visit. A year earlier, Santos had touched down in a forest near the town of Yuto, not that far from Tadó. There, he had accompanied Colombian defense forces while they blew up several hydraulic excavators caught in the act of "illegal" gold mining. *Chocoanos* (people from Chocó) recounted the anecdote to underscore the inhumanity of their government's policies, which were presumably aimed at doing away with local miners in favor of multinational mining firms. Indeed, it would be an understatement to say that the national government was held in low regard by the residents of Chocó's mining towns and villages. Their communities' livelihoods came from the unlicensed placer mining (the extraction of alluvial mineral deposits) that the Santos administration was bent on removing from the local rainforest. And their gold digging—legal or illegal—was tightly intertwined with their self-understandings of culture, race, and history, with most of them being Afro-descendants whose ancestors had been introduced to Chocó's forest landscapes as enslaved gold panners.

Still, although I had frequently heard the president—and his repression of small-scale miners—being labeled as the instigator of Chocó's current hardship, in Tadó there was no shortage of people carrying balloons, trumpets, drums, and placards of presidential encouragement, one even congratulating "president Santos on the Nobel prize."[2] There were hundreds of attendees and the mood was cheerful. Unlike in Yuto, there were no excavators to be destroyed here. This time, the president would open a new aqueduct. This seemed worth the wait, rain or no rain.

Ten minutes after the tolerable drizzle had been replaced by downpours, we found our waiting rewarded. Three helicopters appeared in the sky and touched down amid the blue fog of smoke grenades and the *chuf-chuf* beat of whirring rotors. They filled the football ground with soldiers, journalists, legislators, and—descending from the third chopper—the head of state. The crowd cheered, the balloons bounced, the trumpets blared, the drummers drummed, the placards rippled, and the furious rainfall began to feel less furious. Unfortunately, we, the umbrella-less spectators standing under the roofs, were hardly able to see through the spectacle of smoke, umbrellas, and phone-raising arms, and spotted nothing but an escort of guards protecting some unseen president. To the dismay of my neighbors and myself, this escort hurried itself within seconds into a fleet of tinted-windowed SUVs, which, on being boarded, hastily departed from the multitude.

Clearly, this rushed visit had anything but satisfied our desire for a word or salute from the head of state—a desire assuredly deepened by the rain-sodden wait. Many of us followed the cars on foot. We rushed and ran for a few hundred meters until we arrived at the gate of the new water control facility where Santos would make an address. The gate, however, was guarded by defense personnel who prevented our entry into the ceremony. Disappointed, I asked the woman standing next to me if the aqueduct inauguration would be followed by some sort of public speech.

"No," she answered. "Apparently, he'll only talk to the mayor and that kind of people." This was confirmed by a second woman, who had overheard

Figure 1. Helicopter arriving in Tadó. Photo by the author.

my question: "They only want to talk to the people who are just like them-selves. Not to us, the people with needs!" As she spat out the words, she waved a hand-scribbled letter in my direction. The day before, a miner had told me that when national politicians visit, some people bring along letters to com-municate their problems to those in power. "If you finish high school, you don't want to work hours for one gram of gold!" the woman with the letter continued. "Here, they have ended all of that. Soon, we'll start killing each other. Without food, you start killing."

After just four weeks in Chocó, I knew all too well what "they have ended all of that" meant. Punitive measures endorsed by the Santos administration (selling limits for gold, the seizure of fuel transports, the incarceration of min-ers, the blowing up of extraction equipment) had paralyzed the regional mining economy and drastically reduced the gold winnings of households that had already been making precarious livelihoods.

Our talking attracted the attention of bystanders, who began to vent their frustrations on me. They complained about their long waiting time and encouraged me to pass on letters and messages to the president, assum-ing that I was part of the political delegation, which consisted mainly of white outsiders.

"They never visit us."

"They think we're delinquents. That's why we're not allowed to enter. But we're only here to talk about our needs."

"We have nothing. We're all miners, but now mining is gone and there is nothing to live off. And despite our hunger, they don't do anything for us."

"They remove the excavators but they don't bring alternatives. So what do people do? They stop working and become delinquents. There are no opportunities, no companies."

Their complaints would not reach Santos. After about fifteen minutes, he left the control facility. I caught no glimpse of him. The escort of guards, the tinted car windows, and the speed of his departure made the president as ephemeral a spirit as he had been upon his arrival. In a matter of minutes, he and his chopper vanished into the sky again, leaving behind a profusion of miners' unheard grievances and unread letters.

But if not Santos, other things became sharply visible in that half-hour helicopter visit. In only a few other fieldwork moments did I perceive institutional abandonment so crushingly as there in Tadó, in the physical proximity of the president. To the Tadó miners, as their quoted grievances testify, the lightning visit was a painful confirmation of the fact that their economic troubles lacked a meaningful political audience. Weathering rain, killing hours, and cheering on helicopters, they partook in a state ceremony. But only on the fringes. Only as passive onlookers. Their letters were unworthy of official time. Their bodies were not wanted at the aqueduct ceremony.[3] And so, by briefly touching down in his hyper-modern aerial vehicle in an out-of-the-way mining town, Santos not only extended the state's material infrastructure (the aqueduct) in the imagined hinterlands, but also accentuated the sensorial distance that the hinterlands themselves experienced vis-à-vis bureaucratic power.

In all its symbolic extremity, the Tadó visit encapsulated the spatial remoteness that, in conversations with me, miners in Chocó so often assigned to state politics. With few exceptions, they described "the state" as something above and beyond them; something that was happening in the capital of Bogotá, in fenced-off spaces, or emerging from the sky in the form of helicopters—bringing either aqueducts or excavator-bombing explosives. Their state was elsewhere. The public institutions they described were characterized by impermanent presence and unwanted penal interventions. These institutions were allegedly all about imposed gold-selling limits, destroyed mining machinery, and seized fuel bins; they had little to do with their "needs," their "hunger," their "opportunities." These needs, so I was told in Tadó and elsewhere, did not reach the ears of faraway politicians, nor the voice-recorders of journalists. Much like their letters, miners experienced their lives as being largely invisible to external powers. As being forgotten.

Underground Politics tells the story of small-scale mining settlements that have become progressively forsaken by formal legislation. It explores ethnographically the question of how gold-mining communities in Chocó navigate state governance in a context of criminalization and political abandonment. In wrestling with this question, the book teases out the daily organizational practices through which a heterogenous mining population renders mundane and lawful a livelihood that official discourses deem destructive and illegal. Examining these practices allows me to go beyond the tropes of social disorder and state absence that generally surround wildcat mining regions such as Chocó. Conversely, in this book, I map out the everyday forms of sociopolitical organization that are emergent in supposedly lawless mining zones, and illustrate how such places are being shaped by, and giving shape to, state regulatory practices. Differently put, through a focus on the lived experience of a gold frontier, I show how the state becomes symbolically meaningful and materially substantive in a region from which it is said to be absent.

An Ethnography of the Underground

From 2008 to 2012, Colombian gold mining boomed, with the registered annual production rate nearly doubling from 34,321 to 66,178 kilograms of bullion.[4] To an extent, the increase was domestically driven. Neoliberal reforms and improved safety conditions rendered Colombia increasingly more attractive to foreign mining companies. Yet the greater catalyst for the boom was the increased allure of gold itself, the globally indexed price of which rose by 91 percent in that same five-year time frame.[5] The truth of the matter is that at the height of the bonanza, in 2012, many of the transnational firms that had recently come to Colombia were still only prospecting for, rather than extracting, mineral deposits. Correspondingly, most gold emanated from small unlicensed miners. Due to these miners' informal operations, it is hard to come up with exact numbers to quantify their influence on the Colombian mining boom. Yet estimates of those days suggest the "small-scale" share to lie around 70 percent of the total gold volume (Sarmiento et al. 2013:54).

The figures of the department of Chocó also tell us a lot. Between 2008 and 2011, the local registration rate mushroomed by 731 percent, making Chocó the country's leading gold producer in 2011, with nearly 28,000 kilograms. This despite the fact that back then, as now, almost all mines in the department were small undertakings that lacked the required mining titles and environmental licenses.[6]

Besides mind-boggling statistics, gold fever also begat more worldly outcomes. In Chocó, it spawned the mass arrival of miners from other departments, and even countries, who brought with them new extraction techniques that relied on hydraulic excavators and, to a lesser degree, suction dredges. It was these outsiders who pocketed the largest share of gold during the boom years, leaving in their wake cratered rainforests, fish-drained rivers, and mineral-depleted subsoils. But then again, the years of abundance are hard to dismiss as simply yet another rapacious land grab. Many residents of mining regions told me they had enjoyed the arrival of the excavator miners. They had enjoyed the land rents they paid and the mining pits they deepened— where local "artisanal" miners (i.e., those using low-tech tools such as wooden pans, spades, and motorized pumps) could now find gravels that were much richer than those they had previously mined in superficial earth layers. They had enjoyed, moreover, employment in the new mines, which enabled a lucky few to save up enough to purchase their own heavy mining machinery. And certainly they had enjoyed stable work in restaurants, hotels, discotheques, bars, workshops, tool shops, pawn shops, motor taxis, and liquor, grocery, and garment stores, all banking on more clientele in the midst of the fattened economy. Ostensibly, financial futures felt bright then. The gold rush implied access to new working methods, mining jobs, and rents, and with all this, increased access to education, health care, roofs and cement for houses, transportation, leisure activities, clothes, and food.

But this book is situated at a different historical conjuncture. Much had changed in 2017, the year in which I did most of my fieldwork. For starters, the numbers. Chocó's gold production was calculated at 9,315 kilograms, representing only 38 percent of the number five years earlier.[7] Translated into ordinary lifeworlds, this decline amounted to a drastic reduction in mines and a regionwide rise in economic austerity. What had happened?

In part, the laws of supply and demand. The gold price was no longer what it used to be,[8] and neither were the forest's gold reserves after a decade of earth moving. Both factors had made mining a less financially attractive enterprise. But the larger explanation was political. When clarifying why their family members, friends, or they themselves had stopped mining, interlocutors un-equivocally pointed to the newfound illegality of extraction. Under the Santos presidency (2010–2018), small-scale gold miners became increasingly typecast as one more branch of the country's criminal economy, with high-ranked officials faulting them for their ruination of nature, connection to organized crime groups, and noncompliance with formal regulations. The Santos government passed numerous decrees and resolutions that paved the way for the penalization of the sector, which took its most dramatic form in police and army operations that detained miners and blew up their equipment.

A department scoring high on biodiversity, public safety issues, and clan-destine mines, Chocó entered the crosshairs of the punitive clampdown. Across the region, destruction operations became the new normal; more so after a historical Constitutional Court ruling in 2016 conferred legal person-hood to the Atrato River, Chocó's main artery, while ordering specific insti-tutions to protect the river from the miners whose mercury was squeezing the life out of it. The new police and army missions dramatically cut the num-ber of operating mines. Some miners were forced to quit because their exca-vators were blown up. Others called it a day before any damage could be inflicted. The times of tolerance were over. In 2017, miners had to run from the police, strategize fuel transportation routes, and use and abuse the cre-dentials of fellow operators to circumvent selling restrictions.

It was not just politicians, though, who began to speak ill of Colombian small-scale gold mining. Ever since the boom years, the activity has frequently surfaced in national and foreign news outlets that take pains to map out the wildness of frontier life. Journalists write about a "wild west" of "deathtrap mines, ramshackle huts, prostitutes, drugs, and narco-paramilitaries" (*In-Sight Crime* 2013) and about "gangs and guerrillas" earning more money with "bloody" gold than with cocaine (*Miami Herald* 2018). At the same time, they highlight the "environmental holocaust" (*Semana* 2015a) and "cancer" (*Semana* 2018) that constitute illegal extraction, while buttressing these di-agnoses with bird's eye views of the lunar landscapes that gold fever leaves behind (see also *El Tiempo* 2015). The news reports also speak for the victims: the hard-pressed communities and artisanal miners who own the deaths-capes and swim and wash and live in the mercury-soaked rivers (*El Especta-dor* 2015; *Newsweek* 2016). The victims, we read, have fallen prey to nonlocal predators and also, sometimes, to their own presumed naivety; to a "lack of awareness" (*El Tiempo* 2015) that renting out lands to excavator miners con-notes ecological suicide.

This story of devastation tells the truth in several respects. It is undeniable that small-scale gold miners clear-cut jungles, decimate subsistence crops, asphyxiate waterways with tailings, and poison themselves and other humans and species with mercury. What's more, gold breeds violence. Paramilitaries and guerrillas extort and manage mines; community leaders opposing extraction have been subject to death threats; and workers have met brutal deaths in labor accidents. It is, thus, no overstatement to say that gold mining kills forests, rivers, and people.

Yet the story of devastation is disturbingly incomplete. When browsing through mining accounts, a cynical reader might wonder whether the authors have looked at gold's problems mostly from afar. We learn awfully little about the miners and landholders who are living in the "doomed" gold frontier. Only minimally do we train our eyes below the bird's eye views provided by drones and helicopters. Here and there we find some quoted lines, but neither miners nor landholders talk much. It is often journalists, state functionaries, and professional experts who do the talking for them.[9] As a matter of fact, while small-scale mining in Colombia and beyond grips the public imagination in a way that renders it synonymous with crime and environmental plunder, popular and political discussions remain largely unmoored from the complex life projects that the activity sets in motion. Considering the tooth-and-claw depictions that Colombian miners in particular evoke, several questions are dawning: How do people understand and organize their gold in the absence of legal recognition? In what ways does the ascribed notoriety of miners contrast with their own values and goals? What causes them to destroy rainforests, pay criminals, and work without the necessary papers? And what of the "victims"? How do the landholders and artisanal miners conceive of their assigned victimhood? Why do some of them accept, albeit grudgingly, that excavators fell their trees, dirty their waters, and make their lands unploughable and unminable? And what do they make of government attempts to save them from such extractive rampage?

Asking all this is not to trivialize the negatives of extraction. These negatives are hard to ignore—and harder to trivialize. I, too, know about gold's multiple regimes of violence. I have seen the ecological havoc that excavators wreak. I have listened to fear-induced anecdotes about paramilitaries, guerrillas, and bandits. But while witnessing from up close the horrific face that mining can assume, I also think that the abovementioned questions about local lifeworlds are often only marginally addressed—if at all—by politicians, journalists, and even academics (though, as I outline below, positive exceptions exist). Quite frequently, their accounts of gold frontiers are accompanied by an uncomfortable silence of local voices. This book seeks to puncture that silence by making visible how people in Chocó live with gold mining as they encounter, undermine, and reconfigure state surveillance.

In light of this, the book's title—*Underground Politics*—is not just a play on the subterranean materiality of gold. In Colombia and other places, small-scale miners often stake their claims to gold and negotiate land and labor relations *beneath the surface* of official recognition. Meanwhile, their life-worlds have remained to large extent unexplored by public and academic attention. Thus, the notion of the "underground" also flags this political in-visibility. Moreover, an additional metaphorical advantage of speaking of "underground politics"—as opposed to, say, "illegal" politics—is that it does not imply a complete disjunction from social processes occurring legally, legitimately, and out in the open. After all, the motions on the surface reso-nate in the stuff lying underneath, and vice versa. Along similar lines, the politics of the underground continually encounters the footprint of *above-ground* markets, governance techniques, and community life, which in their turn are affected by the underground trembles of clandestine mines. In short, by "underground politics," I refer to practices of extractive organization that, while contradicting the formal regulatory framework, may nevertheless be constitutive of state power.

Bottom-Up State-Making

When the state appears in social and political theory, it is often as a more or less centralized legal regime that impinges on local communities from the outside, usually under terms that are not of the latter's choosing.[10] Anthro-pologists, in particular, have drawn attention to the administrative and sym-bolic repertoires through which state entities render local populations legible (Scott 1998), normalize social deprivation (Biehl 2005; Povinelli 2011), enhance bureaucratic power (Ferguson 1990), entrench capitalist relations in marginalized places (Hale 2002; Hirsch 2022), or discount ontologies that are at cross purposes with modern politics (de la Cadena 2010). The state-community opposition that reverberates in much of this work also charac-terizes ethnographies of resource politics. Studies of minerals, oil, natural gas, water, and other substances have argued, repeatedly and convincingly, that neoliberal capitalism is premised on government rationalities that act, at once, in favor of mining and drilling projects and against the people living in extraction's shadows. In these studies, host state institutions tend to assume an identity of extractivist enablers that, by strategy or necessity, disregard community rights due to an overdependence on rents and mine shares (Kirsch 2014; Sawyer 2004); share sovereignty with, and outsource governing duties to, extraction companies (Appel 2019; Bainton and Skrzypek 2021; Rajak 2011); espouse notions of development that are at odds with local understandings of the nonhuman world (Babidge 2018; Davidov 2014; Li 2015); and enforce policies that criminalize small-scale miners who stand in the way of the large-scale industries (Damonte 2016; Jaramillo 2020; Tschakert 2009; Vila Benites 2023).

This book builds on these insights on the nexus of state- and resource-making, but makes a somewhat different theoretical proposition. It shows that an anthropological understanding of state power should account for not only the strategies by which governments and companies establish hegemonic extractive regimes, but also the organizing practices by which local communities frustrate, transform, and invigorate governance. Far from being outside or only on the receiving end of the state, mining communities in Chocó entangled legal categories and institutions in the day-to-day organization of their mines. In doing so, they gave shape to how the state crystallized in their gold frontier. I maintain that a comprehensive ethnography of resource politics should not lose track of such "bottom-up" influence. Contrary to conventional accounts of state regimes affecting local places, I approach state-building as a process that is driven by both top-down interventions and the local populations engaging with them. Naturally, such a proposition requires a more open-minded conceptualization of the state than the common notion of a political agent that externally intervenes in everyday life. To be more precise, it requires an ethnographically informed approach that accentuates the disaggregated, emplaced, and contradictory manifestations of politics; one that studies the state not as an autonomous source of power, but as a multifaceted societal construct whose symbolic and material qualities are contingent on mundane actions.[11]

As such, this ethnography is consistent with a burgeoning anthropological literature that has unsettled assumptions about cohesive state bureaucracies superseding society, and instead has opted for a view of the state as "composed of bundles of social practices, every bit as local in their materiality and social situatedness as any other" (Ferguson and Gupta 2002:992).[12] Much of this thinking goes back to a pioneering article by sociologist Philip

Abrams from the late 1970s. Debunking the idea that the state enjoys a singular agency, Abrams (1988[1977]:82) proposed a distinction between the state-system—"a palpable nexus of practice and institutional structure"—and the state-idea—"an overt symbolic identity progressively divorced from practice." He warned us not to confuse the former with the latter; that is, not to depict the state-system as the unified organization the state-idea claims it to be. Several anthropologists and allied scholars have followed this scrutiny of both the ideational and material dimensions of state power. Yet rather than, *pace* Abrams, simply clarifying the distinction between ideology and praxis, they have primarily sought to tease out the iterative performances that allow the "state-idea" to become an affective reality in the first place. While approaching the state "simultaneously as material force and as ideological construct" (Mitchell 2006:169), or as "both illusory as well as a set of concrete institutions" (Hansen and Stepputat 2001:5), one of the major contentions of the anthropology of the state has been that the state's symbolic representation—the *idea* of an impartial and effective apparatus standing over the citizenry—acquires salience through the regulatory rituals of the "state-system."[13]

I engage with this literature by illustrating that the cultural and material construction of the state depends on not just bureaucratic governing techniques, but also the everyday applications and understandings of law by non-state actors. As other anthropologists have shown, laws and policies are continually upended by the people they seek to regulate, whose mobilizations (Holston 2008), documentary readings (Das 2004; Nuijten 2003), and receptiveness to political interventions (Campbell 2015; Nugent 1994) all affect how biopolitical institutions manifest themselves in daily life. In effect, even illegalized actors who contravene formal law sometimes transform into collaborators in official modalities of rule, in that they provide the bureaucracy with opportunities to tax, police, redistribute wealth, and perform public authority (Civico 2012; Jaffe 2013; Roitman 2004).

In a somewhat similar vein, participants in Chocó's mining economy were quintessential in the local unfolding of state power, the forbidden status of their gold notwithstanding. Although formal legislation did a thorough job in regulating, surveilling, and informalizing mining stakeholders, the latter also used laws, documents, and official discourses in ways that exceeded original administrative purposes. In confronting a law-spitting state machinery, small-scale miners and Afro-Colombian community leaders conferred a plethora of fantasies, doubts, and misreadings on the legalities that were thrown at them. They reappropriated state law in ways that were conductive to their informal extractive activities, and consequently played a pivotal role in how statehood materialized in their mines. What's more, miners and community leaders laid the groundwork for the expansion of centralized bureaucracy, inasmuch as their "underground" extractive organization emerged from, and was formative of, the governing practices of public servants.

Thus, to invoke Janet Roitman's (2004) analytical distinction, this book demonstrates that an economy that exists largely outside "state regulatory authority" nevertheless helps to give form to "state power." While state emissaries may recur to abstract conceptual knowledges to render specific populations legible for governance (Scott 1998), my ethnography foregrounds the concrete practices by which these populations themselves act on governance as they seek to legitimize their involvement in an otherwise illegal economy. By engaging with the material apparatus and the cultural idea of the state, small-scale mining practitioners make it easier for state officials to identify their potential for formalization. In this way, they help bring purportedly stateless regions into the realm of formal politics.

The Politics of Small-Scale Mining Geographies—and the Geography of Mining Politics

The decision to look at state politics through the lens of small-scale gold mining is, I feel, a timely one. Artisanal and small-scale mining is a prominent industry in large parts of the world, most notably sub-Saharan Africa, Latin America, and South and Southeast Asia. Although most extraction escapes the registries of public bookkeepers, estimates suggest that small-scale mining employs more than 44 million people the world over (World Bank 2020:1), excluding the goods and services industries blossoming in its shadows. Gold is the most important mineral driving this growth. Small-scale gold mines account for an estimated 15 to 20 million practitioners worldwide, who between them account for 20 percent of global gold production (World Gold Council 2022:13).

In most countries, this expansion has sparked serious public debates on environmental preservation and law enforcement. Politicians and other opinionmakers routinely portray small-scale gold miners as outlaws who make a quick buck at the expense of law, nature, and moral decency. Nonetheless, in-depth research of small-scale mining is in short supply, as the subject is difficult to study quantitatively, because of unreliable or absent statistics, as well as qualitatively, since extraction takes place in secluded and conflictive places. Academics who do write about the sector tend to focus on one of its predicaments, such as mercury pollution (Güiza and Aristizábal 2013), deforestation (Swenson et al. 2011), malaria outbreaks (Pommier de Santi et al. 2016), child labor (Potter and Lupilya 2016), and violence toward women (Cohen 2014) and Indigenous populations (Ramos 2010). Research on Colombia has specifically scrutinized the relation between extraction and armed conflict, as gold is a crucial source of revenue for armed groups (Cohen 2014; Franco and Ali 2017; Rettberg and Ortiz-Riomalo 2016; Vélez-Torres 2014).

In recent years, though, a more miner-friendly body of work has surfaced in and outside Colombia. Writing against the popular idea of miners as predatory gold seekers, social scholars have highlighted that mining rationales are often "poverty-driven" (Hilson 2010:304), while endorsing an image of small-scale miners that might be best defined, in the words of Tschakert (2009:732), as "individuals or groups who, due to persistent devaluation, disenfranchisement, and exclusion from flourishing, have been essentially forced into destructive and illegal activities." Such scholarship has voiced preoccupation with the legal exclusion that miners suffer in national property regimes, criticizing governments in South America (Damonte 2016; Heemskerk 2004) and elsewhere (Hilson 2010; Siegel and Veiga 2009) for endorsing legislation that is tailored to multinational corporations and tone-deaf to the socioeconomic features of small domestic mines. This critique of formalization barriers is specifically pronounced in Colombia, where the informality of the sector has ostensibly strengthened criminals' grip on local mining geographies (Giraldo Ramírez 2013; Idrobo et al. 2013) and facilitated mercury spillage whose scale has no parallel in any other country (Cordy et al. 2011; Siegel 2013).

To recap, analyses of small-scale gold mining have been mostly aimed at larger environmental and legal conflicts. But while writing on what is lost with outlawed extraction, or what is won with legalizing it, neither critics nor advocates have extensively dealt with the sociopolitics to which the gold mines themselves give shape. The recurring motif is one of informal settlements where conflicts thrive and rules are lacking.[14] Colombian mining regions especially have been equated with an imagery of "poverty and lawlessness" (Güiza and Aristizábal 2013:34), with one study even going so far as to suggest that they suffer from a "culture of conflict" and a "breakdown of both public authority and traditional folkways" (Siegel 2013:9, 12). Even if most critics of miner informalization use less spectacular language, in their similar insistence on conflicts, exclusions, and absences—of formality, the law, the state—they, too, have remained somewhat inattentive to the local governing regimes and political subjectivities that gold engenders.[15]

Yet as a growing number of ethnographic studies reveals, gold-mining zones are host to complex socialities and moralities. They are places that are guided not by the laws of tooth and claw, but by strategies of conflict escalation (Salman and de Theije 2017), arrangements of wealth sharing (Jonkman and de Theije 2022; Luning and Pijpers 2017), resourceful material practices (d'Avignon 2022; Jaramillo 2020), and culturally mediated ideas about freedom (Tubb 2020), tradition (Jonkman forthcoming), and the spiritual world (Coyle Rosen 2020; High 2017; Peluso 2018). Much of this certainly holds true for the towns and villages that take center stage in this book. Therefore, rather than making one more economic argument for why miners deserve inclusion in political regimes, or one more environmental argument for why they maybe do not, this book charts out the underground political formations in which they already participate.

Mind you, I view the aforementioned critiques on formalization barriers a valuable addition to the stereotypes that miners suffer in scientific and non-scientific texts. Nevertheless, I also believe that such scholarship has paid insufficient attention to the social heterogeneity of mining areas, as well as to the variegated policy effects to which they are subject. Like Boris Verbrugge (2015:1029), I observe that informality critiques often characterize small-scale mining as a "poverty-driven subsistence sector" and "fail to account for its heterogenous and segmented character." What prevails are legalist explanations of informality that propose that costly license systems sentence impoverished miners to work without formal recognition. Although these concerns are well taken, they evoke the impression, to varying degrees, of a sole downtrodden economy that is systematically excluded from legal frameworks. Doing so, they leave important questions unasked: How is legislation experienced by differently situated mining participants? How does it impact local power relations? And who wins and loses in the transition to formal legal regimes? I explore these questions ethnographically in the goldfields of Chocó.

Visualizing these grounded governing effects serves the additional purpose of making the "state" reappear in gold country. In small-scale mining literature, the weakness of the state has become something of a truism. Critical studies of different governmental failures (e.g., to legalize miners, curtail environmental destruction, curb the mine rents of criminals) include passing comments about "weak state capacity" (Fisher 2008:210), "the weak state apparatus" (Salo et al. 2016:1065), and even "the total absence of any kind of government authority" (Hoogbergen and Kruijt 2004:3). More fine-grained accounts observe that in Indonesia "small-scale gold mining largely eschews the state and its specific forms of territorialization" (Peluso 2018:401), that in Ghana the goldfields have "little state presence" (Luning and Pijpers 2017:765), and that "in Mongolian gold mines state powers seem distant, if not irrelevant, to how life is lived" (High 2017:20).

Applied to Colombia, the language inflates. Those chronicling the exacerbated scale of mercury pollution associate mining regions with "a failed state" (Güiza and Aristizábal 2013) or a "legal no-man's-land" (Siegel 2013:7). Those analyzing gold as a catalyst for violence suggest that criminal groups tap into extractive economies in a context of "institutional weakness" (Rettberg and Ortiz-Riomalo 2016:87), "very low local institutional capacity" (Giraldo Ramírez 2013:46), or "minimal state presence in many areas of the country" (Idrobo et al. 2013:27). And those protesting the informality of domestic practitioners likewise identify a "mining frontier beyond state control" (Vélez-Torres 2016:243) and "areas with relatively poor control from the state" (Álvarez 2016:58).

Inspired by the rich anthropology of Colombian state formation (e.g., Ballvé 2012; Bocarejo 2018; Ramírez 2011; Serje 2013; Uribe 2017), in what follows I offer an ethnographic corrective to these assumptions of state absence. By situating the underground politics of extraction regions within processes of statecraft, I seek not only to accentuate the limitations of top-down government control—as mentioned in the previous section—but also to reject the argument that these limitations are somehow symptomatic of an absent or failed state. The reasoning for my rejection is twofold. On the one hand, the discourse of absence masks the myriad ways in which inhabitants of mining areas encounter state configurations. People in Chocó and elsewhere continually engage with "the idea of the state" (Abrams 1988) through their run-ins with documents, institutions, and public servants. Certainly, nuanced analyses of places as diverse as Burkina Faso (Côte and Korf 2018), Colombia (Rozo 2022), and Ghana (Coyle Rosen 2020) reveal that, despite blatant informalization, the cultural symbols and regulatory structures of the state present themselves in gold country in subtle and unexpected ways.

On the other hand, the idea that social neglect constitutes a symptom of state dysfunction (of weakness, failure, absence) is guilty of making normative assumptions about what the body politic should a priori look like. The characterization of the state apparatus as a coherent juridico-legal regime that has yet to arrive in frontier zones is not grounded in empirics, but rather conforms to, borrowing from Penelope Harvey (2005:127), "the state's own version of itself." While the objection I present is most obviously one of epistemology—an objection to centering scientific analysis on practices that are missing, rather than those that are actually happening—it also holds political ramifications. Insisting on lawlessness and state weakness cements the idea that social destitution exists in contrast to formal policy. The problem, so the claim of absence appears to suggest, is no longer the law but the lawlessness of the resource frontier. Indeed, when taken at face value, the notion may convince us to believe that material deprivation lies outside state intervention and, ipso facto, that the latter is the necessary fix for the former (see also Serje 2013).

This book proposes we believe neither. Rather, it offers everyday snapshots that show that the sociopolitical life of chocoano mining—even if mostly taking place outside the formal legal framework—interlaces with the cultural and material formation of the state. To this end, my ethnography bolsters the claim that "political peripheries" are the places "where the reinterpretation of state policies is most extreme" (Tsing 1993:27). Were we, with Philip Abrams, to entertain the idea that the state is not an established political fact but an unstable ideological project, then peripheralized places such as Chocó become privileged sites to look at all the hard labor that goes into this project. This is because the so-called "margins of the state" (Das and Poole 2004) expose best the disconnect between the desires and achievements of centralized rule, for it is here where laws, symbols, and institutions continually function in ways that run contrary to formal aspirations.

Colombian small-scale gold mines are particularly well-positioned margins from which to look at state power. The obvious reason is the brazen extralegal character of the mines, showcasing—through all the illicitly felled trees, the spilled mercury, the off-the-the-books economics—the undeniable limits of administrative planning. But illegalization, in and of itself, is not the only reason. Rather, what makes Colombian gold such a relevant venue to study politics is that, in spite of its outlawed status, it retains the possibility of law. Unlike coca production in Colombia—that other illicit economy that causes so many headaches for policymakers—gold extraction has always held the promise of formalization.[16] While, as the coming chapters make clear, this promise often falls short in practice, it does have a performative effect, insofar as state law acts as an important organizational mechanism in

mining. If anything, this performance is only amplified by the rampant illegality of extraction, because it is the ever-present menaces that accompany
unlawful work that stimulate miners to search out legislation. That is to say,
the menaces of imprisonment, destroyed equipment, and gold-selling restrictions help explain why illegalized miners invest so much time and money in
legalization procedures, as well as why they administer their informal mines
in accordance with formal criteria. It is, thus, the peculiar combination of
the political present with the politically possible—of actual illegality with potential legality—that allows Colombian gold to shine its light on the contingent workings of state symbols.

There is, further, another appeal that gold has as an analytical window
onto politics, which has less to do with its legality than materiality. Amid contemporary environmental destruction in the so-called Anthropocene, it is
clearer than ever that humans are not the masters of their worlds but only one
element in more-than-human ecologies, who must negotiate the possibilities
and restrictions afforded by their built and nonbuilt environments. In this
light, recent neomaterialist studies in political geography and anthropology
have urged us to stop treating the biophysical world as some inert backbone to
social life, and to start considering it as a restless space that exceeds human
intentionality.[17] These studies have alerted us to the fact that nonhuman geographies are active participants in, opposed to passive recipients of, politico-
economic regimes, whose physical affordances make possible, or not, the
realization of anthropogenic projects—statist projects or otherwise.

As an economy that relies heavily on local matter (trees are tunnels, water
is washing material, stones are channels, and, yes, gold is capital), small-scale
mining is surely an instructive example of how more-than-human geography differentiates human political economy. The corollary of this is that the
physicality of the goldfields (trees, excavators, dredges, and much more) forms
an essential component of the power regimes that are portrayed in the chapters to come. Indeed, much of the beef that state officials claim to have with
miners is the latter's lamentable treatment of their environmental surroundings. And just as the jungle is invoked by the officials as explanation for the
persecution of miners, so too do the miners recur to performative appeals of
ecological care to convince the officials of their potential for legal recognition (see Chapters 3 and 6).

However, it's not just the case that this book's human protagonists po-
liticize mining landscapes; these affective landscapes themselves also lay their
imprint on sociopolitical formations. Part of the attraction of "underground

politics" as an interpretive device for miners' participation in state power stems from the fact that subsurface materiality actively mediates the participation that is at stake. For example, as Chapter 1 shows, the increased scarcity of gold reserves drives local desires for bigger mining machines and, concomitantly, helps account for local rejections of government interventions aimed at removing the machines. Then there is also the not insignificant matter that subterranean geological formations are invisible to the naked eye. Before being wrested from the alluvium, gold's location is largely a mystery to those who mine and regulate it. This epistemic uncertainty of gold is productive of strongly fluctuating production levels, and as a result of the former, of moral evaluations about the beauty/futility of working a "lottery" economy (Chapter 1); of local criticism on the disconnect between rigid selling regulations and the underground's variable yields (Chapters 1 and 3); of contentious percentage agreements through which people share the volatile risks and rewards of extraction (Chapters 5 and 6); and of a myopia among community leaders (Chapter 5) and public officials (Chapter 6) regarding how much gold is extracted from the imperceptible subsoils they govern. The "underground" in "underground politics," then, is more than just a metaphor, for the political and economic subjectivities that this book explores only make sense when situated in the sensorial proximity of extraction.[18]

Cultural Rights, Neoliberalism, and Natural Resources

The mining organization that I describe unfolds in lands that are collectively owned under multicultural legislation. Consequently, to speak about the former, I cannot leave the latter unmentioned. In 1991, Colombia adopted a constitution that recognized its nation as multicultural and pluriethnic. The new constitution not only promoted the institutionalization of Indigenous rights, but also adopted Transitory Article 55, which encouraged legislators to create legislation for Black Colombians. This affirmation of Black cultural identity eventually resulted in the passing of Law 70 in 1993. Popularly known as the *ley de las comunidades negras*, Law 70 assigned collective lands to rural Afro-descendants in riparian zones of Chocó and the other three departments (Valle del Cauca, Cauca, Nariño) in the Pacific coastal region. It also acknowledged the state's responsibility for protecting the culture and fostering the economic development of Afro-Colombians at large. In the aftermath of the law's passage, local initiatives for collective land tenure sprang up across the Pacific. In line with state criteria, riverine Black communities started to organize themselves into "community councils" (*consejos comunitarios*), with each landholding council being represented by its *junta directiva*, an elected administrative body of community leaders.

Colombia's shift to multicultural rights occurred in tandem with similar patterns in other parts of Latin America. Over the course of the 1990s and early 2000s, many national governments adopted ethno-cultural reforms through which they granted differentiated citizenship to Indigenous and Afro-descendant populations. Entailing a strong disjunction with preceding nationalisms, which celebrated cultural sameness and miscegenation, the reforms took on diverse shapes across different countries, ranging from linguistic rights to provisions of land ownership and substantive access to government bodies. Scholars have put forward different explanations to account for this multicultural turn. Some understand cultural politics as the result of effective social mobilization, catapulted in turn by neoliberal policies that undermined rural livelihoods and organizational forms (Brysk and Wise 1997; Yashar 1999). Others maintain that state governments gave in to Afro/Indigenous demands as a way to solve their legitimacy crises in an era when citizenship had become devoid of substance. In this perspective, cultural recognition formed part of wider decentralization agendas that planned to integrate regions and populations in the thrall of state ordering (Asher and Ojeda 2009; Ng'weno 2007; Van Cott 2000).

While such explanations tend to acknowledge ethno-cultural rights as a productive retreat from hitherto political exclusions, a growing number of authors has adopted a less sanguine view. Countering depictions of multicultural policies as a "postliberal challenge" to "neoliberal citizenship" (Yashar 1999:88) or a "friendly liquidation of the past" (Van Cott 2000), this more skeptical scholarship views cultural recognition as concomitant with late-liberal rationalities of governance. In this view, "neoliberal multiculturalism" (Hale 2002), or "neoliberal interculturalism" (Gustafson 2002), involves the endorsement of policies that "do not . . . overhaul structures of economic inequality," but, much more deceptively, "seek to insulate centralised power . . . from various forms of 'Indigenous' and other 'popular' forms of political engagement" (Gustafson 2002:270). In other words, policymakers promote a stripped-down set of rights that leaves material deprivation untouched and keeps most economic and natural resources in the hands of the private sector.

Arguably the most prominent advocate of this line of reasoning is Charles Hale. In several well-cited articles, Hale (2002, 2005, 2006) argues that cultural reforms fit the neoliberal dogma of delegating governance to civil society. Adopting multicultural legislation, he suggests, enables states to harness the political power of Indigenous movements: "the state does not merely 'recognise' community, civil society, indigenous culture and the like, but actively re-constitutes them in its own image, sheering [*sic*] them of radical excesses, inciting them to do the work of subject-formation that would otherwise fall to the state itself" (2002:496). Put another way, by distinguishing between subjects that are sufficiently and insufficiently cultural, political elites mitigate the transformative potential of grassroots mobilization and, in this way, re-entrench capitalist relations of subordination. For example, Hale shows how mestizo elites in Guatemala celebrate a docile Indigenous subject, while Maya demands that oppose dominant development models are defamed as "radical."

Other authors, too, underscore that multicultural policies have not undone but rather reconfigured relations of domination. For different Latin American countries, they show how claims to cultural difference by Indigenous and Black peoples become challenged when they pursue agendas of resource redistribution or carry out activities that mismatch with their ascribed environmental guardianship.[19] Regarding Colombia, for instance, Roosbelinda Cárdenas (2012) shows how business ventures endorse ideas of "green" Afro-Colombian culture to groom Pacific farmers for participation in risky oil-palm cultivation: "Black and indigenous subjects are recruited (both through consent and coercion) into green capitalist ventures and, subsequently, their very involvement in these undertakings serves to legitimize these endeavors as environmentally sound" (329). As Cárdenas sets out, the tragic flip side of such "green multiculturalism" is that "the conditions of cultural recognition get . . . tied to . . . [displaying] appropriately 'green' behavior" (329). People who choose to eschew the green economy "are construed as unruly, or beyond the pale" (321).

However, arguments of neoliberal governmentality have not gone unchallenged. They have received slack for downgrading the role that social movements played in setting policy agendas (Anthias 2014), and for disregarding the opposition movements faced from elites in seeing their demands instituted in laws and constitutions (Van Cott 2006). In this light, several authors choose a middle-ground perspective, perceiving the emergence of ethnocultural reforms as the result of *both* grassroots mobilization and elite efforts to synchronize such mobilization with neoliberal capitalism (Anthias and Radcliffe 2015; Domínguez Mejía 2017; Escobar 2008; Paschel 2016).[20]

Here, my interest does not lie so much in assessing the redistributive potential of multicultural regulation, or, to quote Hale (2002:485), its "underlying principles." Rather, I wish to draw attention to the chasm that separates the "underlying principles" of policies from the unfolding of multiculturalism in specific times and places, and, by extension, to the *protagonismo* of governed subjects in bringing about this governance chasm. Hence, the upcoming chapters reveal not one more case study of how neoliberal multiculturalism subverts grassroots organizing, but, instead, an exploration of how the latter subverts the former; specifically, how Afro-Colombian communities steer multicultural statehood into new, unexpected directions through their practical engagements with law.

Whereas "neoliberal" analyses have been helpful in unearthing the predatory undertones of supposedly empowering reforms, they have also been fairly silent on how multicultural subjects shape governance in ways that cannot be reduced to acquiescence to neoliberalism. Though some analyses do recognize "the potential for negotiation around the concessions of neoliberal multiculturalism" (Hale 2002:522), or the "unexpected outcomes" stemming from "new forms of social mobilization and paradoxes of the reforms themselves" (Gustafson 2002:270), the overall tendency is to theorize governance as something that happens to Black and Indigenous peoples; an external force that rules, seduces, excludes, or (in the spirit of Hale's argument) permissively includes. Yet as proposed above, state-making is a two-way street that encompasses not only bureaucratic protocols and institutions, but also the localized practices of the target populations of governing interventions.

Clearly, the same is true for interventions inspired by neoliberal doctrine. By neoliberalism, I mean a rationality of rule that takes entrepreneurial criteria as fundamental to government effectiveness (Burchell 1993:274), and with that, promotes the minimization of state regulatory functions as a precondition for safeguarding the presumed neutrality of financial markets (Postero 2007:15). In being a governing *rationality*—rather than a totalizing system—neoliberalism, as Aihwa Ong (2007:4) reminds us, always "co-exists with other political rationalities." Therefore, whichever way neoliberal policies attempt to remodel the formal legal framework—say, privatization, trade liberalization, self-regulation (multicultural or otherwise)—their outcomes are varied and partial. Policies often produce what Rivke Jaffe (2013:745) calls "hybrid" political formations, which are "not purely neoliberal" but "the unstable, ambivalent outcome of an ongoing power struggle that takes place at different sites," including in "nonformal systems of rule." Such hybridization, as I outline below, equally pervades neoliberalism's cultural politics. While official schemes might foster an ambition to map Afro/Indigenous territories more firmly within the grid of hegemonic rule, they often have different outcomes on the ground, especially in sites of contested public authority. When confronting the messiness of local power relations, ethno-cultural regulation routinely produces "hybrid, 'not-quite-neoliberal' and potentially double-edged spaces" (Anthias and Radcliffe 2015:268).

This ethnography pays special attention to the "not-quite-neoliberal" spaces that emerged in Chocó amid the convergence of legal cultural rights and illegalized mining. To an extent, my analysis is in sync with studies that show how Black and Indigenous peoples in Colombia (Vélez-Torres 2014; Weitzner 2017) and Latin America (Rasch 2012; Sawyer 2004) contest formal parameters of ethnicity in their endeavor to access natural resources. That said, those analyses mostly describe situations in which people repurpose legislation to defend land and water against mining and drilling. Instead, my focus is on the moments when extractive expansion and grassroots organizing are not opposing forces but find themselves in a constructive relation to one another. In the mining regions of this research, Afro-descendant leaders invoked their cultural rights not so much to safeguard traditional economic customs as to claim participation in an expansionist gold frontier.

A Road- and Rivermap

The host of this frontier, Chocó, is a vast and sparsely populated department in the Colombian northwest. Although it is the country's ninth largest political subdivision in area (of a total of thirty-three), it ranks twenty-third in population size, being home to slightly over half a million of the nation's population of 52 million. Chocó comprises roughly the northern half of Colombia's Pacific lowlands, a tropical wetland region that is wedged between the Pacific Ocean and the Andes and stretches from the Ecuadorian to the Panamanian border. Popular descriptions often imagine the Pacific as a place of natural wildness and social difference. Colombians from the interior and foreigners often dwell on its rich biodiversity, merciless rainfall (Chocó is the second wettest ecosystem in the world), and Black and Indigenous inhabitants; or, in less favorable accounts, on poverty, armed groups, illegal mines, and coca crops. Of the four Pacific departments, Chocó arguably fits best these tropes of "otherness." Its estimates of Afro-descendant population (73.6 percent)[21] and people living below the monetary poverty line (63.4 percent)[22] are respectively the highest and second-highest of all Colombian departments, tying well into the popular imagery of the Pacific as a nexus of poverty and Blackness.[23] What's more, whereas the southern departments of Valle, Cauca, and Nariño are made up of large highland areas that are home to their capitals and the greater part of their populations, Chocó is almost completely covered by rainforest and accommodates its administrative seat in the lowland city of Quibdó.

Yet while Chocó is by all means a sylvan place, its capital Quibdó hosts no less than a quarter of its inhabitants. Located in the geographical heart of the department, the city makes no secret of its tropical origins. Its rain lashes down as intensely as elsewhere, and its central square looks out on the majestic Atrato River—and behind it, you get a glimpse of the vast jungle that blankets the Pacific coastal region. Still, there is no denying Quibdó's urbanity. This is the place where Chocó's university-educated and well-connected find jobs in government or nongovernmental organizations (NGOs), and where large numbers of rural young adults migrate to in order to work off the books in construction and commerce, much of which is controlled by white migrants from the Colombian interior. Quibdó is also where most primary and manufactured goods arrive from external markets, and where you can buy them cheaper than in the village stores that resell them. And Quibdó is where mining meetings with the national government are held, where gold diggers purchase their fuel cheapest, and where precious metals start their export journeys to other departments by air and road.

But Quibdó is also the urban exception to a region whose life mostly takes place in the countryside. While strongly connected to the capital through family, work, or other factors, the larger share of Chocó's population lives in towns and hamlets along the rainforest's myriad rivers. Among these, the Atrato is the largest. Originating in the lower Andes, the Atrato enters Quibdó from the south, from where it snakes four hundred kilometers northward to the Gulf of Urabá on the Caribbean coast, getting wider with each tributary it swallows. Most villages in the Medio (Middle) and Bajo (Lower) Atrato regions—the regions north of Quibdó—can be reached only by aquatic transportation. Local economies are based on subsistence gardening, timber, and fishing, although in certain parts of the basin people also rear livestock (Bajo Atrato) and mine gold (Medio Atrato).

Nevertheless, most gold is found south of Quibdó. At the snail's pace of deep-time erosion, mineral-rich gravels and sands began traveling thousands of years ago from the Andes into the rainforest. Specks and flakes of gold settled in the upper and middle sections of the drainage basins of the San Juan and Atrato Rivers,[24] where contemporary villages continue to search for them. There is less need for boats to reach these mining zones. An asphalted road connects Quibdó with larger towns in the higher parts of the San Juan and Atrato, while many smaller towns and villages are linked by dirt and gravel roads of varying upkeep.

Chocó's divergent geographies, economies, and transportation possibilities produce palpable differences in terms of basic amenities. Places without a terrestrial connection, such as the villages north of Quibdó, are the ones most likely to lack aqueducts and sewage systems. Additionally, their residents depend on diesel-driven generators for electrical power, and, in some cases, on traveling to their municipal capitals for telephone and internet communication. By contrast, the southern road-connected territories of the San Juan and the Alto (Upper) Atrato enjoy greater access to sewerage, telecommunication, and electrical grids, while most of their inhabitants live in cement-plastered houses—a form of housing that tends to be held in higher esteem than the wooden buildings that prevail in the (roadless) hamlets of the Bajo and Medio Atrato. Then again, while the south enjoys faster transportation and more accessible public services, it also experiences most acutely the loss of timber, fertile soil, and precious metals. It is in the San Juan where most extraction took place in colonial and postcolonial times. Likewise, it was there where in recent decades the excavators arrived first, and therefore where trees, subsistence plots, and surface gold have been the most dramatically mined away.

Enslaved, Emancipated, Enclaved

To better comprehend all this—Chocó's gold mines, Afro-Colombian population, infrastructural paucity, poverty, and imagined alterity—it is necessary to delve into history. At the beginning of the 1500s, enslaved Africans started to arrive at what was then the Kingdom of the New Granada. After they had survived the horrors of the Atlantic passage, they were forced to work in domestic labor, plantations, and commerce. By the mid-1600s, most enslaved people worked in gold-mining pits near the Andean city of Popayán, and slavery gold gradually became New Granada's most important export. In fact, from the sixteenth until the early eighteenth century, the region today known as Colombia produced more gold than any other Spanish colony (West 1952a:323).

Chocó's slavery was more recent than the mines of Popayán. It was not until the 1680s that the Spanish gained control over the region, after a string of violent expeditions had killed most of the Indigenous population.[25] From then onward, a colonial economy developed that was almost entirely dedicated to gold production, with 90 percent of the bullion being mined through the pans and sluices of enslaved Africans and their descendants (Sharp 1975). Mining camps were set up and abandoned according to the location of productive auriferous bodies, and stayed the most substantial form of settlement in Chocó throughout the colonial period. Towns remained undeveloped for lack of elite habitation, for most mine owners resided and invested their slavery riches in the Andes, preferring their highland haciendas over the remote and humid rainforest (Wade 1993:99).

Life in the colonial mines has been poorly documented.[26] Yet historical studies show us that miners, even while sharing the inhumane predicament of bondage, had different degrees of mobility. Chocó's placer mines were subdivided into several mining groups (cuadrillas). Whereas the mine as a whole was administered by a white overseer, the individual cuadrillas were headed by enslaved "cuadrilla captains" who were in charge of the distribution of food and the collection of gold. On weekends and during religious festivities, when workers were allowed to work for themselves, these captains amassed the most gold of all cuadrilla members and were in the best position to accumulate enough wealth to buy their freedom from mine owners (Leal 2018:27–60; West 1952b).

When free, libres remained in the mining areas to pan for gold and cultivate plantains and corn. Apart from self-purchase, or the purchase by loved ones who were already free, there were few other means by which enslaved people could obtain their freedom.[27] Unlike other parts of Colombia, where maroon communities created palenques (fortified settlements) to defend themselves against a hostile white society, escapes from slavery are believed to have been rare in the Pacific (Leal 2018:27–60; Mosquera 2002; Wade 1993:100–102).[28]

After the dissolution of slavery in 1851, Chocó became predominantly inhabited by African-descendant and Indigenous Emberá and Wounaan communities. In the secluded rainforest, as historian Claudia Leal documents, manumitted Afro-descendants enjoyed an independence from wider racist society that was probably unmatched in the rest of the Americas. They created "landscapes of freedom" (Leal 2018) by gardening, hunting, and fishing for subsistence and by participating in various extractive economies. Black *libres* could mine freely for gold by buying, renting, and occupying the mines of ex-slavers. Meanwhile, transitory booms of rubber, vegetable ivory, and platinum spurred their involvement in other commodity chains. Whites who stayed in Chocó stuck to the towns, where they traded the commodities that free Black miners produced (Leal 2018). The one great exception to this dynamic was Chocó Pacífico, a U.S./British conglomerate that extracted gold and platinum from the San Juan basin from the 1910s until the 1970s, for which it relied on a fleet of bucket line mine dredges, a private airport, a village of U.S.-styled houses, and a crew of white U.S. managers who paid local miners bottom dollar for their deposits.[29]

In short, the postemancipation economy continued to be the enclave that it had always been. Gold mined by chocoano artisans and foreign dredges went out; few investments made their way back in (Wade 1993:131–148). Government agencies made little effort to diversify the economy, to regulate local panners and imperialist dredgers, and to invest in terrestrial infrastructure and riverine transportation.[30]

One upshot of such isolation was that for much of the twentieth century, Chocó, like the Pacific at large, remained relatively unharmed by the armed conflict that started to shatter the Colombian countryside in the 1940s.[31] For decades, the Pacific lowlands were one of the few havens of peace in a country of war. This changed in the mid-1990s, when the region progressively became the setting for fighting between the army, guerrillas, and paramilitaries. The interest of these actors in the Pacific has been related to various economic activities, ranging from overseeing drug-trafficking routes to feeding on gold mines, coca cultivation, and agro-industrial projects. The human toll exacted by the armed conflict has been massive. By June 2023, the *Unidad de Víctimas* (Colombia's attention center for conflict victims) registered that since 1985, 487,000 people in Chocó had been victims of forced displacement (nearly equaling the department's contemporary population), and 14,000 people had been victims of homicide.[32]

On September 27, 2016, after four years of negotiating, mostly in the Cuban capital of Havana, the Santos presidency reached a peace deal with the left-wing guerrillas of the Revolutionary Armed Forces of Colombia (FARC), one of the major players in the conflict. The deal included arrangements on land redistribution, reparations for war victims, the military disbandment of the FARC, and amnesty for guerrillas who had not committed severe war crimes. Santos put the agreement to a national plebiscite that asked Colombians to either accept or reject it. Chocó voted in favor with 80 percent, the highest percentage of all departments. Colombia as a whole rejected the deal by a 0.4 percent majority. Subsequently, after making some modest modifications, Santos passed the peace deal through Congress in November 2016 and, accordingly, FARC combatants in and beyond Chocó put down their weapons. Still, in the "post-conflict," Chocó's waters have been anything but quiet. In the aftermath of the Havana agreement, other armed actors—most notably, right-wing paramilitaries of the Gaitanista Self-Defense Forces of Colombia (AGC)[33] and left-wing guerrillas of the National Liberation Army (ELN)—have expanded their territorial dominion. As a result, forced displacement has continued, as has the killing of community leaders.

Having said all this, when research collaborators talked to me about Chocó's political problems, they tended to mention not so much armed violence as more quotidian dilemmas. Like the outsiders viewing their department through lenses of otherness, many chocoanos saw themselves as different from the rest of the country. But the differences they discerned often had less to do with cultural or ecological distinctiveness than with the deficiency of state provisions. Interlocutors repeatedly argued that they were, and had always been, forgotten by their governments. They bemoaned the short reach of the department's electrical grid, the absence of sewerage and potable water in villages, the sorry state of the two (partly asphalted) roads that connect Chocó with the Colombian interior, the lack of political goodwill in Bogotá when villages flood due to rising river levels, and the vulgarity of a prominent politician who allegedly described the department as a "burden for the country."[34] Most often, they lamented the fact that they had no nearby medical care; that they had to travel for hours to see a doctor in Quibdó and for many hours more to receive specialized treatment in the neighboring inland department of Antioquia.

On two separate occasions, in 2016 and 2017, local civil society leaders bundled these laments together in *paros cívicos* (general strikes) against state abandonment. During the two paros, thousands of chocoanos took to the streets of Quibdó for several days, marching, singing, chanting, dancing, displaying banners, playing protest songs from speakers on pickup trucks, and waving departmental flags. In each of the paros, in an attempt to warm national politicians to their cause, the strike leaders shut down the department's economic lifelines. The leaders urged local stores to remain closed and set up roadblocks to prevent goods, no matter how vital, from flowing into Chocó. Their radical measures indeed caught the eye of national legislators, who in both paros flew into Quibdó to negotiate the end of protest by promising investments in infrastructure and health care.

As these general strikes evidence, it is no exaggeration to state that, more than three centuries after the introduction of slavery into the region, political abandonment still characterizes Chocó's relationship with the Colombian interior, regardless of the changed dynamics of this relationship. Neoliberal mining governance, as this book points out, adds one more chapter to this history of abandonment.

Research Methods

The book draws on fifteen months of ethnographic fieldwork. The bulk of this encompassed a one-year period from February 2017 until January 2018, while shorter field visits took place in 2016, 2019, 2022, and 2023. Research was mostly carried out in, yet not restricted to, the town of "Caliche," the village of "La Peña" (both pseudonyms), and the Bebará River. While these three sites share an overarching history of placer mining, they also bring along their own socio-spatial features. For one, they harbor unique political geographies: Caliche is a municipal capital, La Peña a satellite village of a larger town, and the Bebará a river whose shores accommodate four hamlets. Apart from this, the rainforest also varied from one place to the next. Due to the river's inaccessible location, excavator miners had arrived relatively late along the Bebará, which helps explain why gold, crops, and trees were in greater supply than in Caliche and La Peña. And lastly, the three places were differently impacted by violence. Whereas Caliche's excavator miners were obliged to pay "taxes" to a nonstate armed group, miners in Bebará (a former FARC stronghold) and La Peña were largely exempt from this obligation, and had more to fear from bandits as a consequence.

I will not deny that doing research on "underground politics" in these and other places caused several moments of distress. While listening to news about public forces destroying illegal mines, I worried about the economic futures of miners I had befriended. While watching people diving for gold or digging away at the foundations of pit walls, I worried about them being drowned by collapsing slopes of mud. While hanging out in the intestines of mining tunnels, I worried about the durability of the planks supporting the earth overhead. And while walking in the woods by myself, I worried, depending on the time and trail, about getting lost, mugged, stuck in quicksand, or struck by thunder.

At other times, though, I did not fear fieldwork as much as the "field" feared me. The miners who shared their lives with me were in the limelight of different forms of organized violence. Nonstate armed groups demanded their taxes, bandits robbed their winnings, and heavily armed police wrecked their extractive infrastructure. In this context, a Dutch PhD student was the object of gossip about possible secret motives. Some people found it suspicious that I was studying far-flung places all by myself for a European university. How were they to know that I wasn't a spy for the government, the CIA, or, maybe worse, a mining corporation? Hence, not all miners were happy to talk shop on first encounters. A couple of them lied, I later found out, about their involvement in extraction. One person even recommended that I keep my research identity hidden, arguing that the idea of an academic study was bound to scare people away.

I did not heed his advice. Instead, I relied on brokers to make a reliable impression. Before visiting a new place, I would contact the junta directiva of the local community council. The approval of community and mining leaders gave legitimacy to my presence, and their kindness and social connections were pivotal for talking to the wider community. Another factor that helped me build rapport was my methodology. While I conducted countless interviews over the years (with miners, campesinos, community leaders, state officials, NGO workers, lawyers, academics), participant observation formed the linchpin of the study. This was in part an epistemological decision. I set out to explore the everydayness of mining organization and state power. To that end, long-term immersion in the texture of miners' lives seemed an especially suitable form of inquiry. But the choice for participant observation was also a pragmatic one, driven by the polemic nature of the research subject. It should warrant no surprise that I was only able to have in-depth conversations on sensitive topics—e.g., experiences of extortion, strategies to circumvent police surveillance, the history of armed conflict—thanks to prolonged involvement in the lives of the fieldwork community. What's more, these topics lent themselves uneasily to interviews and, in many cases, could only be addressed via run-of-the-mill conversations that sprouted from simply going along in daily life. Miners had no problem with me jotting down their opinions, banter, and gossip, yet felt unsafe when I pulled out my tape recorder, knowing well that with recorded interviews dissident opinions can be easily traced back to the mouths uttering them.

The most important research activities were attending meetings, hanging out at mines, and walking forest trails. The meetings of community councils and mining associations offered an illuminative vantage point from which to analyze the interface of grassroots organizing and state formation. Meetings mimicked the categories, styles, and languages of official democracy, while also enabling miners and community leaders to engage with public officials and learn the content of legislation. Hanging out at gold mines, in turn, allowed me to share time with miners, fathom the technical and geographical intricacies of extraction, and appreciate the sociality of mining work. At the same time, my presence in the mines helped convince interlocutors that I was indeed not a government spy but a zealous student of mining. Encouraged by apprenticeship ethnography (Downey et al. 2015; Stoller and Olkes 1987; Tubb 2020), I carried out rudimentary tasks at several artisanal mines in the first three or four months of fieldwork (predominantly, tossing away stones and mud), though I eventually decided to fully commit myself to more passive hanging out once a doctor had diagnosed a hernia in my left groin—probably aggravated by my heavy lifting in the pits.[35]

The third key fieldwork activity, the banal act of walking, offered similar benefits of knowledge acquisition and relationship building. Since many pits were located deep in the forest, I routinely had to traverse several kilometers on foot. Such walking, like mining, helped me to better "read" extraction geographies—and the more ground I covered, the better I read. I soon developed an elementary forest literacy, reflected by: a trained ability to cross creeks and pools without having my boots fill up with water; a basic understanding of the differences between native and foreign trees and, therewith, between "virgin" and "worked" lands; an improved sensitivity for stepping onto hard ground while steering clear of quagmires; and last, a solid awareness, grown from painful experience, to never leave the village without an umbrella and baseball cap as protection against sun and rain, or football socks, serving, as any miner could tell me, as armor against the propensity of rubber boots to blister the calves of their wearers.

Yet treading through forests revealed not only the physicality of the land, but also its social life. Walking enabled prolonged conversations with hike companions (miners, community leaders). These *walked talks* were instrumental for learning people's relationship with their environmental surroundings, as the landscapes we trod through (e.g., felled forests, mining sites, paths susceptible to robberies) determined our conversation topics. Furthermore, I think that by crossing distance physically, we also crossed it socially. Some of my fellow walkers uttered comments of appreciation (and sometimes surprise) that I accompanied them on lengthy, and occasionally dangerous, routes of mud, planks, and creeks. In view of all these different forms of forest sociability, this book aims to bring to life not only fieldwork dialogue, but also the rainforest (its people, mining pits, encampments, and trails) from which such dialogue sprouted.

Now, in outlining these ethnographic benefits, I am under no illusion that fieldwork somehow reduced my blatant "otherness" as a white man from the Netherlands with a foreign accent and university affiliation. In contrast to the ethnographer who feels that participatory research attenuates sociopolitical differences between the researcher and the fieldwork community, including differences mediated by race (Wacquant 2005), I, instead, agree with Paul Stoller (2005:197) that in contexts of structural power differentials "the non-native anthropologist can never really transcend difference." To be sure, the more time I spent with miners, the less I was feared as an undercover agent, and the more I became accepted as a student of mining who was safe to kill time with. But it should be obvious that I, spy or student, remained an unmistakable outsider, no matter how much time had passed. Throughout my stay in Chocó, differences regarding social and spatial mobility, nationality, and the classed and racialized experience of institutional power never ceased to be important talking points. In conversations with interlocutors—who themselves were differently positioned in terms of gender, class, and ethnicity—it was never up for debate that I did not suffer the marginalization that they suffered, did not have their monetary problems, did not experience their travel restrictions, and, as some argued, did not suffer their insecurity when visiting "dangerous places," owing to the all-too-familiar pathologies of racism and citizenship privilege. "You don't need to worry about traveling," my friend Emiro said when hearing about my upcoming trip to a village with an unsafe reputation. "If they kidnap a Dutchman, it will be on the national news. If they kidnap a chocoano, no one will notice."

Inevitably, these conversations on power asymmetrics were not divorced from discussions of my responsibilities as a storyteller. Several interlocutors informed me of the sensational descriptions of Chocó that had been written by journalists and other visitors from outside the region. They were especially wary that mine would be one more work about "criminal" extraction. In this

light, a great part of miners' and community leaders' willingness to participate in my study stemmed, I believe, from the fact that I declared the desire to
tell a less one-sided story about the mines with which they were implicated.
My aim was—and is—to take seriously the livelihoods and complex moralities to which extraction gave everyday substance, though not eschewing gold's
ugly sides and conflicts. Yet rethinking storytelling meant not only nuancing
the narrative, but also thinking together with mining and community leaders
of ways of sharing it with them. Concretely, it meant we agreed that I would
discuss my analyses by means of informal conversations, written summaries,
and freely accessible publications on Colombian journalistic websites.[36]

Perhaps it goes without saying, given the criminalization of chocoano
mines, that people's worries about my study concerned not just my politics,
but also the extent to which my writing about them could expose their identities. These worries have greatly affected the contours of the scenes that pop-
ulate this book. Save public figures, I use fabricated names when describing
people. Whereas anonymity is etiquette in much political ethnography, it is
specifically pertinent for a study on small-scale mining, which is subject to
serious institutional repression and multiple local conflicts. Therefore, as an
extra guarantee of anonymization, I employ pseudonyms for most places, and
am circumspect in giving social and geographical details that could reveal
these places' identities and jeopardize interlocutors' well-being.[37] Only when
the mining characteristics of a place are too exceptional to be disguised do I
mention, in agreement with local community leaders, the original names of
rivers, towns, and villages.[38]

Structure of the Book

The ethnography consists of seven chapters that are grouped in three overarching parts. Part I, *Underground Lifeworlds*, sets the stage. It includes two
chapters that present a close-up view of how Chocó's miners organize, perceive, and live their gold extraction against a backdrop of constraining state
governance. Chapter 1 acquaints the reader with the afterlife of chocoano
mines, along with the punitive politics precipitating it. It tells the story of leftover landscapes, where local artisanal miners relied on rudimentary techniques (pans, spades, pumps, tunnels) to comb the subsoil for the residual gold
left by earlier extraction. The chapter reveals that many of these miners continued to heap praise on the very same settlers whose excavators had turned

their landscapes inside out. Even though heavy extraction had wreaked havoc on traditional economies of subsistence mining and gardening, many residents of mining villages attributed their new deprivation not to the "illegal" mines, but to the state government that was bringing them to a standstill.

Chapter 2 scales up to those "illegal" mines and explores the extractive lifeworlds that emerge under conditions of state penalization. Facing impossible formalization schemes and hefty punishments for working informally, excavator and dredge miners described themselves as being "abandoned" by the national government. The chapter highlights the affectively charged experience of such abandonment and gives insight into how the "larger" miners made sense of being stigmatized by politicians, persecuted by defense forces, and left to fend for themselves against criminal groups.

After we have observed how state governance impacts mining regions, the book's second part, *Performing the State*, stipulates how these regions themselves give form to state-building. Part II consists of three chapters that together destabilize the imagery of statelessness that pervades much writing on gold frontiers. Chapter 3 details how miners, rather than being solely trampled by legislation, actively influenced how state law revealed itself in everyday life. Although most miners saw their political situation as hopeless, they nevertheless continued to engage with the bureaucracy, while using and interpreting legal categories in ways that were at cross purposes with official designs. One form of such legal appropriation particularly stood out, as it occurred in the places where state law felt most absent: the excavator pits. While lacking the required mining titles, excavator miners anticipated that some simulacrum of legality would reduce the risk of being targeted by police actions. And so they reforested landscapes and accumulated official documents, performing a modicum of a formal property regime in sites where that regime had not yet arrived top-down.

Chapters 4 and 5 extend this argument of bottom-up state-making to Afro-Colombian community councils, whose leaders assumed the governance of informal mining activities. Based on fieldwork along the Bebará River, Chapter 4 shows that such "underground" governance—although consisting of the organization, taxation, and policing of a wildcat economy—was predicated on claims, practices, and documents that made affective appeals to multicultural law. Rather than presenting one more example in which "neoliberal multiculturalism" restrains the autonomy of multicultural subjects, the chapter brings into focus the organizational practices by which local leaders themselves created Black collective territories.

Chapter 5 trains its focus on the village of La Peña to probe deeper into the ordinary social arrangements and conflicts to which ethno-cultural governance gives rise. It lays out the tensions that gold-governing community leaders face in seeing their authority respected. The chapter identifies an unfolding of contentious economic relations in the voids of formal regulatory mechanisms, whereby leaders, miners, and landholders simultaneously work together and against one another in the scramble for gold. Although secrecy and conflict mark these relations, the chapter demonstrates that the micro-politics of gold also foster pragmatic attitudes of compromise and reconciliation.

The third part of the book, *Governing Miners*, puts these underground politics in dialogue with public servants. It demonstrates that the bottom-up state-making of miners and community leaders does not just conjure state power in the interstices of bureaucracy; it is also constitutive of, and depends on, the governing activities of the state apparatus. Chapter 6 fleshes out the role of subnational officials in mining. Written as a rejection of monolithic representations of the state, it paints a picture of local bureaucrats as pragmatic rulers whose governing had more to do with the nuances of local power relations than strict allegiances to legal mandates. The chapter illustrates that gold forged surprising relationships between community leaders, miners, and state agents, which brought clandestine activities into curious compliance with formal law. Widening the analysis to centralized state planning, Chapter 7 makes further visible how small-scale mining straddled the line between legality and illegality. It discusses two formalization schemes that partly resulted from grassroots organizing: a regional formalization pilot made possible by community leaders in Bebará; and the implementation of "traditional mining reserves," propelled by a nationwide miner strike. The chapter reveals that both initiatives eventually mismatched with local expectations and did little to challenge the political status quo.

Finally, the conclusion recapitulates the book's main arguments to make wider reflections on state-making. The people whose lives I document show that the study of resource politics cannot be restricted to formal governing techniques (or their failures), but must also bring into the purview of analysis the desires and actions through which people outside the bureaucracy get a grip on the state. The conclusion also draws on recent visits to Chocó to take stock of the Colombian "post-conflict" and developments in mining and formalization. I caution against an a priori celebratory view of formalization, calling attention to several menaces that accompany initiatives to legalize gold extraction.

PART I

Underground Lifeworlds

CHAPTER 1

═══════

Forests of Afterward

Chocó is one of the departments that
will disappear.

—*Lucho (artisanal miner)*

He trod the makeshift mud trail with admirable agility. I struggled to keep up with him. In these forests, he easily outpaced me. His name was Esteban, but this mattered little in a region where familiarity hinges on nicknames. He told me to call him "Tagachí." He would teach me how to mine, he and his company of four: a teenager and three primary schoolers. It was a Monday, but since Colombia was honoring the Holy Week before Easter, the children had the day off. They used it productively, earning a fistful of pesos by assisting Tagachí in his mine, a diesel-powered pump that awaited us farther ahead. Chocoanos have been mining with these pumps for decades. The pumps deliver the power to suction water, which miners use to hose down gold-bearing walls of earth. But more on those walls later.

A week earlier, Tagachí had been working with a friend at another pump. Fearing that their clandestine work would be discovered by the police, the two men had abandoned the operation, leaving a decent gold deposit unworked. "People told us not to mine there, because you're not allowed to dirty the water," Tagachí said as I trailed along behind him over a forest floor of dirt, roots, and moss. "So, we left. You better leave than have the government damage your pump." His words were peppered with cynicism. "How can they damage our pumps, if this is our subsistence? My wife is pregnant and they want to damage my pump."

That day, he would try his luck with a different water pump at a different spot. As we trudged closer to the pump, and farther away from the village, the jungle oddly began to feel more human. A provisional path of rotten planks unrolled before us. It had been placed there, put to use, and later deserted by excavator miners. The footpath's decay was a tacit reminder of the illicitness of their trade: It had not been maintained since the majority of these wildcatters had abandoned the woods, unwilling to await the police actions that every so often sought to sweep Chocó clean of "illegal" mines.

In addition to being rotten, the planks were slippery. Their low traction slowed me down, increasing the distance between me and Tagachí and the children. The wood's treacherous state was the result of the night's rainfall, a surprising downpour that had ended a multiday drought. But while navigating the wet planks, we encountered nothing but heat. Skin-leaking, shirt-sticking, socks-itching heat. When we had started out on our walk, the leafy trees had still provided a chilly shade. Yet the farther we journeyed along the rain-soaked planks, the easier it became for sunbeams to pierce through the forest roof and hammer down on us. The evidence was irrefutable. We were walking straight into the death of the jungle; we were walking into deforested mining fields. The thinning foliage was only the start of it, as our passage became increasingly lined by graveled slopes, rain-filled craters, and gray swaths of barren land.

And then the forest stopped.

It just stopped.

Standing on a hilltop, a sea of green at our backs, we looked out on a gut-wrenching island of stones. Stones and more stones. Hectares of them. Our naked eyes saw no end in sight.

Tagachí led us down onto the moonscape. Bathed in sunlight, we followed a bifurcated path carved out by the caterpillar tracks of one or more hydraulic excavators. As consequence of its disuse, tall grass and stray water streams had invaded it. Yet, walking the path, I recognized a landscape that was anything but lifeless. In the midst of all the gravel and pebbles, a few hesitant cecropia and balsa saplings had managed to find soil worthy to grow in. Far beyond these infant trees, distant ridges of native bush stood proud and tall on each of our flanks, looking down in all their green splendor on the in-between valley of rocks. (The gold rush, I now know, had left these ridges standing, since the diesel required to dismantle them outweighed the lure of striking underlying gold-filled sands.) There was also a distant sound: the growling excavators of Gerson, one of the few white settlers who had not removed his camp from the forest.

What's more, by walking in good companionship, I discovered that lifelessness lies in the eye of the beholder. Tagachí and I were not sharing the same view. We were not walking the same landscape. To him, the slopes of rocks and diverted creeks were not tokens of nature's death but trophies of past labor. As we passed turquoise, chemical-saturated pools that had been the outcome of heavy excavation, Tagachí pointed out the spots where he had worked as an excavator driver. Naively, I asked him what he thought of the environmental effects of his labor.

"I don't think anything about that," he said. "I think the earth sustains the poor. If not, it's just lowering your head. I don't understand why they're giving us such a hard time. They are harming the good ones. They are screwing over the poor who want to work."

I responded with deafening silence. Driving the diesel-hungry earthmovers, Tagachí had earned over three times the Colombian minimum wage. "How much do you make with your pump?" I eventually ventured to ask.

"Buh, just enough to get by. I used to have money for the wife, the kids, and kept the rest so I could drink my soda pops."

"So, you miss the excavators?"

"Money was good," he said. "That I liked. What I did not like is that they sometimes don't pay you."

"When the mine doesn't produce?"

"Aha! Now we start to understand each other. That is why I like to work alone. Not depending on anyone!"

Later in this chapter, we'll arrive at the gold mines. Here I stick to walking. I mention this vignette in part because it acquaints us with how miners in Chocó perceived their work. More than anything, Tagachí's remarks are illustrative of how they understood their political dislocation, how they coined pragmatic arguments of gold appropriation to counter (insensitive) statements of forest appreciation, and why they preferred certain excavation techniques over others—pesos mattered, but so did "not depending on anyone." But most of all I bring up this walk to introduce the socio-temporal context of this ethnography, being situated after a gold rush. The story of the Chocó of my fieldwork was to a large extent the story of "forests of afterward," where low-tech miners dug up the leftovers of previous extraction, where grievances festered about elapsed years of mineral abundance, and where a few stubborn excavator miners continued their forest-razing work at the risk of legal persecution. The current chapter charts out this extractive afterlife, while foregrounding the vantage point of the local artisanal miners living it. To be more precise, the chapter examines how chocoanos in mining regions made meaning of the "illegal" excavators that had turned up in their forests, as well as of the state politics geared toward eradicating the machines.

The Extractive Locomotive—and Its Discontents

First, a brief elucidation of these politics. In 2001, the Colombian government adopted a new mining code (Law 685), which served to render the country more attractive for investment. Whereas in 1996 a privatization-prescribing World Bank paper had singled out Colombia as one of three "major [Latin American] countries still to be reformed" (World Bank 1996:6), Law 685 read like an unapologetic emblem of neoliberal doctrine. The law validated a private title as the single legal leverage "to explore and exploit mines that are state property" (Congreso de Colombia 2001: Art. 14), limiting the responsibility of state institutions to regulating the industry. Moreover, by defining mining as an activity of "public interest" and permitting "expropriations of immovable properties and other constituted rights over these" (Art. 13), the mining code increased the legal leeway with which mining corporations could dispossess local communities. And in a further wooing of foreign investment, the code extended mining titles to a period of thirty years (Art. 70), during which titleholders were exempted from alterations in royalty regulation (Art. 228) and needed to request an environmental license for their activities only once (Art. 207, 208).

The early 2000s was a time of great extractive expectation for Latin America as a whole. Expanding consumer and industry markets in Asia and elsewhere (Bebbington et al. 2013:244), along with technological innovations (Doughtery 2011:406), had made the unearthing of minerals and hydrocarbons significantly more profitable. Against these odds, Latin American governments on both the "neoextractivist" left (Gudynas 2009) and the hitherto extractivist right envisaged subterranean resources as a panacea for development. A genuine "commodities consensus" (Svampa 2015) took hold in the region, whereby policymakers wagered on projects of mineral, oil, coal, and gas extraction to make good on their promises of social policies and economic growth.[1]

Government expectations in Colombia were not much less. If anything, the impact of the 2001 law was immediate. In the wake of its passing, Colombia witnessed a genuine titles frenzy, which acquired increased force due to transnational (the increased demand for raw materials) and domestic (lowered royalties and taxes, and fewer security risks due to the waning presence of the FARC) factors. Then, the second decade of the new millennium upped the ante dramatically, as mining became one of the key imperatives of the national development agenda. In 2011, the freshly installed Santos government identified the mining and energy sector as one of the country's five "locomotives of growth and employment provision" (PND 2011:13). Mining alone was estimated to contribute to 4.8 percent of economic growth during the coming four years of presidency (43). However, in many parts of Colombia, the extractive locomotive fueled not so much growth as conflicts over land, water, and minerals between the new companies and people living in the vicinity of their projects. In several of these conflicts, tensions took a dramatic turn, with community resistance resulting in violence and enforced displacement at the hands of organized crime groups (PBI 2011; Vélez-Torres 2014).

Amid the turmoil of mine concessions, development plans, and social protest, small-scale alluvial and tunnel miners continued to dig up gold, emeralds, coal, platinum, sand, and other substances. They had washed earth and cloven rocks for decades—or centuries, if we consider their mining bloodlines—in places where during the bloodshed of the war few multinationals had dared to set foot. The new mining code declared many of these domestic miners "illegal" when it removed previous legal distinctions between extraction scales. Mechanized mining began to be treated as a single legal category—"legal" only in the presence of a concession contract (i.e., mining title) and an environmental license—notwithstanding the vast technological differences between multinationals and, say, a water pump miner like Tagachí.

Fast-forward to the second half of the 2010s (the period that covered my fieldwork), and we find miners continuing to work in informality. Estimates at the time indexed 88 percent of Colombian exported gold to derive from "illegal" operations (*Portafolio* 2016). Several factors explain this. First and foremost, complicated formalization procedures mismatched with the resources available to small operators. Domestic miners lacked the technical expertise, relationships, and, above all, finances that were necessary to carry out the geological and environmental studies leading to concession contracts and environmental licenses. It would take a staggering number of hours to dive, spade, or hose together the gold needed for the geologist's fees, lawyer's costs, and traveling expenses inherent to the formalization process.

But there were other complications. For one thing, miners faced an enclosure of workspace. Even if they had the cash and patience to sit through titling procedures, there was little room left to mine formally. In Chocó, much land had been designated as national forest reserve, where no extraction was allowed. An additional enclosure, less specific to Chocó, was the usurpation of subsoil, seeing as multinationals, in contrast to small operators, had acquired concession contracts with relative ease.

For another thing, the governmental bodies tasked with formalizing struggled mightily to process the high number of title requests. This problem reached back further than my fieldwork. In effect, as the demand for concessions exploded in succession of the mining code, so did the Colombian mining cadaster. In 2011, all titling requests were temporarily suspended because the institution charged with processing them collapsed under the avalanche of individual procedures.

With all this being said, small-scale miners' political woes amounted to more than lacking the right papers. In the 2010s, an official discourse emerged that designated informal gold extraction as a mostly criminal activity that was harming the nation. The discourse rested on three pillars. The first was public security. In governing a country struggling to move away from half a century of civil war, Colombian lawmakers cast unlicensed extraction as a hindrance to durable peace. In interviews and press releases, they associated miners with criminal groups, which were well known to tax and run mining operations and use them to launder cocaine profits. In this light, former president Santos classified "illegal mining" as "a cancer that we must extirpate" (El Espectador 2012), "a business . . . that moves more money than narco-trafficking," and "an enemy that is much more powerful, much more dangerous, and one that does much more harm than we initially thought" (Semana 2015c).

The second pillar was nature. Colombia's succeeding ministers of the Environment went out of their way to denounce miners' ecological footprint, decrying especially their deforestation and mercury contamination. Along these lines, the 2016–2018 minister Luis Gilberto Murillo, himself a chocoano, asserted that "the negative impact of illegal mining represents one of the worst attacks against nature and the environment," and accordingly called for "combatting [illegal mining] until eliminating it" (El Tiempo 2016).

Finally, small-scale miners were framed as detrimental to growth. State emissaries invoked miners' unpaid taxes to claim that they were an impediment to Colombia's economic development, and by extension, to bolster the image of the unpopular large-scale mining industry. Take note of the words of Silvana Habib, former president of the National Mining Agency (tasked with formalizing miners), who in a 2016 column in a news daily wrote that "each day legal mining companies lose space and capital because of this atrocious crime [illicit exploitation]." After steering us along the deficits of illegal extraction—"child labor," "labor exploitation," the nonpayment of "taxes and royalties"—Habib's opinion piece declared that "illicit exploitation is nothing but stealing state resources. They are stealing from all of us" (*El Espectador* 2016).

Such framing of gold miners as a three-pronged menace carried consequences that went beyond language, insofar as it offered ideological backing to a judicial regime of punitive measures. Colombian jurisprudence not only informalized, but also very much penalized the smaller pits and tunnels. Already in 2001, the mining code stipulated that mechanized miners working outside a title were working "illicitly" and should be disciplined in accordance with penal law (Congreso de Colombia 2001: Art. 160). However, it was not until 2010, when President Santos took office, that the game was afoot, as heavily armed defense forces began actively arresting miners and seizing their equipment. Two years into the Santos administration, the Ministry of Defense issued Decree 2235, allowing for the destruction of machinery by the police and army. Although few of the chocoanos I spoke to owned machinery that was destroyed under the arrangement, most of them did abhor the police and army missions, for these had meant the painful disintegration of their local gold rush. Lucho was one of the critics.

Forests of Afterward

At Lucho's invitation, I stood waist-deep in the shallow creek swirling in front of his house. The stream represented nothing of the pristine images that Chocó's curling rivers evoke on internet search engines. Soda cans, candy wrappers, and plastic utensils littered both banks, and a preponderance of rocks, swept down from higher-up excavator mines, had reduced to a timid current what had once been the town's aquatic life vein. It was here that I jotted down field notes on how Lucho shuffled up mud, gravel, and rocks, over and over again, only to unload it all, over and over again, onto his *matraca*, a two-meter-long wooden sluice box. The matraca was suspended at a twenty-degree angle over a small dam of rocks. It received an incessant flow of water, meshing the sludge that Lucho released on top of it. Such "washing," as Lucho called it, permitted loosened sand to drift down and gold specks, being heavier than sand, to sink and become trapped in the burlap cloths covering the matraca.

Digging, lifting, dumping. Again. And again. And again and again. Lucho's routine operated like clockwork. Lifting was the hard part. It had to go "*lento*" (slow), he said, dragging out the letter "e" as though to emphasize the slowness of slow. If he lifted too fast, the underwater slit from which he extracted the gold-bearing sludge would fill with rocks, impeding further excavation. In fact, rocks were the nemesis of the whole operation. Quite regularly, Lucho stumbled on river cobbles that prevented him from shuffling further. Though he could remove most cobbles by hand, some were so stubbornly rooted in the streambed that they only loosened up after some vigorous rigging with a four-edged metal bar (*barretón*). Then there were those annoying pebbles that, despite Lucho's slow spading, succeeded, in the following order, to enter the underwater slit, sneak onto his spade, fall down on the sluice box, and block the washing water's flow. To resolve this issue, he had tasked his two adolescent sons with tossing away the pebbles at the sluice's lower end. Every now and then, he told them to keep pace. Their task was after all an indispensable one. If stones stopped the water flow, sediment would be left unmeshed and gold left unsunk. His sons, he said, assisted him each morning, with their mother substituting for them in the afternoon at the start of their school classes. "If you work alone," Lucho preached solemnly, "you work yourself to death."

His insistence on working with others was borne out of experience. He had precedent to fall back on. Two weeks before standing beside him in the creek, I interviewed him at his house about his economic past, present, and future. He explained that a few years back, he had made a killing while operating someone else's excavator. This was apart from the money he had received by renting out his family lands to yet another excavator miner. But these income streams had long run dry, and in the absence of other opportunities for collaboration, Lucho was now back to backbreaking work. And I mean this literally, for each spading cycle appeared to worsen the chronic backaches he suffered due to a life full of mining. Yet at nearly fifty years of age, with a shattered spine and no primary education diploma, Lucho reasoned that he lacked the qualifications to find employment outside mining. "At my age," he asked rhetorically, "which company will give me work?"

And so he stood waist-deep in the creek: digging, lifting, dumping, one spade at a time, one loosened cobble at a time, one possible gold treasure at a time, one twinge of back pain at a time. As on any other weekday, he spaded away the hours until the afternoon was late, the back was sore, and the gold required collecting. Under the dimmed sun, he removed the cloths from his matraca and sponged them in a *batea*, a wooden pan of paella-cooking proportion. He massaged the batea's content smoothly and cautiously, making sure that no gold-carrying sand was lost to the creek. Once the batea had reaped all sand and gravel from the cloths, he subjected it to a two-hand spinning rotation, pausing now and again to remove unwelcome gravel by hand. The centrifugal force pushed the lighter sand out of the batea and allowed the heavier gold to settle down in the pan's belly. Rotation became faster and wilder as the batea's content decreased, until only a fistful of *jagua* (black pay dirt) and gold specks remained. Lucho poured the black-yellow hybrid into a *betadora*, a smaller pan, in which he washed away most of the pay dirt by hand-pouring it with water while tilting the pan. He then took the mixture of gold and remaining jagua to his house next to the stream, where he heated it on a metallic plate above a gas burner. When the mixture dried out, he tapped the plate to separate particles of jagua from the gold, at the same time that he gently blew the particles away. He wrapped the now-purified gold dust, which according to his calculations was worth "no more than 30 thousand pesos" (10 USD), in a small piece of paper, so that it was ready to be taken to one of the town's buyer intermediaries. The latter usually did all the tapping and the blowing, but Lucho was a skilled do-it-yourselfer and, above all, a skeptic about the buyers' blowing precision. At least in his kitchen, he said, there was no chance that no gold would fly away from no plate.

It's fascinating stuff, this jagua. After I shared with him some of the mining lessons I had picked up from Lucho and others, a young man told me that previous generations of miners never threw the pay dirt away, because it always retained a few minuscule bits of gold. He explained that people used to bury the jagua in their yards, in this way building their own gold treasuries, their savings for worse times ahead. I met no one who continued with the practice. Listening to research participants, it felt as though the worse times were no longer ahead. One miner joked that, if jagua had any gold, it made more sense to directly squeeze it out in light of today's poverty. Indeed, the

chance of a gold-filled batea has drastically decreased in recent decades, especially for those who like Lucho work without mechanized equipment. So
how did it come to this? And why was Lucho working his back off for "no
more than thirty thousand pesos," a fraction of what he used to make a few
years ago doing much less demanding work?

For answers, we need to rewind a bit. In the late 1980s, white settler miners
started transporting hydraulic excavators from the Andean highlands into
the far-flung corners of the Chocó rainforest. Initially, the *retreros*, as they
were called (from *retro*, or *retroexcavadora*, which is Spanish for "excavator"),
undertook the El Dorado pilgrimage in small numbers. Yet when the gold
price skyrocketed after the 2008 financial crisis, the white settlers came in
droves. They uncovered parts of the underground that the spades and pumps
of local miners had never been able to reach. In exchange for a portion of the
profits, landholding families permitted the outsiders to mine their lands. The
outsiders turned their lands inside out.

But while the forest wept, the economy prospered. Even though the newcomers kept the lion's share of the gold, smallholder families benefited from
mine rents. Additionally, local men and women were employed in well-paid
jobs as rank-and-file workers, drivers, cooks, and mine administrators, with
a lucky few earning enough to buy their own excavators. And above all, there
was this new thing called *bareque*, a satellite form of extraction whereby miners use hand tools to dig out the mud walls (sometimes several dozen meters
high) of an excavator mining cut. Rather than still having to set up matracas
and dams in the river, the *barequeros* now enjoyed access to deeper and richer
gravels in the slopes of mining pits, all set to be attacked with shovels and
pans.[2] When reminiscing about these golden heydays, people narrated anecdotes that vacillated between the incredible and the hyperbolical. Back
then, I learned, rumors about prosperous excavator pits swept across the department, and barequeros hurried to the remote sources of the rumors.
Back then, lucky barequeros could make as much as 2,000 to 3,000 USD a
day. Back then, one very rich mine was worked by hundreds, if not thousands,
of barequeros at once.

The retreros were still combing the jungle for gold when I lived in Chocó
in 2017. However, as they risked the detonation of their machines at the
hands of public forces, their numbers had fallen significantly. While interlocutors estimated that in 2014–2015 their municipalities had twenty or

thirty excavator mines, by 2017 I encountered municipalities with only five excavators, or ten, or even just three. Though most people understood this decline to be the result of legal persecution alone, some noted that gold itself was a mediating variable. In the depleted lands, fuel costs increasingly outweighed lucky spells, and many retreros found themselves forced to rework the patches that others had already mined. In other words, it seemed it was not only the risk of equipment destruction, but also the decreasing geological rewards the miners received for running this risk, that had led to a significant cutback in excavator mines—and, accordingly, of employment, land rents, and bareque. Amid these circumstances, miners like Lucho lamented that there was little more to do than to resume the same rudimentary techniques they had abandoned during the bonanza.

It is this messy historicity that is missed by outside observers of Chocó who commend manual extraction techniques in a language of cultural continuity. In recent years, I have read and heard policymakers, academics, activists, and journalists heaping praise on panning (or *mazamorreo*, as it's locally known) as a sustainable cultural heritage that has persisted despite the mayhem of illegal excavator mines. However, much of the mazamorreo in my fieldwork was about *discontinuity*. To be sure, ancestral extraction generated a sense of pride. Miners spoke with affection about the time a younger version of themselves had cut their teeth at the artisanal mining streams, pits, and tunnels by working with, looking at, and listening to parents and grandparents. They also expressed admiration for their earliest of forebears, who had endured the monstrosities of slavery while working the same goldfields where they now toiled. Indeed, the spirits of older and newer ancestors continued to inhabit the mines; in anecdotes, in memories, in materials left behind in the subsoil—visible to those who knew how to look. Yet the moral economy of today's miners was a complex one, and their stories were shot through with much more temporal nuance than those told by the nonchocoanos acclaiming their cultural history. Having previously enjoyed direct (employment) or indirect (rents, bareque) gold winnings from excavator mines, many interlocutors described panning less as a laudable cultural constant, than as a *return* to no longer rentable extraction. This return, moreover, did not imply an environmental victory but a reappearance of the poverty of the pre-boom years; or of something worse, as the gold in the underground's uppers layers had now been excavated away. Far from being a time-defying tradition that persevered in the shadow of destructive

Figure 2. The rainforest after the gold rush. Photo by the author.

extraction, manual mining labor demonstrated the confusing time experience of gold frontiers, where booms go bust, dreams fizzle out in deception, new technologies cannibalize older ones (and vice versa), and lines between before and now, past and present, and modern and traditional are not always easy to draw.[3] To many miners, mazamorreo was *both* the traditional work that preceded the retreros and the compulsory stuff that came after.

Lucho is a case in point. When I interviewed him, he drew a bleak picture of his unmechanized operation, and that is putting it mildly: "Imagine working the matraca, every single day. With the excavators I made my two million [pesos] per month, two million-and-a-half. I had food for my kids. And now this, imagine doing this all day, for 12 thousand pesos!" He didn't see himself mining for much longer, not because of his back, but because gold could no longer be found manually, leading him to state that "Chocó is one of the departments that will disappear." Like others, he desired a future for his children outside of the mines. But he also knew that the odds of this hinged on expensive education. And how to mine together the tuition fees? "My son is now finishing secondary school," he said. "And me without money, how am I going to put him through university? So, he is stuck. In Colombia, a high school degree doesn't mean anything."

Other miners spoke similar words of resignation. By and large, perceptions about future livelihoods were gloomy. Most of the upper gold had been exhausted, while the war against excavators was bound to grind on. Stranded in this extractive impasse, Chocó's mining forests seemed to maintain a quality of posteriority. Most evidently, the posteriority was ecological. Having been unearthed year after year by excavators, large chunks of the woods resembled residual ecologies bereft of flora and fauna. Yet these forests also gave the impression of being situated *after* prosperity. In the face of adverse politics, most retreros had disappeared, as had the opportunities to earn on them. What remained were what I came to interpret as "forests of afterward": places where "easy" gold was running out and where worries flourished about a foreseeable future without the mines. In these forests, working the way of the ancestors did not always yield enough money to get by. As such, many chocoanos, and young adults in particular, were no longer motivated to pan in the streams. They opted for higher incomes in more technically advanced forms of extraction (using mechanical water pumps and small dredges) or other segments of the informal economy, building houses, driving motorcycle taxis, or hustling in restaurants, garages, and stores. For example, as we drove on his scooter past a group of panners in a stream, William, a merchant in his early thirties, said: "I would be embarrassed if people saw me like that. Those are only older people who cannot do anything else. I'm a businessman. I make around 800,000 pesos a month. For them in the stream, it's only about food. My parents worked like that. We never had a television or a refrigerator. In my house you do see those kinds of things."

However, mazamorreo was not the only livelihood suffering the economy of afterward. While still producing higher quantities of gold, artisanal miners relying on water pumps also complained about leftover subsoils. At the same time, business was bad in the town. Gold traders had lost grip on their raison d'être, liquor stores and restaurants had emptier pockets to cater to, and motorcycle taxi drivers had seen their miner clientele convert into competition, as an increasing number of people began to fully dedicate themselves to non-extractive jobs. Arguably, the sudden end of the gold rush had made work rationalities increasingly "about food," including for merchants like William. He and others were participating in a post-boom economy that was a far cry from the tropes of peace, law and order, and development "locomotives" that central government functionaries appealed to when explaining the destruction of excavator mines. But before I analyze these local grievances further, I need to give a brief introduction to the mines around which they revolved.

Picturing the Excavator Mines

It was white outsiders who in the late 1980s brought the excavators to Chocó, and some thirty years later, it was still white outsiders who comprised a large share of the retreros. Chocoanos called them *paisas*. In Colombia, "paisa" refers to someone from the department of Antioquia, yet in Chocó the term is equally employed as a racial category denoting whites in general. Apart from people from Antioquia (Chocó's neighbors to the east), paisas may likewise include whites from the central coffee region, Bogotá, Quibdó (Chocó's capital), and even the Netherlands. Nonetheless, many retreros I spoke to self-identified as not paisas but *bajocaucanos*; that is, people from the Bajo Cauca, the northeastern region of Antioquia that lies a six-hour bus journey away from Medellín (the city where, according to the bajocaucanos, the paisas are from). Many bajocaucanos and paisas had traded in Antioquia for Chocó at the height of the mining boom in the late 2000s, early 2010s, being pulled by promises of unworked subsoils and pushed by the violence of paramilitaries and guerrillas, for which Antioquia's mining zones are notorious.

Though articulated in many a fieldwork conversation, the common truth that excavator miners were paisas was actually a half-truth. Chocoanos (mostly men) made up a substantial segment of the retrero population as both owners and workers. Still, there clung an unmistakable foreignness to the excavator mines. Workers, including the chocoano ones, were often brought in from other municipalities, because skillful drivers and motivated rank-and-filers were hard to come by. In being from elsewhere, they remained largely unswayed by the banalities of village life. They played their dominos, forged their friendships, and prayed to their God in their mining encampments above anywhere else. Mine owners, or *dueños*, were even less place-bound, as they enjoyed higher economic mobility and were often settlers from Antioquia. Even on the shores of the Bebará River, where quite exceptionally most excavators were locally owned, the majority of dueños rarely sojourned into the village, instead splitting their time between their remote mines and the comforts of Quibdó.

The dueños were a demographic that defied easy categorization, and not just due to their diverse regional and ethnic identities. Financial fortune had not befallen them equally. A lucky few had more than ten state-of-the-art machines spread across different mines. Others tried their luck with second-, third-, or fourth-hand vehicles, bought via quota payments or with money borrowed from gold buyers, who in exchange demanded the sole right to purchase their gold. Yet whatever the dueños' inventory, their workforces largely shared the same characteristics. At the top of the labor hierarchy stood the administrator. Habit dictated that this was the same person as the dueño, for many owners had been miners "since being in the bellies of their mothers," to use their jargon. In addition, a mine camp had one or two cooks, often women, as well as two operators per excavator who interchanged day and night shifts. The majority of workers, though, carried out various auxiliary tasks (*oficios varios*), such as hosing earth, repairing equipment, and assisting operators. Many aspired to become operators themselves, because driving the excavators was less tiresome and rewarded with higher pay.[4]

The work cycle of retreros follows more or less the same steps as Lucho's extraction: preparing the site, extracting the sediments, and washing the sediments to collect the gold. At the beginning, miners pan earth samples to decide on a possibly productive location. When a site is chosen, their excavators remove superimposed layers of vegetation and dirt, resulting in a large pit (*plana*), the volume of one or several swimming pools. From inside this pit, a chain of excavators moves gold-bearing earth upward and outward. The lowest-positioned machine stacks earth on a pile (*mochila*), which is collected by a second machine that passes it onto a possible third, and so forth. Power is in numbers: the more excavators, the larger the chain, the deeper the dig, the higher the yield. (However, most dueños I met owned two vehicles.) The chain's destination is the classification device. In clayey lands, miners rely on a system of contiguous sluice boxes placed diagonally on a slope. In rocky lands, stones are more easily separated with a "classifier" (*clasificadora*), a metal trough three stories high that crisscrosses downward. With both separation systems, water pumped up from nearby creeks and pools flushes away gravel and sand, while gold attaches to plastic cloths, which in the final stage of washing are rinsed in buckets and bateas.

This work cycle has a deleterious impact on the rainforest. To prepare the pit, retreros tear down plants and trees. Later, when washing has begun, they discard tailings in creeks and rivers, thereby clogging water bodies and disturbing the reproductive cycles of fish. And in the mine's afterlife, retreros almost invariably leave their exhausted pits unfilled, preferring to spend their time and fuel on carving out new cuts into the earth surface. The abandoned craters dotted throughout the forest fill up with rain and soil water, and become breeding grounds for malaria-carrying mosquitos. Then of course there is also mercury, the most controversial ill of all. Retreros sprinkle the silverish liquid on the cloths of sluice boxes. Although this helps to trap gold, mercury itself inevitably slips away from the sluice. In this escape, it washes into waterscapes, rendering people who consume local water and fish vulnerable to brain and kidney poisoning, to which mercury ingestion progressively correlates.[5] Yet miners themselves are specifically vulnerable to intoxication. Once their wash operations are concluded, they roast their gold-mercury amalgams and inhale a toxic gaseous mercury that oxidizes in their kidneys.

Mercury ingestion is symptomatic of the wider labor hardship that retrero workers face on a day-to-day basis. By all means, their mines are the wildcat frontier incarnate. Excavator operators maneuver their machines treacherously close to the crater's edge, towering a dozen, or several dozen, meters above the surface. For their part, *chorristas* (charged with hosing down earth on classifiers) hold a water tube in each hand, an outstandingly exhausting task that because of the water pressure requires exceptional arm muscles. In the meantime, they put their bodies at the mercy of heat, downpours, and even thunderstorms, since most dueños expect them to climb on their classifiers come rain or shine. What's more, excavator engines are not turned off at night. Miners rotate nocturnal shifts, with half of the workforce resting during the hot hours of the day. And resting is a daunting task in these treeless wastelands! Miners sleep between the mud and rock of their operations, in hammocks slung inside sun-blasted plastic shacks. This provisional accommodation is befitting of miners' impermanent settlement patterns, whereby camps are routinely built and abandoned according to the logistics of production.

Before visiting Chocó, a stint of desk research had made me expect that local communities would have an adversarial relationship with such mining. Newspaper and civil society accounts usually paint a picture of invasion in their coverage of Colombian gold frontiers. These accounts speak of timber-felling, mercury pollution, river sedimentation, and armed violence. They speak, on some occasions, of excavators and dredges that "day in day out rip out the treasures from the Chocó rainforest" (*Semana* 2013), of "hellish underworlds of deforestation, sex trafficking, forced displacement and child labor" (*Miami Herald* 2018), and of armed groups that "intimidate and forcibly recruit [local residents] to search for gold, or subject them to extortion" (*Newsweek* 2016).

Much social research echoes this tenor of coercion. Tianna Paschel (2016:194) describes "illegal and state-sanctioned extractive mining operations" inside a community council in the Upper Atrato in Chocó. She discerns an "increasingly entangled relationship between community members who were either coerced at gunpoint or understandably lured by the prospect of extracting in one day what took weeks using traditional methods" (194). Along similar lines, Irene Vélez-Torres (2016) documents how Afro-descendant community leaders in the southwestern Cauca department protest an invasive resource regime consisting of illegal excavator pits and multinational companies. She documents a situation of "accumulation by dispossession" (243), which is founded on the violence of "illegal armed groups that have guarded both legal mining operations and illegal mining backhoes" (241).

There is no doubt that the narrative of invasion is an urgent one. The wrenching pains of excavators are impossible to miss. The dentures of their buckets maim trees. Their spillage plunges rivers into carnage. Their gold has a mercury pull on armed groups. And yet, at least in Chocó, invasion is by no means the whole story of retrero-community relations. To be sure, I met people in mining villages who described similar scenes as those rendered by the journalistic sources cited above. These people condemned what was perceived as the deterioration of traditional life at the hands of paisas, who had ruined their lands and replaced values of companionship and soberness—germane to artisanal mining—with land conflicts, alcoholism, laziness, and childhood pregnancies. Nevertheless, lots of research participants told a different story, one that favored the excavators. They, too, had recognized the corrosion of the social fabric, but linked it not to the arrival of intensified extraction but to its subsequent demise. When they yearned for the past, they did not reach very far back into history. Rather than the once-abundant mazamorreo and tunnel mines, they missed the excavators that had succeeded the artisanal techniques.

Such extractive nostalgia makes a jarring contrast with conventional portrayals of coercion and resistance. These were artisanal miners who weren't "[intimidated] and forcibly [recruited]," "lured," or "coerced at gunpoint." On the contrary, they welcomed the new extraction. Compared with grassroots resistance against the gold frontier, these welcoming stances have remained rather unaccounted for in scholarly and popular accounts. As anthropologist Daniel Tubb (2015:723) points out, "the literature fails to make clear . . . what people see in various scales of mining."[6] In view of the similar deprivation and political marginality of those people embracing excavator mining, analytical scrutiny feels long overdue. Such scrutiny, I believe, should start not by describing landholders as being solely preyed upon by outsiders, but by taking seriously how they view their relationship with retreros, as well as what they hope to obtain from it. As a way to conduct such textured scrutiny, it helps to take a closer look at the economic and ecological attractions of bareque and land rents.

Praising the Excavator Mines

"Don't get in there!" Luz yelled at the group of a dozen men who, some ten meters away from us, were thrusting their spades into an earth slope, nearly vertical in inclination and at least five times as high as the men were tall. "Can't you see that peak is cracked?!" she continued, before she turned to me and mumbled, "People are stubborn."

Her worries concerned a thick, squishy layer of mud that lay atop the earth wall. It was destined to slide down. In fact, in spading out the wall's foundation, the men only brought forward the moment of breakdown. These "stubborn" barequeros encompassed the front row of an ensemble of bareque duos. The men worked in pairs with a back row of predominantly women, whose bateas washed the earth that the men loosened in a nearby silver-colored pool. Neither back nor front row paid much attention to Luz. They were goldbound. Most had started as early as 6 A.M. They had arrived in boats, readied and boarded in the full darkness of night, as this excavator pit was only accessible by river. In the first three hours, all their shoveling had been in vain. But now it seemed that waking up early and risking a nocturnal fluvial passage had not been for nothing after all. One man had successfully sampled gold. This had encouraged others to assemble in the spot of discovery, and not long after—and not minding the layer of descending mud—to combatively push and pull each other away from that spot so as to conquer the square meter of pit wall that appeared to contain most yellow-colored specks.

Along with a handful of other cautious miners, Luz had decided not to engage in the extractive rugby. Yet they were not the only observers of, rather than participants in, the danger-riddled work. Standing with us in the pit was also Romario, one of the river's *líderes de bareque*. He was among several men who had been assigned by the community councils of Bebará to maintain order during the bareque, meaning they had to ensure no one got into fights or was caught out by landslides. With his gaze fixed on the pit wall, Romario revealed that his job motivation was personal. Two years earlier his brother had been killed by a land collapse while mining. As he was telling me this, we watched the front row of barequeros making occasional backward leaps, dodging pebbles and patches of mud that had started to slide down. Several minor landslides later, the shouts of one bystander announced what everyone knew would eventually happen: "Careful, that peak is going to fall!"

A mini-glacier of bronze-colored slurry slid toward the excavation spot. The barequeros shot off, all in good time. After checking that everyone was okay, they burst out laughing. Annoyed, Romario and two other líderes de bareque came over to scold them. Standing on top of the pit wall, one of the leaders shouted that work could only continue once all remaining mud had slid down.

Not many listened. But Francia did. A *barequera* of old age, she was hesitant to defy fate and gave me company from a safe distance. "Just now people were leaving," she said, as we watched roughly the same group of spade-handling men assaulting the same death-defying pit wall. "But someone found gold, and now look at them go. Gold has its mystery."

I nodded my agreement and uttered a platitude—"*Así es* [that's right]."

"Last week in the bareque, people found a *castellano* per person,"[7] Francia added, as if to give substance to her assessment of gold's mysteriousness.

"Really?" I said. "Did you also find a castellano?"

"Nah, I wasn't there. The motor of our boat did not start."

One castellano of gold. That equaled more or less a monthly wage in a Quibdó restaurant. It puts into perspective why several barequeros did not show Francia's and Luz's restraint and instead gouged away at the pit wall, laughing land collapses in the face. Excavator pits lower barequeros to geological depths that river panners can only dream of. Though landslides and hotheaded competition make some people avoid the pits, the bareque has the power to draw many miners away from their matracas, motorized pumps, and even excavators, especially when the subsoil starts "giving." There is barely any economic risk in the bareque. There are no fuel expenditures. It's principally one's body that is at stake. In places with limited economic alternatives, many are willing to accept this trade-off with safety.

Two days after my conversation with Francia, Colombian national television reported that six barequeros had been killed by a landslide in Chocó's municipality of Tadó. To my relief, Andrés, a befriended barequero from Tadó, had remained unharmed. When I asked him later that week if he was planning on resuming his work in the pits, he was resolute: "Of course. With two children, what else can I do? It's not that I want to be there. But you must risk your life, otherwise you don't have an income."

The relationship that barequeros like Andrés, Francia, and Luz had forged with excavators was less one of invasion than one of *access*—as in, "the ability to benefit from things" (Ribot and Peluso 2003:153). They cherished the bareque for bringing them closer to gold. In point of fact, they were cherished by the retreros for exactly the same reason. By scraping out the pit walls, barequeros were doing the prospecting work for the larger miners. Their scraping and lucky spells served as leads for retreros in search of subterranean gold reserves.

Arguments of access also informed the explanations of the people who had invited the excavator miners to work their forestlands. Quite often, the landholders mentioned their lack of access to a sales market for their produce to explain why they had allowed excavators to eat away their gardening grounds in exchange for minority percentages of mine profits (12–18 percent). History had taught them that mines, and especially lucky mines, made way more money than plots of yuccas and plantains. Elongated transportation routes via land or river implied that market crops from rural Chocó were sold at bottom prices.

Of course, these justifications left unexplained the matter of why excavators were favored over more modest extractive methods. But explanations there were, and most of them focused on access to gold. Much like the barequeros, retrero-taxing landowners mentioned the depth of underground mineral deposits when clarifying the need for bigger machinery. Akin to barequeros, they—not sporadically barequeros themselves—reckoned it was no longer possible to reach productive gold bodies with pans and pumps. In the leftover status of their goldfields, they needed horsepower. Excavators delivered just that.

These arguments of access depended on individual circumstance. More or less accepting attitudes toward excavators were colored by personal histories, memories, and skills. Some had invited retreros because their old age and frail physique inhibited them from mining themselves. Some lived far away from their goldfields and presented their inactivity in farming and mining as a valid reason to have outsiders mine their plots. Some feared that unscrupulous neighboring families would lay claim to their land, and wooed miners as a way to mark off territory and secure access to gold. Some feared the future enclosure to come from the government, which presumably clamped down on Chocó's gold mines because it wanted to sell the department to mining multinationals. This last argument suggested a "before it's too late" attitude. Interlocutors felt that at least the excavator miners—unlike the multinationals—allowed them to partake in the profits.

To recap, whether driven by bareque or land rents, by limited access to gold reserves or food consumption markets, local villagers were hardly always adversaries of the migrant miners. To a large extent, villagers and retreros were washing and weighing gold together, while finding a common enemy in the punitive surveillance of the Colombian government. Digging deeper had borne fruit. In their conversations with me, residents of mining villages indexed the benefits that excavators had ceded to them. They cited plastered houses, zinc roofs, and newly bought furniture as trophies of the golden years. The more isolated the village, so it seemed, the more materially contrastive the "pre-retrero" situation. For example, on the shores of the Bebará, people mentioned that excavator mining had brought them refrigerators, cell phones, televisions, porcelain toilets, and other convenient home utilities. To them, the gold frontier did not symbolize chaos and violence. Rather, they depicted mining as the economy that had breathed life into their solitary villages during the height of the war, when the presence of the FARC had prevented NGOs, civil servants, and family members from stopping by the river. Community leader Moisés articulated well this common sentiment: "In 2000, the villages were deserted. There was no source of employment. After the excavators arrive, in 2003 more or less, people start returning to their communities. Today the villages are full of people. If you look at the houses, they are not deteriorated. They have a nice zinc roof and are painted. In the nineties, houses were made out of palm wood with roofs made from leaves."

In Bebará and elsewhere, the combination of mine employment, bareque, and land rents had also paid hospital bills and financed school uniforms, birthday parties, and funerals. Better yet, retrero gold had enabled people to send their children to university and, in the case of more remote villages, secondary schools. "The day they close down the mines, a peasant can no longer send his kid to university!" *bebareño* Manuel said. "Who will pay for it? The children of the poor don't go to university. They die at the doors of the hospital. We have lived it!"

Research participants generally agreed that excavator mining was not the extractive sin that politicians and journalists made it out to be. Many felt the government, in penalizing the regional mining economy, was denying Chocó the right to advance. As Moisés argued: "The state wants us to do traditional mining: a batea, a bar, and a spade. All legislation focuses on this. But this is only going backward. Artisanal mining is no longer possible. We have passed that stage. We also want to progress. That's what they're denying us: progress."

Still, while evoking extensive praise, the retrero revolution did have its local critics. Ultimately, the newcomers had generated not only prosperity but also forest destruction. Local concerns for this only partially touched on mercury spilling and biodiversity loss, the themes that news coverage of Chocó dwells upon. More than anything, people worried about the disappearance of the forest's resources, articulating an economic pragmatism that was akin to what ecological economist Joan Martínez-Alier (2002) defines as the "environmentalism of the poor": an environmentalism guided less by "a sacred reverence for nature" than by "a material interest in the environment as a source and a requirement for livelihood" (11).

Ecological grievances primarily centered on the disappearance of gold. The inaccessibility of gold-rich gravels that retrero advocates like Moisés brought up when pleading for "progress" was similarly noted by retrero opponents. The latter were quick to associate the exhaustion of gold deposits with the preceding years of intensive mining, pointing fingers of blame toward the families that had endorsed the arrival of the new machinery. Some critics proudly said they had resisted the temptation to engage with the paisas and boasted that their tracts continued to rely on "easy" gold. Sure enough, just as renting out lands dovetailed with the ambition to have one's tract mined before it was too late—before greedy neighbors or the greedy government confiscated one's gold—so too was the rejecting of retrero offers motivated by arguments of austerity; of keeping gold in the ground, of saving up for future generations or worse times to come.

Besides gold, excavators were criticized for robbing the land of other gems. In today's forests of afterward, there were fewer fish to catch, trees to cut, game to hunt, and plantains, yuccas, corn, and rice to harvest. Excavator mining had put under strain traditional subsistence production, most notably the gardening activities through which people had historically complemented their income from mining. Serena, who was in her sixties, was weary of the loss of vegetable crops and other forest resources. On my invitation, she participated in a group discussion in La Peña. When barequera Flor remarked that excavators had pulled the village out of poverty, Serena offered a stern reaction: "For me they did not! For me they did not! I have also worked this type of mining [bareque], but I don't like it. It has destroyed a lot. Before the excavators, you could find gold in the river right next to your house. Everything was artisanal! No dredges, no pumps, no excavators! People were cultivating their crops and wild animals still showed up. There, you had your food! Now the *guaguas* have left because of the sounds of the machines.[8] There was no hunger and living was cheap. With a grain of gold, you could buy your clothes."

Once she had finished, Flor offered some counterweight: "But there was less money."

"Yes, Flor, but the peso had more value," Serena resisted determinedly. "Many say life has improved, but I like the way we were before. You had your lot where you grew basil, pennyroyals, coriander, and onions. You had your finca and did not have to buy your tomatoes in the village."

"Yes, Serena, but it's people's own obligation to not spoil their lands with excavators," Flor said. "Gold lets me buy rice and *agua de panela* (sugarcane water), but I still have my hills of plantains and yuccas."

Discussions such as this one allow for a productive conversation with the anthropology of dispossession. In many accounts, dispossession is studied in situations in which external pressures encroach on rural communities, albeit in the form of an ill-intentioned corporate industry, organized crime groups, or enabling legal regimes (e.g., Ballvé 2012; Escobar 2008; Kirsch 2014). Rural communities, in other words, tend to be situated on the receiving end of land loss, if not as victims, then as opponents. One provocative exception comes from Tania Li's (2014) ethnography *Land's End*. Li contends that Indigenous Lauje from highland Sulawesi became immersed in capitalist relations, not through state planning or corporate creed, but through their own aspirations for change. In their attempt to escape poverty, Lauje highlanders traded in subsistence crops for the production of cloves and cacao, a choice that gradually impelled a situation of land loss (148). Cloves and cacao decreased the land available for subsistence production, which pressured farmers to fully dedicate themselves to market crops. This transformation set in motion a cycle of debt accumulation that, combined with declining soil fertility, forced many Lauje to sell their lands. However, though the decision to switch to market crops had proven unfavorable in hindsight, Li notes that even after land loss few households desired a return to their previous economies of food production: "they insisted that their future lay in cacao and announced their hope and intention of pursuing the same course that had enabled some of their neighbors to prosper" (154).

Despite the particularities of her study, Li's observations on the contentious workings of dispossession ring significantly true with chocoanos' engagement with excavators. In Chocó, many households had not been passive bystanders to the settlers who had taken their gold and crops and trees. Land as an economic resource had started to "come to an end" (Li 2014:17) partly because landowners and barequeros had taken a liking to the excavators. When interpreting this process of dispossession, research participants were very articulate in describing the harms of the excavators. They did not like their fruit trees being smashed to the ground, their fish being poisoned, and their crop gardens being devoured. Few had anticipated the vastness of the ecological catastrophe at the beginning of the extraction bonanza a decade earlier. People insisted that the decision to accept the outsiders had seemed right at the time. They only found out about the intensity of devastation after the damage had been done and after the retreros had left. And yet, contemporary attitudes displayed anything but unequivocal remorse. Despite today's ample evidence of destruction, many people expressed the hope that someday their bareque would return, their lands would be excavated again, and their money would be sufficient to buy their own yellow vehicles.

All in all, critique of forest degradation rarely translated into a complete rejection of the retreros. In the places of this research, there was a lot of gray between the skepticism of environmental defenders like Serena and the positivism of mining believers like Flor. People often lamented some of the ecological pathologies of excavators, but argued that these downsides were subordinate to everyday survival. On several occasions, the hydraulic diggers were described as "a necessary evil," which acknowledged the fact that they supplied both destruction and development. If anything, it seemed that the machinery's necessity became more urgent when the destruction was at its most evil. The perverse corollary of the gold frontier was that the retreros had set the ecological stage for their own inevitability. Of my fieldwork locales, it was in the municipality of Caliche, the place where retreros had consumed land the most avidly, where articulated wishes for bareque and mining rents appeared most numerous. The fact that excavators had done away with farmable lands and gold reserves was likely only fueling desires for high-tech excavation.

It was this pragmatism of everyday survival, so I was repeatedly informed, that national politicians had failed to fathom in their insistence to save the rainforest from the retreros. The government was seen as taking without returning, removing mines without bringing in economic alternatives, blowing up excavators without factoring in that these were poor municipalities lacking in construction equipment and infrastructure. Government discourses had presented the persecution of illegal mining as the salvation of Chocó, but here there were many chocoanos who did not require saving. In fact, even artisanal miners who held low opinions about the excavators saw the new mining regulations as an infringement on their autonomy.

Producing Autonomy

"Watch out!" Darwinson exclaimed, while making a dire facial expression. "If you look at it for too long, it will fall down."

I had just lowered myself into the *guache* (traditional tunnel mine) of which Darwinson was the administrator. He caught me gaping at a vertical wooden beam. It was an old foundation pole, the remnant of an ancient guache that he and his coworkers had tunneled into, built, by their estimates, fifty or so years ago by the *viejos*, the ancestors.[9] Soil water was gushing alongside the pole's decayed wood. Meanwhile, the rickety wooden walls of the contemporary guache—the one the miners were extending that very moment—were creaking and leaking too. Here, eight meters into the dimly lit bowels of the earth, where past was meeting present, geology made itself felt. It unnerved me.

Darwinson's creaking and leaking guache was an impressive feat of engineering. He and his team had pierced into the earth a rectangular wooden shaft about eight meters long and two meters wide. It consisted of four contiguous holes, each one diving a short two meters deeper than the last, creating the effect of a giant-stepped staircase that zigzagged into the underworld. A tricky descent over the staircase to the lowest of the four holes—whereby protruding planks served as handgrips and stepping stones—led to the entrance of a tunnel that was high enough for standing upright and wide enough for lying sideways. This subterranean passage comprised a meshwork of variously sized boards, planks, and poles, which together sheltered a muddy pathway that was enveloped in the hesitant glow of overhanging light bulbs. The tunnel was shaped in a horizontal Z-structure: It went straight for three meters, took a ninety-degree turn to the left, covered another two meters, then turned similarly drastically to the right, after which it finally arrived five meters farther at a pitch-black wall of mud. It was into this wall that Darwinson and his companion Miguel launched their metal bars, extending the artisanal mine little by little, swing by swing, in the hope of locating a gold deposit somewhere ahead. And artisanal it all was! No nail had been hammered into either staircase or tunnel; the stability and compression of the mine's timber were fully ensured by the pressure of the alluvium.

Darwinson burst out laughing. He was chiding me. Nothing would fall down. Pleased with his joke, he repeated it to his guache companions, who heartily laughed at my expense. Apart from Miguel, they were all women. Whereas Miguel and Darwinson were picking down earth chunks from the end of the tunnel, the women were in charge of disposing of the loosened chunks. Sixteen women formed two lines that started at the wall, traversed the four steps of the mine's wooden staircase, and ended outside the shaft some eight meters higher. The human chains functioned like finely tuned machines. Wooden pans were filled up and tossed over, until they could be unloaded at the top end of the chain on a ridged canal. In synchronous tandem, empty pans moved in the opposite direction shaft-inward, thus requiring the women to throw along one pan overhand while receiving the other underhand, and vice versa.

Encouraged by the miners, I too participated in the operation. To no one's surprise, and to everyone's amusement, I was the chain's weakest link. The weight of the mud made throwing the pans startlingly exhausting, while the rotation of the pans occurred at a breakneck speed I couldn't keep up with. As my undexterous hands drew the scorn of the miners' laughter, I inquired about their guache. For their part, they inquired about my stay in Chocó, my family, and my girlfriend. They asked when I would bring development projects, money, or at least a few bottles of soda pop. We settled on soda pop.

Working against the décor of the antique mining tunnel, physically akin to the one they were building themselves, the work of the *guacheros* displayed an irrefutable connection with the past. As discussed above, artisanal miners not infrequently spoke of this connection with reluctance, viewing themselves as condemned to performing the same backbreaking work as their ancestors, but with lower returns. These guacheros were not much different. Talking with them in the tunnel—but also at other moments during

Figure 3. Entering the guache. Photo by the author.

breakfast and lunch hours—they stressed how much they missed going to the excavator pits for their bareque.

"The government has killed us all at once," Liliana said, as we discussed the police crackdown on excavators over lunch. As no gold had been found so far in Darwinson's tunnel, she was only working for free lunches. This was hardly worth the many hours of tossing pans, especially considering that she had to pay for transportation to get to the shaft.

But talking to her and others, I noticed that artisanal forms of extraction had another, more positive side. Economic productivity, or the lack thereof, was not all there was to them. They also produced autonomy, tradition, and community. The guacheros took pride in continuing the livelihood of their parents, which permitted them—as it had permitted their parents—to work with, and for, their loved ones without having to punch any boss's clock. They also took delight in the camaraderie that such work entailed. After railing against the disappearance of excavators, Liliana noted certain advantages that guaches have over bareque: "In the bareque we always fight for the same spots. Here, everyone gets their wheelbarrow of [gold-bearing] earth. We are great companions. Here, everyone is friends or family." Several of her coworkers even expressed a preference for the tunnels. Altanacio, one of the mine's carpenters, would choose the comradery at Darwinson's mine over a better-paid job in an excavator pit on any day. "With the excavators, there is always someone giving orders. Here no one tells me what to do. I work independently. If I say, 'I'm going home,' they will tell me: 'Go ahead.' No one will say: 'Don't come back.'"

He was spot-on. Guaches attract a rotating workforce in which kinship and friendship often matter more than labor capacities and production necessity. Miners come and go, weighing up the prospects of the tunnel against the ebbs and flows of alternative sources of income.[10] Administrators accept fellow villagers in the mine, even when the latter's labor is surplus to production. Eventually, when the mine starts "to give," and each worker is allowed to wash their individual portion of gold-specked earth, the fullness of one's wheelbarrow—the size of one's rewarded portion of earth—is estimated on the basis of the number of days worked during the preparation phase. Miners invest their labor, so to speak. The investment is risky. Reaching a rich deposit may take months. Therefore, administrators like Darwinson motivate miners with free lunches, minimal financial compensations, and, naturally, weighty arguments of friendship. It's them who have the most at stake, because, along with the landholding family and a possible financing entrepreneur, they are the mine's *socios*, meaning they are entitled to more gold-bearing earth.

Now that gold has become harder to find, money for food and wages often runs out before a respectable deposit is reached, inciting workers to drift away until a tunnel becomes abandoned. Hence, in the current aftermath of the gold rush, guaches have become something of a dying breed. Darwinson dreaded this disappearance. On multiple occasions, he extolled to me the communal virtues of the guache. A staunch critic of the get-rich-quick mentality of excavator extraction, he emphasized how building tunnels allowed him to help other people's families. One time he explained that when a tunnel starts producing, women in the chain purposely drop some of their pans' gold-bearing content near their feet, so that they can later wash it in secret. Captivated by the story, I asked if these secret earth drops result in conflict upon discovery.

"No! I love it! Let them bring gold to their families!" he said, curling his lips into a generous smile.

His response confounded my expectations. "But aren't they stealing from you?"

"Of course they are, and they shouldn't do it too much. But what I like most about these holes is the moment when people benefit. I am poor, you understand? But there are people poorer than me. That's what it's all about."

Excavator mines enabled bareque, well-paid employment, and land rents. Yet they also spawned foreign profiteering and family conflicts; perils that were less numerous in artisanal mines. If excavators were missed for their higher returns, guaches and other low-tech techniques were desired for their independence and companionship. This is why, like Darwinson and Altanacio, some people applauded the current demise of excavators, noting that their advance had trimmed down traditional methods of extraction and, conterminously, the family values and horizontal working relations adjoining these methods. When working in human chains, streams, and pump mines, you were working alongside people who were close to heart. There, arriving late, or not arriving at all, was not subject to severe punishment; at best to a comradely sneer or joke to which you were always allowed—better yet, encouraged—to offer a reply. There, winning gold occurred through collective effort, and winning respect through beating friends in card games, dominos, and heated discussions of politics, music, football, and more football. There, you shared labor duties as much as you shared food, gossip, digitalized salsa songs, advice on personal hardship, and thunderous laughter when someone did something foolish (like fearing a leak or struggling in the guache chain).

In critical social science, mines often appear as an analytical entry point into the predations of industrial capitalism, in that they are archetypical illustrations of how capitalist enterprise steamrolls over peripheralized bodies and ecologies in its pursuit for maximized profit (Arboleda 2020; Kirsch 2014; Li 2015; Nash 1979; Taussig 1980). Yet the internal social life of Chocó's artisanal mines was all but a straightforward metonym for capitalist relations. Even if gold miners were at the producing end of global supply chains of jewelry, electronics, and other items—and undoubtedly exploited in the Marxian sense (by the chains' "downstream" retailers and traders enjoying the surplus value extracted from undervalued mining labor)—they nonetheless tended to describe their everyday digging not in tropes of exploitation, or even profit maximization, but in the language of autonomy.[11] Miners were well aware of the low socioeconomic status of their work. Yet they also found joy in working with peers and took great pleasure in not having someone bossing them around. Gold revenues were important to them, but so were the sensibilities of coming and going when they pleased, of not having to work in the rain and with an empty stomach, and of not being someone else's beast of burden. As such, when miners explained why they favored their pans and pumps over working for excavator dueños, they didn't mention gold (or money), which many reckoned to be more abundant in retrero employment. Rather, they insisted on the joy of working as autonomous agents; of "*no tener que rendir cuentas con nadie*" (not having to report back to anyone) and "*no tener a nadie atrás*" (not having someone behind you).

"Not having to report back to anyone" is at loggerheads with government surveillance. Artisanal miners were well aware. They badmouthed their national politicians not only for the legal persecution of the retreros—whose bareque and land rents they relied on, and with whose livelihood struggles they sympathized—but also for the removal of other extractive liberties. After all, besides bombing excavators, the government's strategy against illegal mining also comprised restrictions that directly affected the smaller miners: law-enforcement personnel had begun impounding fuel transports, while stringent legislation prohibited the unlimited and undocumented sale of manually mined gold. In this regulatory climate, even retrero skeptics like Darwinson and Altanacio did not evaluate governmental politics positively. Theirs was an economy of independence, of sustaining the family day after day, autonomously, with no larger authorities helping out or setting the rules. Theirs was an economy that was driven by "empirical knowledge" and "empirical work"—terms miners used to stress they had acquired their skills not through formalized schooling, but through the hard routinized labor of actual extraction. Theirs was an economy that had been with them since slavery, and sustained them in subsequent centuries of political neglect. It required a specific kind of evil to put such an economy under state regulation.

But what rubbed the artisanal miners the wrong way wasn't just the top-down curtailment of a labor of autonomy, but also the fact that the government completely misunderstood the irregular logic of such labor. I admit that I too had once failed to grasp this. At the beginning of my stay in Chocó, I asked interlocutors to indicate how many pesos they made per month. I soon realized I had made a mistake in soliciting a precise number. Talking and working with them taught me that searching for gold has strongly indeterminate outcomes. In the opaque underground, gold flecks may be resting anywhere. Owing to this unpredictability, miners do not perceive their earnings as a return on labor. Instead, they receive what the earth decides to offer. Their mines have agency. They are spoken of as "giving" and "catching on." Accordingly, from the miners' viewpoint, it's not just effort but also luck that fosters success.

Although such earthly authorship means that miners sometimes spend more money on fuel than they get back in gold, indeterminacy also has a seductive side. Because of the landscape's unpredictability, there is no telling when luck will bring you riches, and such geological chance partly explains why miners continue entering their tunnels and pits. Certainly, just as that the subsoil's mineral scarcity may have reduced the economic attraction of mining, so too does the subsoil's quality of invisibility ensure that, despite lower yields, the mines retain some of their lottery appeal. Concealed underground gold specks—being simultaneously everywhere and nowhere to those who mean to find them—allow miners to fantasize about an improved tomorrow in a way that other economies cannot. Whereas city jobs and farming provide some degree of financial stability, they are unlikely to lift you out of poverty the way a lucky day in the mines can. As pump miner Didier said: "This is my art. I wouldn't want to work in anything else. In the town hall people earn high salaries, but I tell you what: In the mine, I can triple in a single day what they make in a month."

The standardizing vision of centralized bureaucracy looked straight past these arguments of contingency. As part of its effort to restrain the illegal commercialization of gold, the Ministry of Mines and Energy introduced in 2017 a selling maximum for nonmechanical producers (the only miners who do not require a title), consisting of a monthly thirty-five grams—or, in Chocó's measuring standard, a rough seven castellanos. Because of the policy, excavator miners found it harder to pass off their unlawfully mined gold as legit bullion. The production levels of panners and water pump miners, on the other hand, rarely reached the seven-castellano maximum. But while in my mind's eye these smaller operators had little to fear from the new legislation, they bombarded me with concerns and described the selling restriction as an abhorrent injustice. They argued it was not for the government, but for the mine or God to decide how much they made. In the end, a gold strike was always imminent and luck could befall them at any given moment. "The government is taking away our liberty to produce," Didier said. "If you make twelve, ten castellanos completely legally, why do they need to put a maximum on how much you can sell?"

Postulating these concerns to state-employed formalization experts was a hard sell. Many of them laughed off the concerns as irrational, deceptive even. When I hypothesized to an official of the National Mining Agency about manual-based miners topping seven castellanos in the face of favorable geological odds, his reply was: "If they tell you that is what they make, they are lying. If they're making more than seven castellanos per month, you know they're not artisanal miners."

Officials like him have spent little time in Chocó's mining forests, where independent work thrives on a restless underground. What they fail to see is that finding gold in these forests has less to do with monthly averages than with chance, God, and the willingness of the mines. Finding gold, in other words, is not so much about maximizing profits as bumping into them.[12] Instead of trying to reach production maximums, alluvial artisanal miners envision their labor as simply being more or less lucky when sampling their way through an undefined whole of underground gold specks. From this vantage point, government-imposed production limits hamper not only the lauded autonomy of mining work, but also the autonomy and agency of gold itself.

Conclusion

Anthropologists have long shown that the popular portrayal of a sharply demarcated world of crime—whereby illicit economies (e.g., contraband,

drugs, gold) exist separately from legit, informal, and small-scale economies—
has little grounding in lived economic experience. Rather, the logistical operations of the "underworld" alloy with the mundane actions of "ordinary"
people, whose search for livelihood requires them to participate in variously
moral economies in variously substantive forms (Muehlmann 2015; Nordstrom 2000; Ramírez 2011). Such critical nuancing has clear traction for the
mining villages of Chocó, where artisanal miners experienced, first, a wildcat gold rush of unprecedented scale and, later, a set of punitive politics that
put this gold rush to a halt. In a remarkably short period of time, excavator
mining operations took the rainforest by storm, depleting mineral deposits,
culling trees, and disarraying local extractive and subsistence production
economies. These operations happened with the blessing of large parts of local communities, which rode the wave of a mining boom that improved
their access to placer gold (through bareque, rents, and employment), and,
as an outcome of the former, their ability to live up to cultural standards of
successful personhood, especially in terms of material well-being.

Residents of mining areas were not indifferent about the ecological price
they had paid for their access to gold. But they also presented themselves as
being more than their lands. They desired to remodel houses, pay for tuition
fees, have money for leisure activities, and dream of better futures. To accomplish these goals, many continued to view excavator mines, now diminished
in number, as the preferred model for development—despite, or rather
because of, the damage these mines had inflicted on traditional economies.
Now that environmental degradation had entered an advanced stage, artisanal mining methods and subsistence gardens simply felt too little, too late.

Against this material backdrop, Colombian police forces were refuted not
so much for their failure to combat illegal extraction (a criticism commonly
heard outside mining villages) as for their callous insistence on eradicating
the mines that provided local income. Many people begrudged the extractive afterlife the national government had subjected them to. They were destined to the same Herculean labor as their parents, but now for lower returns
and with less freedom—no longer could they sell gold, transport fuel, and
set up mines however they pleased. Still, it was the larger excavator and dredge
miners who suffered government measures most directly. Their experiences
are the subject of the next chapter.

CHAPTER 2

Being Abandoned

When they call me illegal, I feel so sad
that I start to feel sick.

—*Claudio (retrero)*

"We're not illegal. It's only the government that calls us that." Evelio gazed at me intently. "Did you know that we were brought here as slaves? Do you know why?"

As I swallowed one more spoonful of rice, the mine dueño answered for me. "To mine! This is our tradition. How can a tradition be illegal?"

"You just don't get it, Evelio," a voice behind us said. "The government doesn't say: 'Don't work.' *He* just says that you should change *how* you work, so you don't affect the environment." The voice belonged to Rigoberto, Evelio's brother, one of the four workers who accompanied us for lunch in the open kitchen shed, but who, unlike the rest of us at the picnic table, ate his rice dish while seated on the shed's wooden floor.

With a face ready for battle, Evelio stood up from the table, paced toward his brother and, inconsistent with the lesser distance now separating the two men, raised his voice. "The government wants us to abandon these machines! That we work with our hands again!" He pointed in the direction of the far-off pit that his two excavators had carved out, deep enough to bury a house. "Who can dig a hole like that by hand?" He laughed energetically, then switched his gaze back to me. "We are worse off than slaves, don't you think?"

Not willing to make polemical statements, I opted for a conciliatory answer. "Well, the government allows some miners to work with machinery,"

I conceded to Rigoberto, "but for miners like Evelio, getting a title is very difficult."

"But that's what I'm trying to say," Rigoberto said. "But you don't listen, Evelio."

Seated again, opposite me, Evelio rejected my explanation with aplomb. "It's not difficult to get a title. If the government wants, he can change everything, just send over some people and organize us: 'We'll let you work and if you don't follow the rules, we'll burn your machines.'[1] But now they're burning us without even knowing how we work. A new machine costs 400 million pesos. That's money you have to borrow from others. So, tell me, if they set fire to that, aren't they killing you in cold blood?"

"With all due respect, Evelio," Rigoberto said, "I feel that we miners sometimes burn our own fingers. If we cultivate trees and tap holes, they may not burn—"

Evelio cut his brother off. "Did I not just say that I want to take care of the environment?!" His recurring rhetorical questions did not require answers. The immorality of state politics was a self-evident truth on the mine-filled shores of the Bebará River. Every time native bebareño Evelio spoke, his words were rewarded with approving nods and encouraging comments from the three other workers. They had chosen his side in the discussion, sharing the conviction that their illegality was unjust.

Evelio shot one more pensive frown in my direction. "Tell me, *holandés*, if you did not have money for fuel, would you tap your holes? Well?" As I was still mulling an appropriate response, he again answered on my behalf. "Of course not! We all want to be environmentally friendly, but when you own excavators, you soon discover what is possible. It's not like you don't want to. You must think of your family, your workers."

A smile plastered across his face. He strapped his feet in a pair of rubber boots. There was gold to be won.

Whereas the previous chapter laid out how local communities related to "illegal" excavator mines and their politicization, here I give insight into how the illegalized themselves experienced—in word and deed—the government's punitive measures. Compared to artisanal miners (panners, guacheros, pump miners), those working with high-end machinery (*retreros* like Evelio, but also *dragueros*, or dredge miners) were at the forefront of criminalization. Their upscaled extraction had made them more likely to be blamed for environmental degradation, to be associated with and extorted by nonstate armed groups, and to be subject to equipment destruction and police detention. This chapter wrestles with the question of which fragmentary forms of citizen-ship arose under such politico-legal conditions. In broaching this ques-tion, I do not set out a narrative of liberating resistance. Rather, I chronicle burned-out excavators, worksites raided by bandits, and men like Evelio claiming to be "killed in cold blood." The narrative I propose is one of "aban-donment," an analytic that echoes the phrasing of miners themselves.

Though the chapter takes some backroads to dredge mines, its true pro-tagonists are retreros, because it was this category of "larger" miners that was active in the three places of my fieldwork. By recounting my conversations with these miners, the chapter serves a secondary purpose of painting a more complex picture of people designated as "illegal." When politicians and me-dia outlets depict illegalized miners, they generally characterize them as na-ture destroyers or associates of criminal structures. In the course of fieldwork, I learned that there are other, lesser-told stories about them. I discovered their friendships with (and participation in) local communities, desires for legal protections, worries about sustaining their families, and fears of bandits, paramilitaries, and guerrillas. I discovered, thus, what Carolyn Nordstrom (2007:143) calls the "disconnect" between popular portrayals of "criminals" and the latter's actual adherence to moral values and enmeshment in social relations. While insisting on these values and relations, this chapter presents an up-close account of the human actors who work with forest-killing min-ing infrastructure.

Being Abandoned

While dueño Evelio, Rigoberto, and two other workers headed for the pit, a fourth worker, Claudio, and I stayed behind in the kitchen to finish our beans and rice. As the voices of the departing miners began to fade out, Claudio made a surprising confession: "I didn't engage in the discussion, because they were talking. But with all due respect to Evelio, I think he and the other due-ños are also to blame for our situation."

"What do you mean?" I asked.

"They are working here in hiding. But when you hide, you accept that you're a criminal, just like the government says. When they call me illegal, I feel so sad that I start to feel sick. Journalists call us criminals without even coming here! Are we perhaps killing people? Are we robbing? Do we finance armed groups? No! This is honest work. Chocó lives off mining. If they continue like this, they will turn us chocoanos into delinquents. They're looking for peace with the FARC, but here they're creating another armed group."

I mentioned the irony that government officials also invoke armed groups when they rationalize the need to attack miners like him. Naturally, Claudio disapproved of this logic. "The government is to blame for the money we pay these groups. Tell me: Who wants to give money away? No one. But who has us in abandonment here? If someone says: 'Give me one percent of what you make,' you give it, because there's no protection. The government does nothing for us. But we are human beings. We're like any other people in the world. The only thing we do is work the earth that sustains our children. And they want to stop us from doing that. Our government has us in abandonment."

Political abandonment, as brought up by Claudio, has in the past decades come under intense scrutiny by anthropologists and other social scientists, largely owing to the tendency of present-day governments to zealously abandon those parts of national populations that are of low value to capitalist production processes. In this regard, Tania Li (2009:66) examines what drives "governing authorities . . . [to] select one subset of the population for life enhancement while abandoning another." She contends that many of the world's poor have become "surplus populations" that "are in fact abandoned," given that in a hyper-industrialized global economy their labor is no longer vital "to the requirements of capital accumulation" (67). Meanwhile, focusing on the "zones of abandonment" of late liberalism, Elizabeth Povinelli (2011) goes one step further. Departing from Michel Foucault's seminal thinking on the politics of *faire vivre* and *laisser mourir*, Povinelli observes that under neoliberal doctrine, people who do "not produce values according to market logic" are not just cut off from life-enhancing politics (faire vivre)—and governed through a politics of "letting die" (laisser mourir)—but are even, "in situations in which the security of the market . . . [seems] at stake," proactively subjected to sovereign manifestations of state violence.

Colombia is a high-profile example of the variegated citizenships to which Li and Povinelli alert us. The second most unequal country in Latin America, Colombia can arguably be dichotomized, as one prominent sociologist has done, into a "*sociedad civil*" and a "*sociedad incivil*" (Pécaut 2004:46), whereby the second category has historically lacked the access to land, physical integrity, and political participation that the first has. While this national imbalance is in itself not new (Serje 2005), it has acquired certain "neoliberal" undertones in the past twenty to thirty years, marked as they were by the elimination of social policies (Hristov 2014), the dismantling of trade unions (Gill 2007), and violence against rural populations standing in the way of legally sanctioned agribusiness and extractive projects (Rojas 2009).

What is new, moreover, is the symbolism that official discourses ascribe to the abandoned. Though in the nineteenth and larger part of the twentieth century, campesinos were associated with the expansion of agricultural frontiers, and the "civilization" of the Indigenous peoples who suffered the frontiers' violence (Appelbaum 2003; Roldán 2003), this *colono* imagery has gradually given way to government tropes that portray smallholders as guerrillas, environmental destroyers, henchmen for drug lords, and other identities that resemble obstacles to industrial development and national security (Ramírez 2011; Ojeda 2012).[2] As Chapter 1 discussed, comparable administrative rationalities affected miners in Chocó, whose unsustainable labor, assumed criminal links, and obstructiveness to large-scale extraction were frequently cited to explain their political detriment. As such, although miners' environmental degradation and (involuntary) contributions to criminal organizations may not have won them the sympathy reserved for other segments of the rural poor, I find it not far-fetched to conceive of them as one more example of late-liberal abandonment. They, too, failed to secure a place in a pro-corporate governing framework. They, too, lacked formal work, physical safety, and economic security.

Speaking of abandonment comes with two rhetorical advantages. For starters, it invokes political agency. In its concrete allusion to institutional neglect, the notion of abandonment links the deprivation of out-of-the-way populations to a government that abandons them. Accordingly, the notion should not be confused with state absence, a discourse frequently applied to Colombia. As Margarita Serje (2013) contends, the "myth of state absence" ignores that rural violence in the Colombian margins has been premised on the establishment of state sovereignty. Conversely, the alternative analytic of abandonment views marginalization not as being outside of liberal political formation, but as "a state effect" (Rasmussen 2015:181) and "an active choice" (Rasmussen 2017:352). The analytic channels attention to miners' sporadic and arbitrary encounters with a state apparatus that presents itself as both viciously real, through its legal persecution, and deceptively illusory, regarding its promises of development and security.

A second advantage of the concept harks back to Claudio's self-identification as being "in abandonment." His comment illustrates that abandonment as an analytical category indexes not only material deprivation but also the affective experience thereof. It is a language used by governed people who desire to be governed differently. As Mattias Rasmussen (2017:328) puts it, "figurations of abandonment . . . serve as a critique of governance and an exercise of citizenship." Rather than "[describing] the level of state involvement in either absolute or relative terms" (352), the claim of being abandoned "suggests . . . expectations of what the state should be by framing ideal-types of state authorities and citizens" (352–353).

Much like Claudio, most excavator miners I met considered themselves poor, hardworking people who were left behind, unseen, and abandoned by the state government. These self-analyses were intriguing, because they not infrequently came just before or after miners bemoaned the restrictive actions of what they saw as a malevolent, and very much present, state. Theirs, it seemed, was a Janus-faced state: at once out to get them and "absent" in its role of caregiver. Therefore, miners' reference to abandonment was "a matter not of the state's presence but rather of the conditions of state presence" (Rasmussen 2015:110); it questioned less the morality of state rule than the current template of governance. By insisting on their entitlements from a state that abandoned them (to respect, property, security), miners tentatively expressed the expectation of an alternative political treatment. In doing so, they invested emotionally in a bureaucracy that had allegedly shortchanged them.

In sum, in writing about "abandoned" miners, I am mindful of both the detrimental fulfillment of their everyday citizenship and their own understanding of this. While foregrounding these material and sensorial aspects of political belonging through ethnographic snippets, the subsequent sections examine empirically how miners deal with being abandoned—and more specifically, in the following order, with being stigmatized, penalized, and forsaken to the whims of criminals.

Being Stigmatized

Through television, newspapers, and word of mouth, retreros heard and read the Santos government repeatedly mention how much they were failing in their moral obligations as citizens. They were the "unauthorized," the "criminal," the "illegal." Their labor inflicted unrivaled harms on nature and peace and the national treasury. Clearly, such language festered, especially when pronounced by one's president. In conversations with me—predominantly held at the kitchen tables of mining camps—miners took great pains to counter the admonishing comments of their government. In order for me

Figure 4. Excavator mine. Photo by the author.

to understand the severity of their abandonment, they appealed to what James Holston (2011:346) calls "insurgent conceptualizations of rights." That is to say, they claimed entitlement to an improved form of citizenship in a language that was often more normative than legal; one that defended their extraction, not so much by citing specific legal categories, which mostly operated against them, as by articulating a working-class identity built on the values of tradition, honesty, and contribution (yet as Chapter 3 shows, the law did pop up in mining camps in unexpected ways).

To begin with, retreros highlighted their traditionality. They argued they had been miners "since [being in their] mother's belly," "since lying in the cradle," or, as Evelio had put it, since "we were brought here as slaves." To many, it mattered little that hand tools had been replaced by excavators. They were artisanal miners by birth, retreros only by choice. Mining was histori- cally ingrained in them. How, they asked me, could politicians conflate such cultural heritage with crime?

In addition, retreros breathlessly stated that they were working honest jobs. They had to scrape together their gold in the face of many hardships: the inhospitable chocoano heat, the slashing rain, the uncompromising length of the informal working week, the physical distance separating them from their families in other parts of Chocó or Colombia. Such work, they maintained, was *not* illegal. Their gold was a virtuous commodity, belonging to God, the land, and the salt of the earth working the land. Who were these politicians, they asked, to decide otherwise?

In underlining the honesty of their work, excavator miners accentuated their distance from the paramilitaries and guerrillas with whom they were associated. The dueños of the mines self-identified as victims of extortion rackets. They painstakingly explained that without paying the *vacuna*, the obligatory extortion tax, they would not be able to work. This, the dueños protested, was not just their economic reality, but also that of many local businesses. Yet despite the ubiquity of extortion in Chocó, they were the only economic sector the government had mixed up with the armed actors. In light of this grave misrecognition, questions beckoned. "The state, with all the authority it has, why does it not combat the real delinquents?" paisa miner Alejandro asked. "Instead, they leave them be and oblige us to pay the little we have to someone who says: 'If you don't pay vacuna, I'll kill you and your family.'"

Furthermore, the dueños and workers of excavator mines considered their work not only traditional and honest, but also as contributing to local development. Rebutting official discourses that described their mines as an obstacle to economic growth, they pointed to all the local shops that had profited from their gold, and listed all the community buildings and roads they had donated to. Often, they sustained their right to work by claiming—on personal account or on behalf of excavator mining in general—to have done more for Chocó than the government itself, citing the buildings, infrastructure, and education that local villages had been able to pay for thanks to the excavators. There was no shame in gold digging. To the contrary. "It gives me pride and satisfaction to be a miner," said dueño Fabio, himself a chocoano. "You know why? Because we help people with their necessities, people who have their houses in poor shape; or we build a community work; or we pay for groceries."

Dueños like him were quick to nip in the bud the prevailing critique that they were living off the riches of impoverished communities. When I brought up the impossibility of subsistence gardening as a result of their labor, they spoke of the absence of consumer markets for local produce. When I hinted at the diminishing of gold reserves accessible to artisanal miners, they replied that these reserves had been depleted prior to their arrival. They saw their relationship with local communities as harmonious. Dueños who were natives to Chocó rarely made an effort to substantiate this claim. Their being from Chocó, or even from the municipality where they were working, seemed enough reason in and of itself. Alternatively, white dueños from out-side the department tended to resort to racist and geographical stereotypes when defending themselves against insinuations of exploitation. The paisas reasoned their presence was warranted, because they had a work ethic that was supposedly lacking among the local population. Yet whether chocoanos or paisas, and whether dueños or workers, excavator miners by and large agreed that the government was crushing the regional economy by crushing their machines. With all these barequeros, workers, and landowners depend-ing on their gold, the mine-bombing defense forces were believed to achieve nothing but unemployment and crime. Miners suggested—sometimes jok-ingly, sometimes seriously—that in the event of a shutdown of their encamp-ments, they would start robbing or join the guerrillas. Drastic times called for drastic measures.

Now, while the identity of the working miner (traditional, honest, con-tributory) offered retreros a solid counternarrative to stigmas of delinquency and tax evasion, it did little to challenge accusations of environmental deg-radation. It's no surprise, then, that when discussing these accusations, re-treros were much more multivocal than they had been in their rejection of being stereotyped as criminal henchmen. Positions on mercury varied strongly. Some saw little harm in the liquid and sprinkled it freely, saying they had never experienced bodily complaints. Others agreed with the govern-ment's diagnosis of mercury being a health hazard, and claimed compliance with community council guidelines that either prohibited it or permitted it only in the final stage of washing (in the batea). A couple of miners even re-nounced the quicksilver altogether, opting instead to amalgamate gold through the bonding juices of local plants.

Stances on deforestation were equally hard to generalize. A few retreros rejected the government's assertion that they had a negative ecological foot-print, and argued that their excavation actually helped to regenerate the for-est. Most, however, did admit to their own forest-felling, but saw this as a necessary evil in contributing to the well-being of local communities and themselves. While spinning fervently a sand-filled batea, the sexagenarian José said: "When we started to work in these five cuts, I proposed to culti-vate something like grass, so that the people here could graze cattle. You think it doesn't hurt me to cut trees? It hurts, but I do it anyway. Because this is how I've looked for food since I was a little boy."

Whether due to pressures from the local community council, or in the hope of becoming less susceptible to police and army actions (see Chapter 3), many dueños made at least some attempt at reforestation. They built tree nurseries or paid forest experts to seed plants for them. Truth be told, the planted saplings nearly always covered a limited section of the forest-cleansed land. Confronted with this, dueños emphasized financial limitations. As Evelio indicated a couple of pages ago, there were more important expenses to think of. Several dueños defended themselves by saying that the desertified landscape I inquired about was mainly the result of people who had mined there previously. Why, they wondered, were they responsible for cleaning up the mess of others?

But even if retreros held a wide array of opinions about the impact of extracting, they were univocal in their mistrust of the government's preoccupation with nature. Overall, they experienced that their original sin was not being harmful to the forest, but being poor in a country that favored the white-collared and the rich. They reckoned that the official narrative of forest protection was nothing but a political stick to hit them with, a shameless valve for resource appropriation. They laid out stories about mining corporations staffing the executive branch of government; about Chocó's subsoil being sold off to multinationals whose ecological carnage was a thousand-fold worse than theirs; about a conglomerate of oligarchic families who ruled their country at the expense of the downtrodden.

Their feelings of political abandonment were of course not just based on stories but also grounded in firsthand experience. After all, their work involved avoiding a security apparatus that set fire to their subsistence, literally. It is to this affective and political experience of being "burned down" that the next two sections turn.

Being Burned Down: The Friendly Dragon of San Miguel

An eighty-horsepower engine suggests dazzling speed. Yet our engine pushed forward a steel-hulled boat, jam-packed with five human-sized diesel tanks, so our speed was anything but dazzling. Our eyes could absorb the land and water sights nonetheless. And what sights to be seen on the San Juan River! In navigating down it, we navigated down history. After passing the town of Andagoya, we steered past a rusty chunk of metal sticking out of the water (which, frankly, I had failed to spot and was only told about afterward). My travel companion Aurilio explained that it had once belonged to a pontoon of Chocó Pacífico, the U.S./British mining business that had dredged the surroundings of Andagoya for half a century and had left in 1974, leaving in its wake a legacy of foreign-looking wooden houses, a few pensioned workers, and a subsoil filled with mercury and emptied of gold and platinum. As we continued down the river, more recent remnants of predatory extraction unfolded. With increasing frequency, the river flow was interrupted by sandbars, produced a decade ago by Brazilian *dragones*—the same "dragons" that had gained a notorious reputation in Colombia for their mercury pollution and, as witnessed here, river sedimentation.[3]

In a way, the sandbars and metal scrap provided material clues to the San Juan River's larger history of prolonged abandonment, a history in which the story of San Miguel, the village to which we and the diesel tanks were heading, was only one more episode. Aurilio was shepherding me to his village so I could learn about a two-story suction dredge. It had been blown up, or "burned down" (as miners in Chocó say), by a special forces squad two months earlier, but was now up and running again. The fire itself was not newsworthy. Burning down dragons had become common practice in Chocó. Every few months, the police and army took a couple of them out. However, when it came to dredges, the San Miguel one was an anomaly. This was a friendly dragon. Half the money needed for its construction had come from the pockets of eighty villagers, who were also in charge of the mine's administration. They had assigned Aurilio, a son of the village, as their "legal representative." And if I were to believe him, the joint venture had spawned employment, community buildings, and a collective sense of pride in a context of structural state oblivion.

That morning, before traveling, he had sketched this context out to me over an early lunch. In the previous two decades, the village had been subjected to the military dominion of different armed groups: paramilitaries of the United Self-Defense Forces of Colombia (AUC), FARC guerrillas, and currently, guerrillas again, but now from the ELN. It was against this backdrop of "state abandonment," as Aurilio called it, that the tragic displacement of July 21, 2004, happened. In anticipation of a possible clash between AUC and FARC combatants, the entire population of San Miguel had been forced to flee to nearby towns. The fighting never occurred, but on their return to the village the *sanmigueleños* found their houses looted.

Aurilio's account of state abandonment didn't end there. In the aftermath of the 2004 displacement, a growing number of villagers began to dedicate themselves to the cultivation of coca, because they lacked nearby consumer markets for their "legal" crops. Money multiplied, but only until 2012, when the Antinarcotics Unit of the Colombian police doused the coca crops with herbicides. It was from the ashes of this second collective trauma that the idea of the community dragon arose. With the assistance of two paisa investors, the eighty local socios registered their mine with the Chamber of Commerce in 2015. "There was no compensation from the government for the fumigation," Aurilio said. "So, many people migrated to other places in search of work. Those who stayed, in their desperation, saw mining as an alternative for subsistence. And they risked everything, all their capital, to let luck decide."

After we disembarked in San Miguel, Aurilio had me see with my own eyes that luck had decided in their favor. He offered a tour that guided us past a school classroom, a children's playground, and a market square. All of it was new. All of it lacked the trademark mold that Chocó's concrete buildings display when exposed to the rainforest's moisture for too long. Aurilio proudly remarked that these "public works," along with the cemented pathways and bridges leading up to them, had been paid for with dragon gold. One by one, he presented the works as physical testimony to the dredge's success; as exhibits of a proper public space, fully financed by their mine. But while the concrete constructions—in the explanations of Aurilio and passing villagers—were metaphors for progress, they were also a stark reminder of the unfulfilled promises of modernity.[4] Putting it differently, here cement was not so much performing the far reach of the modernist Colombian state (Zeiderman 2020) as exposing its limitations and filling its infrastructural cracks. In fact, walking and talking around San Miguel taught me that many local buildings had been built with the earnings of successive illegalized economies, of which dredging was merely the latest. Villagers boasted that their community council had used previous coca and mining profits to build a school, a community hall, and a house in which to hold wakes.

Aurilio's tour ended at the mine itself, on the outskirts of the village, where it became visible how the sanmigueleños curtailed the environmental costs of their newfound progress. Instead of dredging away a river, as these machines tend to do, the dragon was working land-inward. What's more, no holes or slopes could be detected at the rear. It resembled an operation by the book: Excavated lands had been smoothed by a bulldozer and decorated with an impressive number of young acacia trees, planted three meters apart.

Before mounting the dredge, I got to meet some of the socios. Aurilio took me into a large hut abutting the extraction site. It had numerous bedrooms, equipped with mattresses, as well as a spacious kitchen, equipped with a smart television. I was slack-jawed. In terms of comfort, the building easily beat the shacks of green debris-netting I had grown accustomed to in excavator mining camps. In the kitchen, co-founder Jorge and administrator Mauricio responded to my expressed amazement by listing the mine's social contributions. They said that people who had previously migrated elsewhere were now returning to San Miguel to find employment at the mine as cooks, mechanics, and administrators. In addition, the socios gave food rations to elderly villagers and ran a training program that helped local men become dredge operators. And most importantly, as Jorge noted, they generated multiplier effects. "He who has bananas, sells them here. He who has lemons, chicken, we consume everything from our own people."

They said that the explosion two months previously had taken them by surprise. The day before, the dredgers had received a visit from a military regiment. The soldiers had congratulated them on their work, designating it as the "best mining in Chocó," and assuring them they would be spared in a forthcoming destruction operation. But they had not been spared. Their dredge had been mercilessly taken out, dynamited away along with the rest of the department's dragons. Mauricio said: "What happened to us, personally, tears flowed from my eyes. It was something we had fought for. When you have a dream and you achieve it, and then someone comes along and destroys it without giving you a single opportunity. . . . It's terrorism to take your machine out like that! That they decommission it, or give you a fine, but to take you out and blow you up like that?! Bum!"

The two socios and Aurilio explained that after this event, they had bent over backward to convince fellow villagers to not throw in the towel and to chip in for a new engine. They had succeeded, but were under no illusions: This was the final straw. The three men were adamant that a new police mission would mean the death of the dragon. There was no money left, nor arguments to encourage people to save up once more for something that would likely be blown up again. So they continued working, but with the threat of the police hanging like a Damoclean sword over their heads. Because the end of the dragon, as Jorge made clear, would be the end of San Miguel: "We would have to leave, because what else would we live off? What does the government pretend? Only because we're trying to survive, they attack us like this. Who would have thought that we could build a company like this? Just by uniting as a community. We are entrepreneurs and the government should value that and not destroy what we have! Here the state arrives with nothing!"

A few anecdotes later, Aurilio and I were outside again, boarding the dredge and witnessing the effects of the explosion from up close. The steel construction was blackened with carbonation, the upper deck denuded of its

Figure 5. The San Miguel dredge. Photo by the author.

sleeping quarters. What remained was a skeletal frame. Still, this dragon skeleton encased a well-functioning heart. On the bottom deck, a rust-free iron contraption, not much smaller than a kitchen table, was roaring a deafening noise. This was it: the brand-new engine that, in generating power for the dredge's suction crane, sparked a final glimmer of hope in those socios in the kitchen. After listening to their proud stories, and after walking the paved pathways of their village, I couldn't help but sympathize with them. Admittedly, standing inside that carcass of rust, the eradication of illegal mines started to feel less like environmental care and more like a rejection of citizenship on the part of a government that, as Aurilio had put it in our interview, "doesn't build public works and doesn't let us build them."

Being Burned Down (II): On the Denial of Property and Citizenship

I met other *dragueros* in Chocó.

One afternoon, while having lunch in a canteen in the town of Istmina, I began chatting fortuitously with three men who were drinking beer at the contiguous table. Two of them, a paisa and a Brazilian, owned dredges that were mining the Quito River. Upon learning about my research, they readily included me in their conversation and rounds of beer. A ceaseless stream of damp 330-ml bottles arrived, lubricating our tongues. The men shared with me their takes on mercury pollution ("That's all theory, I believe in practice"), their experiences with police operations ("I already spent one month in La Modelo prison[5] and another month here in Quibdó"), and their opinions about the futility of suing "the state" for dismantling their dredges ("They always have better lawyers than we do"). They were angry with their government. But I did not share their anger in the way I shared the anger of Aurilio, Jorge, and Mauricio. I knew of the environmental reputation of the Quito dredges, outlined to me by local community leaders who, in the face of gold-levying paramilitaries, were powerless to halt the dragueros' entry.

After we had shared several beers and cemented our mutual confidence, the paisa played a cell-phone video of his pontoon going up in flames. In an inebriated tone of voice, he said: "Imagine that in the Netherlands you have a vegetable garden and your state destroys it. That's what's happening here. This is my subsistence. You work and then *pram*." He stretched out the five fingers of his left hand, indicating an explosion. "Your own compatriots destroy it! Now I'm broke. I don't have a single peso!"

This declaration of hardship surprised me. I had listened to the two dredgers boasting about their incomes and priding themselves on their persistence in rebuilding their machines, explosion after explosion. I was also physically experiencing their insistence on buying drinks. These men did not come across as being stretched thin. "So, many dragueros are broke now?" I asked. "What does that mean? I mean, we're still drinking beers, right?" My alcohol-soaked tongue was no longer subtle, and my questions sounded far too judgmental than in non-tipsy retrospect I would like them to have sounded. The paisa took them as an insult. He sneered at me—"You're only one more politician!"—then got up and drove off on his scooter.

Though not my finest moment as an ethnographer, this conversation captures well the emotional affect that extraction equipment bestows on its owners. When I talked with retreros and—in lesser quantity—dragueros, it felt as though the government was not only destroying their excavators and dredges, but also, in a way, these miners themselves, along with their rights as Colombian citizens. It felt as if they *were* their machinery. Herein, miners of the Quito River were not so different from those of San Miguel.

How to understand this nexus of having and being?

Writing on land rights in Africa, Christian Lund (2011) argues that property and citizenship are mutually constitutive. For Lund, property can be "distinguished from . . . momentary possession or longer-term access by virtue of being recognized by others, through enforcement by society or government, and by custom, convention, or law" (72). Thus, in understanding property as "sanctioned by some form of public authority" (72), Lund views claims to property as closely intertwined with claims to citizenship—"the relationship between individuals and an institution of public authority" (73). Whereas "citizenship and belonging can be avenues to secure property," at the same time "property may bolster claims of belonging and citizenship" (74).

With Lund's ideas in mind, we may wonder what happens to political subjectivity when, as in the case of wildcat miners, institutions decline to authorize possession as property—and instead blast it to pieces. When discussing the injustices of police missions, miners in Chocó equated the ruination of their equipment with their own ruination. "If they set fire to that, aren't they killing you in cold blood?" Evelio asked in this chapter's introduction. In other words, they depicted their affect-laden machinery, scraped together by years of arduous labor, as a material extension of self. In blowing this up, the Colombian government also blew up their historical trajectories, savings, and aspirations for the future. Interlocutors took this mechanical personification to the extreme in their usage of auto-referential pronouns when identifying the recipients of explosions (e.g., "If they burn *me*, I don't have a Plan B"), suggesting that in the elimination of their possessions, their actual personhood was also on the line.

Yet the identity at stake was as personal as it was political. With their claims of being "killed" and "burned" by their own government, miners declared their dead as citizens. In an inverted twist to Lund's dialectics—of property producing citizenship, and vice versa—miners saw the demolition of their excavator and dredge stock—the misrecognition of their property—as an unmistakable denial of their citizen entitlements. They reckoned the explosions to be unlawful treatment by a government that trampled their rights to property, labor, and protection. It was as if, with the region-wide sprees of mine explosions, their social contract with the Colombian state was also going up in smoke.

The case of Óscar is telling. A year before I interviewed him, a police helicopter had touched down next to his mine to blow up his three excavators. He had refused to flee. "Subversive groups run. Why should I run from the state if I haven't killed anyone? Working is not a crime. So, when they came, I shook their hands and made sure that no one ran."

Later in our interview, he added another reason for deserving a fairer legal treatment: the ownership of his mining gear. "The last thing that the state should do is burn the machinery of people. It's an injustice. It's damage to someone else's property. Why do they damage my machines? It's not theirs!"

Effectively, to counter what they saw as their political abandonment, miners like Óscar underlined not only the honesty of their labor, as argued earlier, but also the lawful possession of their excavators. More than once, I listened to them bringing up the legal documents for their excavators as evidence of their right to work. Unluckily for them, these property pleas were often to no effect. Dutiful policemen had bombed Óscar's excavators to uselessness, all before the crying eyes of his children, who worked as employees of the mine. In recounting the event, he described the loss of the equipment as a loss of self. As a result of the police mission, he had needed to sell off all his cars and motorbikes and had lost twenty kilos in weight. With no money to repair his excavators, he was now fooling around in a water pump mine that was running low on fuel. He was truly living the destruction in the flesh. "I was accustomed to three good meals a day. I used to be fat. Look at me now. How do you see that, Jes? When they brought me to Bogotá by helicopter, I told them: 'Better you put me in jail, because without these machines, I don't have anything to eat.'"

His personal drama epitomizes how property destruction can be a deeply visceral experience of political impotence and dismissed citizenship. When confronting descending helicopters (and possibly thereafter, criminal investigators and trials), retreros' claims to honest work and proprietorship usually fall on deaf ears. As Roberto, who likewise had lost three of his machines in a police operation, said: "What can you do when they burn you? You cannot complain to anyone. They don't ask for paperwork. You just stand there like an ass. The two things you can do are run or get yourself killed. I was not there when they burned me, but had I been, those sons of bitches would have had to kill me."

Unlike Roberto and Óscar, most miners did run. Retreros shared memories of dashing into the woods on the arrival of choppers, while dragueros remembered how the approaching sounds of police speedboats had prompted them to jump into the river. Of course, although running away precluded detention, it did nothing to stop machinery from being "burned." And miners agreed that having equipment blown up was worse than being detained.

Where tales of running from the police were usually met with laughter, the loss of machinery was never a joking matter. When excavators disappeared, so did the employment of workers and the capital of dueños. That hurt more than a few wrists in handcuffs.

It was, however, not just the actual moment of machinery destruction but also its sheer possibility that marked miners' strained citizenship. Ultimately, to minimize the risk of having their equipment impaired, retreros had to remain invisible to public intelligence. Therefore, they avoided excavating too close to urban hubs and busy roads and rivers. Some did not even like the nearby presence of fellow miners, arguing that clustered excavators were eye-catchers in the bird's eye vision of aerial surveillance. The fear of explosives, though, never went away completely. Few, if any, excavator dueños held the conviction that their machines were completely invisible to the government. They knew their mine was blinking on some state radar, having seen helicopters, airplanes, and drones flying overhead.

The "art of not being governed" (Scott 2009) became more refined when police and army operations loomed large. Once they had been called or texted by fellow retreros about a rumored explosion spree (there was always some-one knowing someone at the police or public prosecutor), dueños and administrators ordered workers to remove excavators from the pits. Since danger came from the sky, some placed the vehicles under roofs or dense parts of the forest canopy, often using additional black sheets to conceal the machines' conspicuous yellow and orange. Others simply left the machinery at the side of the road, attempting to grant it the impression of construction equipment that was resting after performing legitimate roadwork. Usually, danger passed and business could continue. Yet there was no telling when and where the public forces would strike again. It was this arbitrariness that made the operations so relentlessly effective in instilling fear. Because of the unpredictability of state surveillance—because of the imminent possibility that this time they were coming for you—retreros time and again put their work on hold when destruction missions were happening elsewhere.[6]

When I visited dueño Gerson at his mining camp, he received a text message saying they were "burning" again. It instantly blackened the mood at the campsite. While one worker phoned other miners to investigate the veracity of the rumor, Gerson summoned the rest of his crew to fetch his excavators from the pit and cover them with plastic sheets. As the men departed for the vehicles, I asked Gerson about the when and the where of the police action that had been just called in. "*Hermano* [brother], we don't know," he answered. "It's all a mystery. Maybe it was yesterday or maybe tomorrow. But although they're just rumors, they make you uncomfortable. That's their goal. That we hide like criminals."

Compared with excavators, dredges are lousy hiders. Their robust structure prevents them from retreating quickly and sheltering under forest cover. Yet what the dragons lack in mobility and stealth, they make up in money. Interlocutors who had worked in either dredge mining or government told me that mine owners bribe soldiers and policemen to be excluded from eradication operations, or to gain the latter's approval to remove the engine—the crown jewel of the device—before the explosion. There was also a more innovative strategy, as I first learned in an interview with dredge operator Sebastián. In a Portuguese accent picked up from a decade of working alongside Brazilians, the young paisa man explained that the dragueros had started to dig out pools in the banks of the Quito River, large enough to store their machines in the event of a police operation. He estimated the entire procedure could be done in less than two minutes. "We usually do it one or two days before an operation. Someone from the police or army informs us and then we sink the machine at night. Sometimes only half of it, because it's more difficult to get it out when all of it is underwater. Also, sometimes they say they are going to burn but then they don't. So you only sink the lower floor, where the engine is. The engine you seal. Then, when they pass, they see the sunk dragon but they cannot do anything."

On initial review, I found the explanation too spectacular to be true. Nonetheless, I had it later confirmed by the director of the Unidad Nacional contra la Minería Ilegal y Antiterrorismo (UNIMIL)—the police unit tasked with blowing up mines—who added that in reaction to the miners' astuteness, his task force now relied on divers to place the explosives underwater.

The violence that miners endured, however, went beyond police dynamite. In their "abandoned" mines, in the voids of formal regulatory protections, there were also nonstate armed groups to worry about. Few places visualize these voids as well as "Consuelo."

Being Unprotected: Working in Zones of Abandonment

There wasn't much village left of the village of Consuelo. Its dozen wooden houses were no longer desired for living space. The families once residing there had traded them in for cement-plastered homes in or near the munici-pal capital, where the prospects of work were more appealing. And who could blame them for their departure? The village's abandonment was a fitting an-alogue of its postapocalyptic surroundings: a gray-brown no man's land that offered pebbled dunes where once palms and plantains must have grown, a silted current where once a free creek must have tumbled, silence where once birds must have twittered. The past decade of heavy excavation meant there was little to mine here, less to cultivate, nothing to fish, nothing to hunt. In-frastructure didn't offer much solace either. The gravel road that connected Consuelo to the rest of the world was one of potholes and rickety plank bridges that needed vigorous inspection before they could be crossed on motorbike. The road's condition evidenced a decline of traveling, of mining, of life.

But not all was afterlife here. Consuelo was also the place where paisa Ramiro had set up camp and where, half a kilometer away from the residen-tial area, his two excavators were mining the scraps from a surface subsoil that had once been rich in gold. Although the purpose of my visit was to see his mine, Ramiro had summoned me to meet him at his house in the village. His explanation had been that the short journey from village to mine was an unsafe one. On undertaking the passage with him, I understood why he had been cautious.

After trudging out of the creek that flanked the village, Ramiro and I walked toward a short line of balsa saplings. On getting closer, he said that in treeless lands like these, balsas are the perfect hideout for bandits. All of a sudden, he pulled an automatic pistol from his jeans, while assuring me in a hushed voice not to be scared. I had seen my fair share of firearms during fieldwork. Lying on kitchen tables, leaning against jerry cans, or grasped in miners' hands, pistols and shotguns popped up as compelling reminders of the bandits who haunt these forests, and who, according to miners, can only be warded off with gunpowder. But to see Ramiro carrying a piece that was all set for firing and to see him walking his predator walk—slow-paced, bent over, his left hand covering the sun-reflecting silver of the pistol resting in his right hand—was a whole different experience. His message that all was fine didn't soothe me. The whispering tone in which he communicated his assurance only made matters more urgent. Of course, I was scared.

Ramiro explained, still whispering, that a week earlier three unknown men had been asking for him. He had not since dared to leave the surround-ings of Consuelo, and each time he walked to his mine he took a different route. He believed the three men to be the same ones who, a few months previous, faces concealed with ski masks, pistols in hand, had snatched ten thousand US dollars' worth of gold from him just outside Consuelo.

There were no men in ski masks this time. So once we had passed the balsa trees, Ramiro and I raised our voices again, reassured by the exposed desert of rocks and grasses encircling us. We spoke about his miner history. He was from a rural town in Antioquia, where he had started panning for gold at eight years old. He came to Chocó in his mid-twenties, in the 1990s, following a dueño who had convinced him that the department was "virgin in gold." He worked for the man for two decades, until the latter was murdered a few years back. No one knew who was responsible, though it most likely had to do with the man being previously kidnapped by guerillas. In the wake of the killing, Ramiro received from the dueño's widow several sluice boxes, water tubes, and a high-caliber motor pump as compensation for payment due. He took out a loan and bought a secondhand excavator, with which, with a bit of luck on his side, he managed to mine together a second excavator. Consequently, he was now a free agent with his own full-fledged mining camp.

He was still summarizing his life history as we made our way through his mine. The place exhibited the gold frontier in all its honest, diesel-driven ugliness. His excavators were chewing away a remaining stretch of trees with their steel beaks, while leaving at their rear a chocolate-colored swamp of water and sludge. After Ramiro showed me a small field of acacias that his own tree nursery had grown, we went into a tent of black and green plastic to do an interview. It became the archetypical conversation of a miner sacrificing one government-endorsed stereotype after another. To Ramiro, retreros were not harming the environment; they were "subsistence miners" who were "reforesting with pure wood." To him, retreros contributed much more to the economy than multinationals. He listed all the good stuff that he and fellow miners had accomplished in Chocó: roads to remote villages, bridges over remote waterways, commerce in remote economies. To him, moreover, retreros were not criminals: "I work so my children can go to university and see a different world than mine, to develop their minds, because the government cannot take away their minds."

Deep into our talk, we were interrupted by the revving of a low-flying police helicopter. Ramiro stuck his head out of the tent to see what was going on. Once the danger had flown over, I asked him what he would have done had the helicopter touched down at his mine. "I can only hope that it doesn't happen," he said, still visibly startled. "Because when it happens, I'll be on the street. I have no money. If they destroy my machines, everything stops.

Can't you see how nervous I am right now? All the time I have to check that there are no soldiers or police coming from the woods. This is no life. And now with these thieves? I never seek problems with anyone. But this makes me want to return to [Antioquia] and do something other than mining. Maybe I'll invest in something legal there. Agriculture. . . . Or I can buy three cows. It's not illegal to have three cows."

Not much later, we took a different route back to the village. Again, we encountered a batch of balsa saplings. Again, Ramiro drew his gun. Again, he walked his predator walk. But this time something was amiss. A sound. A someone or a something maneuvering through the creek behind the balsas. We fell silent as we passed the trees, until, after a few pregnant seconds, two little girls darted into view. They were playing in the water.

"Ah, the scare they gave me," Ramiro said as he lowered the gun. While crossing the creek, I asked how long he would stay in Consuelo to wait out the danger of the bandits.

"I don't know," he answered, shrugging his shoulders. He explained that a couple of men had promised to take care of the problem.

"The police?" I probed, naively.

"No, they do nothing. They catch them and the next day they're back on the streets." He said he meant "the *manes* (guys) further down." He nodded in the direction of a road that connected Consuelo with a few more ghost villages, each accommodating an excavator mining camp. Members of a paramilitary group had entered some of those villages and begun to charge Ramiro and the other encampments five percent of their earnings. "The other day they knocked on doors. They told me they were here to protect the retreros. . . . Let's see what happens."

Academic and policy descriptions of "criminal mining" fall flat when you stroll around with Ramiro in search of bandits, or when you witness his palpable fear of helicopters. Barred from working under conditions of legality, he feared threats from multiple directions: police descending from the sky and ski-masked bandits emerging from behind bushes. In light of this double exposure, it should come as no surprise that retreros like him are skeptical about dealing with the bandits by calling the police. In their tangible "zones of abandonment" (Povinelli 2011), they may very well prefer the alternative systems of law and order of nonstate groups, which supply protection in exchange for gold percentages. Indeed, in Chocó's mining country, the official defense apparatus shares its sovereignty—as in, "the ability and the will . . . to decide on life and death" (Hansen and Stepputat 2005:1)—with AGC paramilitaries and ELN guerrillas, and previously also with the FARC. Amid this scenario of multiple sovereigns, state agents' public authority, monopoly on violence, and fiscal administration are all vehemently challenged. During fieldwork, police and other public functionaries confessed that some of the department's gold areas were off-limits to them because of the threat of organized crime.

Organized crime had its own opinion about this. One day, when visiting a small mining town, I suddenly had to introduce myself to a paramilitary commander. He presented his organization in roughly the following way: "I can tell you who we are because that's no secret to anyone. We are an organization that, let's say, manages the theme of public order here. In Colombia, the state doesn't enter many regions. We're like the state, but a private organization. The state says we're a bunch of terrorists, but that's a lie. We work with the community. Here we have done more for the people than the state."

When mentioning shared sovereignty, I do not insinuate, as the commander did, that excavator and dredge mines are somehow outside state ordering. In the end, police and army operations do "enter many regions." Rather, I mean to designate a situation of various institutional orders, whereby state governance is characterized by intermittent and arbitrary interventions. In the mines of this research, centralized bureaucracy was at once tenaciously present and deceptively absent; just as it instilled fear by blowing up excavators and dredges, so too it fell short in its duty to protect its citizens against bandits. It was this regulatory void that paramilitaries and guerrillas claimed to fill.

Then again, these organizations' provision of supplementary security had much more to do with access to violence than some community-endorsed mandate. To view, like the paramilitary commander, nonstate armed groups as virtuous substitutes for the police is to ignore the violence that local people must suffer when making public their opposition to these groups. Along the same lines, to simply describe miners' payment of vacuna as a voluntary transfer of protection money—as lawmakers are keen to insist—is to overlook that for the involved miners such transactions are tantamount to extortion. The decision to pay or not pay the vacuna often boils down to a choice between paying up or not working. Or worse. There is always the possibility of being kidnapped. I know of two men who, like Ramiro's boss, endured a kidnapping because they had not paid their respective protection sums. In addition, the groups can destroy one's mining equipment. In the course of our interview, one mine administrator recounted how guerrillas had once threatened to burn down his excavator mine if he did not come up with 100 million pesos (25,000 USD) within a week. Being short on such money, he instructed his mining crew to flee the forest where they were at work. In the dead of night, they loaded their expensive water pumps onto their two excavators and drove for eighteen hours straight. Asked about the risk of the operation, the administrator said: "There's only food for us with those machines."

Being Unprotected (II): The Perks of Paying Vacuna

Violence comes in different shapes, though. In the village of La Peña, there were no armed groups charging vacuna. While this power vacuum offered retreros some financial leeway, it also paved the way for a spree of violent robberies at their encampments. Although to my relief I didn't witness the robberies, I did become privy to the spiraling fantasies about them. Retreros and local villagers alike wondered at great length: Why these sudden thefts? Were they triggered by the upcoming expensive Christmas holidays? And who were they, these robbers with ski masks? Villagers? Gang members? Off-duty policemen? Former FARC guerrillas? Ex-miners? Also—as one robbery had happened while gold was being collected (or "washed") from the classifier—who was snitching to the bandits about the washing hours? And the most important question: How to proceed? How to protect the gold? Hide it? Or take on the bandits with guns? Everyone agreed on one thing, though: The village police were of little use. "These hijueputas [sons of bitches] know we don't go there, so they take their chances," a policeman conveyed during one of the many soft-spoken conversations I had about the events.

Four days after the second robbery, one of the junta directiva leaders and I walked from the village to the forest to visit the retreros. On the road leading out of the village, we ran into an army squadron of four soldiers. Their presence was a reaction to other, non-mining-related thefts that had occurred on the road. Even so, considering the recent mine robberies, one of the soldiers guaranteed that the retreros could also count on their protection. "But if you want us to do something, you need to give us a call: 'Now, we're going to wash.' Then we can go out there and hide in the forest for protection. This is how we did it in other areas of Chocó as well."

Walking away from the men and into the bush, the leader and I discussed the protection promise. We evaluated it as good news. After all, this was a problem that demanded resolving—and fast. This was violence, merciless violence. In the first robbery, retrero workers had been rifle-whipped on their heads and forced to wash their classifier at gunpoint. Additionally, in a macabre demonstration of power, the bandits had dug a large grave with one of the excavators, breaking any will to resist among the workforce. In the second robbery, which took place at another camp, the (same?) ski-masked bandits had shown up at the exact time of washing, tied the hands of the entire workforce, and smacked with the sides of their machetes two miners who tried to flee the scene.

Understandably, miners at these campsites were still engrossed in heated conversations about the events. At the camp of the second robbery of four days before, we encountered Rubén, Guzmán, and Édgar eating lunch at a kitchen table. I asked them whether in light of the assault they wanted to remain in La Peña. The question I thought reasonable was answered with down-to-earth resignation.

"In every part of the country you can be assaulted," Rubén snapped.

"You think that Buenaventura is safe? Or Barranquilla?" Guzmán added.

I changed course. "Did you get injured?"

"No," Rubén said, "but one of them wanted to steal my phone." He gently tossed his cell phone on the kitchen table. It was a model that was as small and worn and *smart-less* as they come. Rubén shot me a cheeky grin. "I said to him: 'This will not even earn you 30,000 pesos [10 USD]. For that, you want to leave me cut off from my family?' So, they let me keep it."

"I kept my mouth shut," said Édgar, the third miner. He adopted the pose of a boxer ready to rumble. "But what I actually wanted to say was: 'Drop those guns and let's fight it out with our fists.'"

"None of you were carrying guns?" I asked.

"We have one pistol," Rubén said. "But that was over here [in the camp] and we were out there in the mine. Besides, what are you going to do with one pistol against five armed men?"

"But that is why, I say, we need more weapons," Édgar said. "If we have four weapons, it's an entirely different game."

Rubén favored a more soft-handed solution. "To tell you the truth, Édgar, I'm not going to get myself killed. I'll tell you one thing. The day of the assault, I thought: The washings take too long. Why don't we wash some sheets here and others in the mine, so they can't rob everything at once?"

Édgar drew the conversation back to protection. "Look, I'm also not capable of shooting someone, but we must find someone who has the heart for it." His spirits were visibly lifted when the discussion turned to the news of the soldiers' earlier protection promise. "That sounds good! If this means we have to pay two castellanos per soldier, I don't care. Paying for protection during the washings is better than being the way we are right now."

"But there's no way we can pay," Rubén protested. "The problem is that the moment we've finished washing, we bring the gold to the village. And then, there's no protection and they can attack us at any moment."

A month after this conversation, a gang of bandits tried to rob a third mining camp. Several people informed me that when the dueño of this camp spotted the gang, he indeed phoned the soldiers, who thereupon entered the forest and kept the bandits away by firing at them. The dueño left La Peña after he had received death threats in the wake of the failed attack. Not long after, the army also left La Peña. The miners were on their own again.

The here-described fears of bandits and discussions of protection strategies chime poorly with how national government officials described mining insecurity. In meetings with mining leaders or myself, officials reprimanded miners for not going to the police. If retreros were not the criminals they were accused of being, so the officials asked, why didn't they just denounce the groups extorting them? Such discourse crudely disregarded the restricted territorial control of public forces, which in faraway goldfields offered little to no guarantee of safety. In point of fact, miners generally spoke of "the state"—as in, the public officials who arrested them and blew up their excavators—as one more armed actor to be feared. It's telling, for instance, that when learning of the possibility of calling in the army's help, Édgar and Rubén began discussing the soldiers' payoff. Insofar as army protection was antithetical to their quotidian experiences of citizenship—to their outlawed working lives—it seemed something that warranted a bribe.[7]

While feeling abandoned by state troops, retreros relied on guns, dogs, and walkie-talkies to fend off raids. Nevertheless, even with these auxiliaries, they stood quite powerless when staring robbers in the face, lacking the gunpower and "heart" to meaningfully defend themselves. Given this exposure to violence, it was not uncommon to hear miners express their desire for an external "someone"—to quote Édgar—to protect them from bandits. And thus, while few retreros did not detest the imposed vacuna, I heard a lot of positive comments, particularly when banditry was happening, on the deterrent effect that nonstate armed groups had on robberies. Paramilitaries and guerrillas were considered crooks, yet crooks who rarely stroke with machetes and who didn't steal all one's gold. For retreros, this was worth something. At least with them, you knew what to expect and who you were dealing with. Bandits were a whole different game. These were just faceless ski masks. They had no rules, no arrangements, no empathy for one's difficult financial situation. In short, there was a certain drawback to not paying extortion money. In La Peña, some villagers and excavator miners even sang the praises of the vacuna. "At least those groups look out for you," said Fulton, dueño of a local mine. "I much prefer to pay vacuna than have them kill me or steal from me."

However, these praises were sung loudest in the fieldwork site of Bebará, which used to be governed by the FARC's 34th Front. The guerrillas' military disbandment—celebrated by the Santos administration as a catalyst for peace—had evoked feelings of unsafety among the local retreros. With the FARC no longer supplying security, miners now had to rely on their own weapons. Yet such self-protection paled in comparison with the armed support of one of the world's most famous guerrilla organizations. Besides, there were plenty of indicators suggesting worse times were ahead. Retreros had heard of a violent mine robbery along an adjacent river, of bandits raiding boats on the nearby Atrato headwater, and of cruel gangs wanting to become the new taxer of their mines. These were things to worry about. With the FARC around, payment arrangements had been crystal clear and security well supplied. "We were much calmer with the guerillas," one dueño noted. "It's good, of course, that there's peace, but for our security it's bad. We can now be attacked from all sides."

Mining frontiers produce ambivalent moralities. Although the violence of gold-levying paramilitaries and guerillas was wholeheartedly rejected in places such as La Peña and Bebará, some people (including nonminers who had marginal dealings with such groups) also remarked that at least under the law of the vacuna no robbery or murder got left unpunished. Retreros were among the most vocal in expressing their sympathy for nonstate groups' dealings with thievery and wrongdoing—especially when juxtaposing the latter's nononsense tactics with state forces that were known for corruption, negligence, and, perhaps worst of all, a reluctance to guard informal miners from harm.

Conclusion

This chapter has exposed the impact of criminalization on excavator and—to a lesser extent—dredge miners, the dramatis personae of Chocó's contentious gold rush. To understand their fraught relationship with state governance, I have relied on the analytical notion of "abandonment." In using this term, I don't propose an absolute desertion or blindness of state entities. Rather, the abandonment of excavator and dredge miners was due to a governance of selective withdrawal. On the one hand, these miners remained partly "unseen" by formal bureaucracy. They were—justifiably or not—barred from the formalization framework, and were—not justifiably—excluded from security provisions, having to fend for themselves in their dealings with bandits, guerrillas, and paramilitaries. On the other hand, miners remained very visible in terms of penal and surveillance interventions (aerial and terrestrial supervision, incarceration, property eradication), as well as in demonizing discourses that depicted them as the culprits of their own unsafety.

Such Janus-faced politics sits uneasily with conventional accounts of "state absence" in the Global South. In much political theory, the state is portrayed as a centralized organization, whose sovereignty extends from the nation's political core to the periphery and recedes in potency and presence along the way. Instead, Chocó's goldfields experienced a disjointed unfolding of the state bureaucracy, whose multiple agencies (from the mine-destroying UNIMIL to the immobile La Peña village police) affected gold country in different ways, as they were characterized by varied levels of regulatory efficiency and authority. Speaking of the gold mines' abandonment, thus, is speaking of a multifaceted state apparatus that was present and absent at the same time; one that oscillated between violence and retraction, between disciplinary power and noninterference, between concrete acts of detention and a structural *inaction*—out of choice or inability—regarding miners' problems of unsafety and informality.

Finally, by thinking of miners as being abandoned, I also allude to their own understandings of self. That is to say, the notion of abandonment captures not only material conditions of deprivation, but also the languages of disenfranchisement through which miners made meaning of these conditions. Retreros and dragueros claimed to be abandoned, excluded, and forgotten by their state. By doing so, they were not declaring the virtual nonexistence of governance, but simply pointing out what they saw as its flaws and injustices. They viewed the damning stories that lawmakers spun about them as a misrecognition of their contributions to local economies. They judged the (possible) destruction of their machinery as a grave violation of their rights to work and property. And they perceived the lack of protection against criminal groups as a rejection of their Colombian citizenship.

PART II

Performing the State

CHAPTER 3

===

Putting Mining Law into Practice

You never know what the government
wants.

—*Alex (barequero)*

By early 2017, two weeks into my fieldwork, I scooped an invitation for an impromptu meeting of dragueros and allied mining leaders. It took place at the small and improvised office of a local mining association, which lobbied government officials for the formalization of Chocó's miners. Three days before, a special forces team of the police had dynamited twelve pontoons that had been illegally dredging the Quito River. The dragueros at the meeting, five paisas and one Brazilian, had been victims of the police mission. Not surprisingly, they considered it a grave injustice. A woman (speaking with a marked Portuguese accent, looking about thirty years old) stated that the oil spills and metal rubble produced by the bombing of their machines were more harmful to the environment than the actual devastation wrought from dredging. A man (at least a decade older and betraying the immediately recognizable drawl of Antioquia) agreed and said that Chocó's communities should rise up and protest the police operations, because it was they who were reaping the benefits of a healthy mining economy. Another woman (looking the same age as the man and evincing the same paisa accent) added that there were at least four hundred people employed by their "dragons," while local commerce profited from their consumption of diesel and other products.

This wasn't the first destruction mission they had suffered, nor would it likely be their last, and so the discussion centered on how to go on from here. There were one or two comments about other dragueros who had been left unscathed in the recent clampdown, because they had paid a fair bit of gold to soldiers of influence. For her part, the paisa woman suggested putting computer chips on their machines, so as to inform the government about which of the Quito dredges were owned by miners who belonged to the association, and therefore were serious about formalization. The leader of the meeting saw little use in this strategy. He reminded everyone they had tried this before, to no effect, by attaching Colombian flags to their dredges to distinguish themselves from the nonassociative, and mostly Brazilian, dredgers working in the same river. He concluded the meeting by proposing a more relational strategy: pressuring local politicians to lobby on the association's behalf for less repression with the defense personnel that orchestrated the police missions.

The meeting, in short, addressed a vexing question that preoccupied many miners in Chocó (for obvious practical reasons), as well as myself (for theoretical reasons): How to navigate state law in a context of blatant illegality? Observers of small-scale mining have repeatedly called out state entities for their myopia toward the lived complexities of extraction regions (e.g., Idrobo et al. 2013; Siegel 2013; Siegel and Veiga 2009). These diagnoses of regulatory blindness often interlace with arguments that such places suffer from "minimal state presence" (Idrobo et al. 2013:27) or "the absence of a functional state" (Siegel 2013:12). Although such analyses provide well-founded critiques on government neglect, their suggestions of state absence fail to account for the bottom-up practices of state formation that emerge in mining zones. Through their lobbying, flags, formality-aspiring association, and proposed computer chips and bribes, the dragueros of the Quito River actively engaged the state bureaucracy in their criminalized mode of production. This chapter looks into such engagement. It provides ethnographic snapshots that illustrate that small-scale miners are not just outlawed or abandoned by governing schemes, as shown in the preceding chapters, but also give shape to how these schemes materialize through their alternative performances of law. But before delving into these underground legalities, I first introduce—with a bit of support from Monique Nuijten's work—the backdrop of bureaucratic despair that set the stage for miners' own enactment of legislation.

Lost in Legalization: The Despair-Generating Machine

In what is now a landmark monograph on state formation—*Power, Community, and the State*—Monique Nuijten (2003) maps out the organizational activities of a Mexican *ejido*. She shows how the *ejidatarios* of her study, in their endeavor to resolve a land conflict, undertake an endless search for brokers to get a foot inside the bureaucracy. Nuijten connects this never-giving-up attitude to the capacity of state agencies to convince "that everything is possible, that cases are never closed and that things will be different from now on" (16). She perceives the state as a "hope-generating machine," endowed with the ability "to overcome people's scepticism" (197). From this standpoint, she positions herself "against a view of the state as an almighty apparatus with almost top-down control," and instead theorizes it as "a collection of decentered practices without a central agency, or core project" (15). In Nuijten's thought-provoking account, it's the fantasies engendered by bureaucracy, rather than efficient centralized control, that enable the reproduction of state power. She reveals that in her research site, state documents acquired meanings beyond their original purpose. Land tax receipts ended up serving as proof of land usage in communication with officials, while a lost village map evolved into a fetishized object around which ejidatarios mobilized. This appropriation of government techniques leads Nuijten to propose that the "culture of the state" consists as much of bureaucratic rituals of representation as of the "practices of interpretation and reading" of the people targeted by these rituals (117).

Other scholars have applied Nuijten's ideas to places beyond Mexico. Sandra Martínez Basallo (2013) calls on the case of Afro-Colombian land titling in Chocó to argue that the Colombian state is likewise a hope-generating machine. While recounting the difficulties of a community council in obtaining a land title, Martínez Basallo notices how titling agencies "reproduce the fetishized image of the state as a central locus of power" (178). When rejecting title requests, officials insist on the failure of applicants to comply with formal protocol, an administrative "punishment" that consolidates the image of the state as a coherent and top-down machinery (179).

However, the interpretive device of the hope-generating machine does not land very smoothly in the gold mines of Chocó, where state regulation generated despair and fear above anything else. The region's miners, too, were confronting "officials . . . always willing to initiate procedures" (Nuijten

2003:16). But to most miners, the constant arrival of new legislation was evidence of the fact that solutions were *not* forthcoming. For example, Camilo, an excavator dueño who was a native of the department, certainly did not expect much from state law. "They say: 'You have to fulfill this and this.' Then, you've fulfilled these requisites and they say: 'It's not that, it's this.' If you eventually get your paper, your title, the government comes up with a new law two years later. You'll never get there. Because the government doesn't help you. They destroy you."

Facing the stranglehold of formalization procedures, miners did not express a belief in a state system of "coherence, coordination, and consistent top-down working" (Nuijten 2003:116). Instead, retreros and artisanal miners alike confessed to being completely lost in the maddening red tape of mining law. They were in the dark regarding how to acquire a concession contract, why title requests were rejected, and which combination of papers they needed to sell gold. They did not view the paper bureaucracy as one of coherency, one that gave "the message that everything [was] possible" (Nuijten 2003:196–197), but one that discouraged them from continuing to try. If anything, it was because of the experienced *incoherency* of the state—because of years of waiting, being shuttled from pillar to post, and seeing application forms magically disappear in government offices—that some of the retreros had abandoned their efforts to seek mining concessions. These skeptics saw working legally as something unfeasible, arguing that even the best-organized among them had seen their machinery blown to bits. In being the losers of today's regulatory framework, they simply desired to proceed with their labor while it was still possible. "No one will provide us with a title," bebareño Alfredo said. "In Quibdó, they tell you to go to Bogotá. In Bogotá, they say: 'Go somewhere else.' You get tired of the runaround; that no one gives you a solution."

In effect, it was arguably in the excavator mines where the hopelessness of bureaucracy became most evident. Rather than upholding much faith in formal proceedings, retreros collectively self-identified as the victims of law. Early on in my research, I had wondered why they still bothered to head into the forest, working unholy hours, with almost no prospect of formality and public forces breathing down their necks. After a few conversations at mining camps, I realized that my wondering betrayed my privileged positionality. Whereas some research participants insisted on the freedoms of mining to explain their ongoing presence in the goldfields (e.g., not being bossed around, the imminent chance of striking it rich; see Chapter 1), most posited arguments of economic pragmatism. There were no good-paying jobs in commerce or agriculture. There were no construction companies taking their résumés seriously. There was amid the current political ambience no one willing to buy their excavators. Above all, there were bills to pay and families to feed and machinery debts to settle. They were here, in a zero-sum face-off with their government, simply because there was no *there* affording a more attractive alternative. But with the persecution of excavator mines likely to grind on, retreros' perspectives about formalization were not at all hopeful. Rather, they continued mining *despite* the bureaucracy—despite selling restrictions, despite police choppers, despite army speedboats, despite their diagnosis as "illegal." As James, a paisa mine administrator, laid out: "The way things are now, mining will definitely end. We won't throw in the towel until the government stops us, but the truth is, this has a very uncertain future. We live in uncertainty day after day. It's better to think of the present, because who knows if we'll still be here tomorrow."

In view of the dead end of formalizing, and so the ever-pending threat of destruction operations, a couple of the "larger" miners had given up on mining altogether. Aurilio, whom we met in the previous chapter, had eventually retired from his coordinating position at the San Miguel dredge because incarceration would wreak havoc on his political aspirations. Yet the most-cited reason to leave mining was equipment destruction. The risk of losing excavators had encouraged some retreros to temporarily use them outside the gold mines, in more legitimate construction work. Others continued mining but expressed remorse for their decision to invest in excavators a few years back, in a day and age in which no one foresaw the vastness of the police missions to come. "When we proposed putting our money into mining, things were not so difficult," Fernando remembered. Four years before our conversation, he had pooled resources with five other chocoanos to buy an excavator. "But if you were to ask me today, I wouldn't have done it. There's always the fear of them coming to burn you. So, we're not going to invest anymore in our mine. We will continue as long as we can, until the machine breaks down."

Still, despite such widespread disillusion, the seductive pull of bureaucracy that is the focus of Nuijten's study wasn't completely absent in miners' discourse. Because even if expectations of public policy were low, there were many people who did still take an interest in legislation, as they fetched selling documents, registered with mining associations, and honed their legal knowledge in government meetings. Just as failed titling attempts prompted some miners to give up on working inside the law, so too they inspired others to formulate new strategies and find new allies with access to the formalization process: investors with the muscle to pay for a part of the expensive titling process, or professional middlemen (engineers, accountants, lawyers, state employees) who were better equipped than they—in terms of political savviness and relations—to navigate the bureaucracy. Even miners with damning visions about the government did not always cease their efforts at legalizing their businesses. Take retrero Everson, who when interviewed said the following about a titling procedure he had initiated a few years ago: "When we asked about it, they told us that it lay beneath ten thousand other request forms. We never heard more about it. The government does not want to see who works well and who doesn't. They never come to see if we are filling the holes. Our government doesn't want the common good to be for all of us; they want those on the bottom to stay at the bottom."

A couple of minutes later, though, he said he had recently registered his mine with the Chamber of Commerce and started to pay for social benefits for his workers, as part of a new title application. Asked why he thought that this time things would turn out differently, he answered: "Because you never know what happens with the state. Colombia is the country that has the highest number of laws. Every time you think that you can become formal, they pull out another law. It always changes. So maybe the next time with a new president the laws will help us."

To be sure, statements such as this one underwrite the argument that the "hope-generating characteristic of the bureaucracy is . . . based on the fact that the bureaucracy offers endless openings" (Nuijten 2003:16). And yet, it would be crude to make such a proposition without addressing the specific freedoms that regulatory "openings" provide: in the case of Everson, the freedoms of selling gold without restriction, working without detention, and enjoying property without its destruction. Each time police actions loomed large, Everson had to halt production and hide his excavators. The point being, the bureaucracy's capacity to peddle hope in miners like him was premised on a parallel capacity to peddle fear and despair. Or to put it another way, Everson and other formalization-seekers persisted in their legal quest not just because they were pulled by the state apparatus's enticing promises, but also because they were pushed by its punitive interventions.

As I see it, it is these latter interventions that the concept of the "hope-generating machine" has little to say about. Nuijten views the state as being "made up of thousands of uncoordinated actions without a centre of control" (119–200), which nevertheless manage to solidify the *idea* of a "centre . . . of . . . control in which power is concentrated" (15). I concur with her that stringent bureaucrats often seek to convince governed populations of an illusory governmental coherence. However, I fear that if we follow her strong emphasis on the discursive aspects of domination, and her concomitant emphasis on the inefficiency of state disciplinary control, we run the risk of confining political subordination to the ideational—to the fantasies of the governed—and miss out on the vicious underbelly of biopolitical life. Though Nuijten is right to note that the state machine lacks a unified agency, her theorizing remains rather silent as to the fact that statutory regimes are often violently effective in subjugating people to their rule, and with that, as to the fact that such subjugation affects people's decisions on whether, and if so, how to engage with public institutions. I maintain that we can only grasp how miners are "enticed" by rules and laws by taking into account the material context of penalization from which these arise. Miners' insistence to keep investing time and money in formalization schemes results not only from the bureaucracy's ability "to overcome people's scepticism" (Nuijten 2003:197), but also from very real punishments that dissuade them from choosing the alternative of nonengagement. Through pursuing formality, miners hope to be relieved of equipment destruction, the threat of incarceration, and limitations on gold selling. "They demand and we follow," artisanal miner Héctor said, as we talked about the paperwork that he needed to sell his gold legally. "But what else can I do? If I don't get those papers, I can't sell gold and my family dies."[1]

With this being said, I believe that the greater value of Nuijten's analysis lies not so much in her explanation of the attraction of bureaucracy, as in her refined ethnographic effort to replace the common image of nonstate actors as recipients of state power with one that portrays them as participants in it. Because whether driven by hope or fear (and often it is both), the mundane practices of people outside bureaucracy constantly reconfigure the governing interventions of those within. The following section examines how this came about in Chocó.

The Mayor's Certificate

Over the course of my fieldwork, miners frequently notified me about ongoing developments in mining regulation. They mentioned the restrictions put in place by some new resolution, urged me to read up on one more formalization initiative, and sent text messages with hyperlinks to freshly issued decrees. Amid this circulation of documents, bills, and legislation, I had a hard time keeping up and often felt clueless about all the legalities miners threw at me.

I soon discovered they also struggled. Though mining law and its paper paraphernalia generated grandiose thrills and fears, there was little consensus on what the law meant. People continually misread legislation or envisioned it to be unreadable. Panners were unsure about which certificates and ID cards they needed to sell their gold. Pump miners had no idea which paper allowed them to move their fuel legally. And excavator miners invested efforts and money in becoming recognized under an *Área de Reserva Especial*, a legal category that formalized "traditional" operators, yet, in contrast to the hopes of many, offered no direct juridical protections to those working with excavators (see Chapter 7). Yet few government interventions created as much buzz as Decree 1102.

In June 2017, Colombia's Ministry of Mines and Energy issued the decree as part of, to quote then-minister Germán Arce, "a strategy to control illegality" (*Semana* 2017b). This roughly meant preventing the widespread phenomenon of gold buyers registering illegal gold as though it came from manual-based subsistence miners—who were exempted from the requirement of a mining title. Decree 1102 regulated an earlier established selling maximum for subsistence operators (thirty-five grams a month), which had been implemented to discourage the fraudulent declarations.[2] More concretely, the decree declared that subsistence miners could commercialize their metals only if they presented buyers with two documents: a "Mayor's Certificate" [*Constancia de la Alcaldía*]—a document issued by a miner's municipal office acknowledging their status as a local subsistence miner—and a "Declaration of Production" form—on which a miner declared the origin and weight of their merchandised gold.[3] Further, Decree 1102 stipulated that miners surpassing the production ceiling, as well as those not possessing a Mayor's Certificate within six months from the decree's publication, would be removed from the register of the National Mining Agency and cut off from the possibility of gold selling.[4]

I didn't know all this when I accompanied my friend Emiro on a motor trip to his town hall to apply for the Mayor's Certificate. Neither did he. "I know we need a paper, but I don't know which one," he told me. He knew, though, that the paper was important. Without the proper documentation, he could not sell his gold legally and would be forced to do business with *aventureros* (local middlemen), who paid 25 percent less.

Emiro did his mining with a so-called *minidraga* [mini-dredge]. This is basically a scaled-down version of the larger "dragons," although in lieu of a mechanical crane it relies for dredging on a human diver with a suction hose. It is lethally dangerous work, because divers are vulnerable to being flooded by subaquatic landslides. Yet as Emiro often impressed on me, the work generates more gold than low-tech forms of extraction above the water. In view of this productivity, he planned to apply for an extra certificate for his wife, Sandra. She did not mine, but Emiro figured a second registration would prove useful when he reached his own selling limit (quite likely with a minidraga), or if other *minidragueros* reached theirs and required Emiro's papers to sell their gold—in exchange for a few pesos.

On reaching the municipal capital, we first dropped by Emiro's regular buyer, who gave him an application form, along with a piece of paper bearing his registration number at the National Mining Agency. Emiro took the two papers to the town hall, where he presented them at the desk of the municipal employee who—a long investigation around the building had clarified—was tasked with all matters related to the Mayor's Certificate. Seated at his desk, and not looking up from a pile of papers he was flipping through, the officer told us he was only in charge of *approving* certificates. He scoffed some hasty directions to the booth where we could locate the woman processing *requests*. Yet at the respective booth, we only found two of the woman's colleagues, who had us know she would be back in no less than a few hours. "They always tell you to come back," Emiro said while walking out of the building. "They do that to wear you out, Jes, because this government doesn't want you to mine."

A lunch and two-and-a-half hours later, we did encounter the official at her booth. She told Emiro to get photocopies of his and Sandra's ID cards, because only then could she commence the request procedure. Emiro began to lose his patience. "They always invent something to limit traditional miners," he protested, now storming out of the town hall. "This is why I'm thinking of moving to Bogotá and working in construction."

Once we got our hands on Emiro's photocopy at a nearby printing shop (in the absence of Sandra's ID card, he would now apply only for his certificate), we once more entered the town hall. We joined a long line of people waiting to exchange their photocopies for "payment forms," which authorized them to pay the 14,000 pesos (5 USD) the municipality charged for processing the certificates. On receiving this form, we needed to wait in a second line to make the actual payment, after which we could finally return to the request booth and hand over the payment receipt, along with the initial application document we had received from the buyer. "This government tries to prevent us from mining!" Emiro fumed when we were outside again, in reference to the paperwork treadmill we had just survived.

But while many papers had passed through his hands, the mother document had not. To receive the Mayor's Certificate, he had to come back another day. The first time he returned, there was no document with his name on it. The second time, he was denied entry to the town hall for wearing shorts. The third time: no document. Finally, after several weeks, he obtained the certificate. "Each time they told me to come back next week. So I asked: 'What do I have to do to get this done?' I paid him a bribe. Nothing big. A lunch. And that's how I got the document." While telling me about these futile visits to the town hall, Emiro once more linked the slow pace of the municipal bureaucracy to a bigger political master plan to kill off Chocó's mining trade: "The government says we need this paper and then they say we need another one. They do this because we don't pay taxes. They try to stop us from selling gold, just so that we'll leave mining."

Emiro was not alone in indulging in fantasies about a hidden rationale behind the Mayor's Certificate. When miners discussed the document, they generally didn't mention mean-spirited merchants or armed groups abusing the data of subsistence miners—as their legislators did. Instead, they perceived the document to be one more trick up the government's sleeve to do away with them in favor of multinationals. Even the artisanal miners whom the decree was supposed to protect from fraudulent registrations shared this critique. And yet, while the news of the certificate and the decree behind it had spread around Chocó like wildfire, miners knew little about their specifics. Almost no one had read the decree. Although many perceived it as unjust, they did so by erroneously assuming it had introduced a selling limit—which had already been in force for five months (Decree 1102 and the Mayor's Certificate were merely intended to enforce this limit). The selling maximum itself created similar misapprehensions. There was much confusion regarding whether the ceiling was annual or monthly, as regarding what the consequences would be on reaching it. Some imagined that their selling accounts would be blocked. Others reckoned the government would start taxing their earnings. It was especially these taxes that frightened miners. They worried about having to pay huge sums of undeclared gold earnings, about seeing their personal belongings impounded, about facing incarceration.

Though mostly unsure about all this, they were careful not to push their luck and surpass the selling cap.

Along the Bebará River, the Mayor's Certificate harbored an additional threat. For more than twenty years, the river had fallen victim to the coercive tutelage of various nonstate armed groups, most notably and recently the FARC's 34th Front. In the aftermath of the 2016 demilitarization of the FARC, many bebareños harbored the hope that they would receive financial compensation for their suffering during the war. They had registered themselves with the *Unidad de Víctimas*, the national agency offering redress to victims of the armed conflict. For this reason, many people had become averse to the idea of applying for the Mayor's Certificate. They knew that the paper surveilled their gold production and feared that using it (and making public their income from their bareque mining) would lead the government to negatively evaluate their need to be monetarily compensated for their victimhood.

In one village, these worries had been largely bolstered by community leader Breiner. In a village meeting I attended, he had sternly warned his neighbors against applying for the document:

> There are those here who for a difference of 50,000 [pesos] [14 USD] want to get their papers and sell to legal buyers in Quibdó.[5] But just so you know, when you sell your gold legally, who owns the data on your income? The government! And here we know that when the government wants to control you, it's always to take away your benefits. What I am trying to explain: Here we all say we are poor and have lived in extreme poverty. But when you earn four castellanos per month, that is four times the minimum wage, for the government you're not poor anymore. Since we have registered ourselves as victims of the war, humanitarian help will not come here, because the government looks at our gold incomes and says we're not that poor. Another thing: If you do intend to get the paper, don't throw away your gold receipts. If you make too many castellanos, the DIAN (the Colombian tax authority) will come after you. And if you cannot justify that you have made your money with bareque, you'll go to jail and they'll take away your house. That's why I will keep searching for my gold, but I don't sell legally to no one!

Breiner's concerns found resonance among fellow barequeros, who, especially after this speech, were betwixt and between getting the Mayor's Certificate, implying the higher price of the legal market, and preserving tomorrow's war victim returns. One night, I discussed the sanity of Breiner's advice with Yulia, her niece Zuleidy, and their neighbor Alex, as the four us were gathered at the house of the two women.

"You know, I almost committed the error," Yulia said. "I almost sold legally. I already had the papers."

"Why didn't you sell with your papers?" I asked.

"Because people say that they will take away your benefits."

Zuleidy, who was roughly the same age as her aunt (late thirties), cracked a smile of disbelief. "So *tía* [auntie], you're not selling because you're a displaced person?"

"That's right," Yulia said.

Zuleidy shot me a look and shook her head. "She thinks that they will interrogate her because of five pounds of gold!"

"Did you get the certificate, Zuleidy?" I asked.

"Of course," she replied. "I sell legally. What I don't agree with is using the paper to sell the gold of others. Because then, when I want to sell my gold, my quota is already full. I will never do that, no matter how much they offer. Because when I sell someone else's 90 million pesos of gold, well, that other person doesn't appear anywhere and the state will think that all that gold is mine. Then comes the DIAN and I must pay, what is it, the IVA tax, I don't know the name.[6] How do I pay these taxes?"

Zuleidy directed herself to her aunt again. "What I don't believe, tía, is what Breiner says. How are they going to take that money away from you? If I'm displaced, I'm a victim! How are they going to leave me with nothing?"

Alex, who had remained silent until then, came to Yulia's rescue. He acknowledged that he, too, didn't trust the certificate. "Here there are people who say the high price is the high price, that the official price is 370 [thousand pesos] per castellano and that aventureros buy for 320 [thousand pesos]. But they're wrong. When you start to analyze, it's the government who has proposed this paper for selling gold. And behind this paper there's got to be something else. Maybe they charge you taxes afterward or maybe they take away your victim money. You never know what the government wants."

The discussion demonstrates how interlocutors' experiences with state governance oscillated between hope and fear, being suspended in what Deborah Poole (2004:38) describes as the "slippage between threat and guarantee" through which state power makes itself felt.[7] While the Mayor's Certificate offered miners the guarantee to sell for official prices, it was also a "source of... vulnerability to the arbitrary power of the state" (Poole 2004:36), as it opened them up to the threat of surveillance. Many people were reluctant to apply for the unfamiliar document. The state apparatus they knew was sleazy. Its laws and paperwork had to be viewed with suspicion, notwithstanding the innocent qualities that policymakers bestowed on these. In deciding whether or not to get the paper, it mattered little what their legislators said about or in the decree endorsing it. Miners said they didn't understand such language, or fantasized about a secret motive about which officials kept their lips sealed. More than anything, it seemed it was not the factual content of the certificate and the decree, but rather their "illegibility" (Das 2004)—their indecipherable language, possible secrets, indeterminate judicial repercussions—that triggered miners to wonder about the wicked ways of state rule. "You never know what the government wants," Alex had said.

Accordingly, miners' documentary practices underscore Monique Nuijten's (2003:117) aforementioned proposition that "the culture of the state" depends as much on state procedure as on how this is interpreted by the population it means to govern. By understanding the Mayor's Certificate as a threat—a danger to "your victim money"; a trick to "take away your benefits"; a strategy "to stop us from selling gold, just so that we'll leave mining"— miners in Chocó, like the ejidatarios in Nuijten's study, ascribed attributes to a legal form that transgressed its original regulatory function. To put it in another way, upon its reception in everyday lifeworlds, the certificate had less to do with "a strategy to control illegality," as the minister of Mines and Energy had stated, than with grievances of abandonment and fantasies of unlimited state control. Correspondingly, it was not just formal legal interventions, but also these grievances and fantasies that gave shape to "the cultural inscription of the idea of the state" (Alonso 1994 in Nuijten 2003:17).

Even so, while recalling that the state exists "simultaneously as material force and as ideological construct" (Mitchell 2006:169)—as an "idea," but also as "a palpable nexus of practice and institutional structure" (Abrams 1988:82)—I wish to emphasize that the role of miners in state-building was not limited to the ideological. While their fear-induced interpretations of the Mayor's Certificate most clearly implied an appropriation of the document's symbolic meaning (of the state as "idea"), such readings also laid their imprint on actual governing practicalities (on the state as "material force"). After all, the perceived threat of the certificate sparked a refusal among many people to apply for it, thwarting the document's potential as an effective tool of knowledge production. This more practical kind of subversion—of the paper's administrative potential—also happened in a subtler way, as my trip with Emiro illustrated. By affording a higher price for gold, the Mayor's Certificate became a source of economic power on which people could secretly capitalize. Municipal functionaries delayed allocation procedures in exchange for petty bribes, whereas miners applied for additional certificates for non-mining family members, either to escape the selling cap or to sell leftover selling space to others for a small profit. Certainly, both these documentary subversions—both the refusal of the certificate because of its *threats* and the exploitation of its selling *guarantees*—give weight to the argument, as posited by Nuijten and others (Das 2004; Navaro-Yashin 2002; Nugent 1994), that state-making is contingent on the mundane understandings of law by non-state actors. Through their alternative readings of the Mayor's Certificate— and through similar alternative readings of mining titles, transportation papers, and other documents—miners actively mediated how mining legislation arrived in their goldfields.

Cumulative Legality

Yet miners' entanglement with state law went beyond the (mis)reading of certificates; it also involved making the law tangible in the sites where it felt most absent: the excavator pits. As outlined in the previous chapter, the retreros were at the forefront of informality, being more likely than smaller miners to fall subject to equipment destruction and detention by public forces, as well as to the violence of nonstate armed groups. However, regardless of these vulnerabilities, the excavator mines were anything but "lawless" places, given their dueños' performance of the mines' quasi-legal character. To illustrate what I mean by this, let me recount a visit to a mine that I'll call "Suerte Divina."

Upon learning about my studies, Suerte Divina's administrator, Jefferson, had suggested a personal tour of his mine's campsite. When I subsequently visited, I understood why he had so readily invited me. Suerte Divina was something to be proud of. All workers wore helmets and uniforms. They were not paid by the customary percentage, but enjoyed contracted wages and social benefits, while a nurse attended to their medical needs. The campsite, in turn, was not the cluster of plastic tents, hammocks, and scattered litter that I knew from other excavator mines. Here, miners rested in a U-shaped mini-village of twenty-three wooden sheds, each designed for single occupancy and each with a water tank and television. In between the sheds, arrowed notices indicated the direction of the mine's evacuation route, whereas other signs motivated workers to use garbage sacks. And then there was the kitchen: a one-story wooden house staffed by no fewer than three cooks and furnished with two lunch tables, a picture-perfect television, and a two-by-one-meter plaque listing the "Internal Labor Regulations of the Suerte Divina Mine." The plaque touched on "Remunerable Vacation Days," "Measures of Sanctioning Labor Harassment," and "Hygiene Regulations and Industrial Safety"; topics that were all smartened up with meticulous references to laws, decrees, and resolutions, down to the specific article.

Yet the high point of Jefferson's tour was a walk across a "recovered" piece of land. In the same area where two years earlier excavators had been grazing for gold, the miners were now planting trees, rice, and sugarcane. Walking ahead of me at a self-assured pace, Jefferson boasted: "You can register there are no holes here. We have smoothed everything. There is not one single pool!" I registered all I could, taking photos, jotting down notes. In the meantime, he apprised me of everything in the site worthy of celebration. "Santos says that it takes five thousand years for a seed to appear in these lands," he commented as we passed a plot of leafy acacia saplings. "But these trees are from one week ago and just look at them."

When we arrived at a large pond, I told Jefferson he needed to retract his promise of "not one single pool." A prompt clarification followed. One of the mine's workers, who had been following us for just this purpose, threw a fistful of granular food in the water. No sooner had it touched the surface than an army of hungry fish emerged. "This pool was very difficult to dry up," Jefferson explained. "So, we introduced some cachama fish. Around eight thousand of them."

To Jefferson, the landscape's second life was irrefutable proof of the seriousness of their labor. "We comply with whatever the government wants," he said as we walked away from the tailing pond turned fish-breeding pool. "The garbage, the acacias, the removal of holes. You could work cheaper by working carelessly, but when you're careless, the government comes and burns your machines."

"So you're not scared of an operation?" I asked, knowing that the mine did not have a mining title.

"Nah, we've been here for twenty years and always with the support of the people. They have never burned us, because we're legal. We have everything."

His reference to legality surprised me. I mentioned their lack of a title, to which he countered: "But if they haven't burned us in all those years, it's because we're well organized. We don't work with fear anymore. We take photos of all of this [the land] and the community leaders give them to the government during their meetings with the Ministry of Mines. That has helped us in not getting burned. We're paying for boots, uniforms, social security. The government likes that. Supposedly, we're legal. If they come, we can say: 'We've done everything you've asked.'"

As the former shows, while Jefferson and his co-workers worked without a formal concession, the state acquired a spectral presence at their goldfields. The retreros mined the way they mined with the criteria of officialdom in mind. Logic held that, someday, some public institution would confront them with their labor. And when that day arrived, as Jefferson explained so clearly, the miners would be prepared. Although this readiness would not per se result in a mining title, it would most definitely save them from an equipment-destroying operation—from "getting burned." In strategizing this way for the future arrival of the state apparatus, the Suerte Divina retreros had begun—so to speak—legalizing themselves, and had animated the state where it had hitherto been quite lifeless.

These anticipatory stances are reminiscent of similar practices in other South American rainforests. In a captivating ethnography, Jeremy Campbell (2015) sets out how colonists in the Brazilian Amazon fabricate documents, histories, and territories in the hope of having their colonized lands recognized as formal property at some future time. Through these speculative strategies, colonists "engage government in . . . a 'proleptic' mode," presenting themselves "as if the state and market [have] already ratified their positions" (7). Campbell maintains that it is by speculating on future government interventions that colonists produce the state before its actual arrival, "making the illegal legal, aligning policies to fit speculations, and exerting influence on the shape of government" (192).

As with Brazilian colonists, the state was never far away from the hearts and minds of retreros when organizing their informal labor. Though almost never as committed as Jefferson, a lot of mine owners and administrators were keen on manifesting some kind of proof of what they presumed to be the workings of a legal enterprise. Even if retreros viewed the odds of formalization

Figure 6. Field of acacia saplings. Photo by the author.

as rigged against them—and usually described their relationship with the bureaucracy as hopeless (see Chapter 2)—many also felt that those most faithful to formal environmental criteria were the ones least likely to undergo the wrath of excavator-smashing police. Owing to such speculation, their consumption of large swaths of rainforest coexisted with more or less limited expressions of ecological goodwill, ranging from filling holes to building tree nurseries and planting acacias and fruit saplings.

What's more, in light of the outlawed status of their work, retreros considered that any document hinting at state law would be useful bargaining power in a future one-on-one with state functionaries. And thus they hoarded tax receipts of gold sales, formalization letters, excavator ownership papers, testimonies of Chamber of Commerce registrations, and written approvals of the Afro-Colombian community councils that owned the lands where they mined Although these papers had little value compared with a mining title, miners suggested that they might prove helpful on a given judgment day. Perhaps their company folders filled with (surrogate) legal papers would one day prompt the police not to demolish their machinery, convince the army not to seize their diesel transports, or maybe, as a few dared to dream, persuade the National Mining Agency to rule in their favor at an upcoming titling process.

The retreros' modest attempts at environmental care and legal documentation articulated what Campbell (2015:129) classifies as "prolepsis": "the representation of something as existing before it actually does." Retreros were mining *before* state recognition, before being formalized. Yet they incorporated a slight hint of the law in their work in preparation for the moment that public officials would show up at their mine, with either a mining title or, more likely, an explosive. Just as the dragueros of this chapter's introduction used Colombian flags to apprise the police of their desire to formalize, so too the dueños of excavator mines relied on symbols of legit entrepreneurship (e.g., legal papers and acacias) to perform their right to work before this right had been officially conceded to them.

Consider paisa Gerson. He had never experienced the trauma of equipment destruction, but on one occasion he had come close. He reckoned that it was only thanks to his portfolio of paperwork that no harm had been done to his two excavators. "Exactly where you are right now, *papá*, there were some guys from the police. They wanted to know what I was doing here. So, I showed them my papers: papers of the machines, of the engines. They saw I was registered with the National Mining Agency, that I had my paper to sell gold, and my Chamber of Commerce [registration]. I think that's how I saved myself."

His registration with the National Mining Agency related to manual-based, not excavator, mining, as did his documentation permitting him to sell gold. Moreover, having his company and inventory registered in the annals of public institutions did not grant him any legal right to dig with excavators. He knew all this. Nevertheless, he also felt that being a serious miner could decrease the likelihood of property destruction and increase his chances of someday obtaining a mining title. Therefore, he had piled up a stack of evidence of his virtuous way of working. Aside from the portfolio of legal papers, he had planted a miniature forest of acacias. He had also hired a "man with a drone" to video-record the already deforested state of a land he was planning on re-mining, thereby documenting, for a possible visit of government officials, that he was not guilty of any environmental crime.

Everson, a bebareño who owned three machines, strategized similarly. He said it was thanks to not using mercury that he had never been singled out for a destruction operation. He also figured that his large file case of "official" documents held convincing sway in an ongoing formalization procedure, as well as in the nerve-racking moments when he was stopped by the navy while transporting excavator fuel by boat. "I have three folders: one for each excavator. I have my Chamber of Commerce [papers], my social security [papers], my RUT [papers],[8] my approval [papers] from the community council. You show this to the navy hoping that they don't confiscate your fuel. And for the title request, I have sent it all to the government. They don't ask for it, but that doesn't matter. You put everything in there, hoping that it will affect them. Because, tell me: How am I illegal if I pay for all of that?"

What was striking about these miners, as it was with Jefferson, was that they continually insisted on being invisible to governance. When bringing up "the state," research participants discussed its absence, its ignorance of their working methods, its lack of intention to sort the bad apples from the rest. However, in preparing themselves for mine-destroying public forces and titling procedures, retreros also acknowledged the plausibility of a benevolent governmental vision. Indeed, the law that they knew was always changing and open to the interpretation of the bureaucratic beholder. In their descriptions, state departments were awash with brokerage, favoritism, and corruption. This being the case, many retreros felt it didn't hurt to act out a sort of makeshift formality, if only as a final straw to positively affect the outcomes of state surveillance.

It follows, then, that amid such a scenario of political bricolage, state legality figured less as a zero-sum game (as simply being either present or absent) than as a variously credible performative project. To some extent, the law enjoyed a cumulative quality in mines such as Jefferson's. For the legitimacy of their extractive labor, while reaching its zenith with a mining title and an environmental license, could be validated and incremented through state-like behavior, most prominently in the form of documentary and territorial practices. While such "cumulative" lawmaking mismatched with the black and the white of official jurisdiction, it played a pivotal role in the localized constellation of state power. By employing tactics of auto-formalization—out of fear of imminent police actions, or due to some stubborn hope for future mining titles—miners put extractive regulation into practice on their own terms, and, albeit marginally, brought their informal territories in compliance with formal modalities of rule. In other words, insofar as they accumulated proof of their bona fide intentions, miners were, in their own resourceful way, mapping the state frontier. With their plaques, documents, acacias, and Colombian flags, they produced a modicum of the state in sites that were presumed to be outside of it.

Conclusion

Much academic literature depicts small-scale mining regions as suffering from an absence or deficiency of the state. In these pages, conversely, I've sought to visualize state power in gold country by showing that Chocó miners, instead of being merely sidelined by state legislation, played a crucial role in its unfolding. As miners faced an entrenched legal apparatus that generated at once hopes and fears, they did not sit idly by waiting for government interventions to happen. Rather, they anticipated, commandeered, and frustrated state governance by means of their own documentary readings and territorial organization. On one hand, by engaging with the Mayor's Certificate and other legal categories, they appropriated the meaning and thwarted the regulatory efficiency of official documentation. On the other, by accumulating paperwork and investing in forest recuperation, they invoked a statutory regime before it had arrived "top-down." These in situ projects of law urge us not to mistake state planning for the messy emergence of statehood "on the ground." Phrased otherwise, the organizational practices analyzed here reveal that formal designs change in meaning and style whenever they appear in the daily minutiae of miner lifeworlds. The next chapter will expand on this by showing how, like miners, Afro-Colombian community leaders partook in insurgent forms of state-building as they invoked ethno-cultural legislation in their underground mining governance.

CHAPTER 4

Underground Multiculturalism

It's a form of control and discipline.
—*Moisés (community leader)*

For more than five hours, community council leaders from up and down the Bebará River had debated a wide array of issues, each in one way or another related to mining. However, the meeting had still one matter pending. Winston, the president of the communities' very own mining association, called forward an elder man who was a stranger to many. The man introduced himself as being from Quibdó, which was a four-hour boat ride away from the Bebará community building where we were gathered. He told the community leaders that he had invited a group of miners to search for gold in a nearby tract of land, inherited by him from his late father, a native bebareño. The miners already had their excavator stationed in the prospective extraction site. The landowner had undertaken the long journey from Quibdó to obtain approval for the operation from the local community councils. Cognizant of their authority, he said he had "always respected the law" and had no intention "to offend anyone." He did not foresee any problems, though. He knew that "a community council has no authority over these matters," and shared with his audience the indisputable wisdom that "everyone has the right to work." More importantly, he claimed the land was "private property" and that he was in possession of a "public deed."

The talk went on for ten minutes or so until Winston cut it short, to the eye-rolling relief of the fatigued crowd. In a cogent rebuttal, he lectured the senior on Law 70, the piece of multicultural jurisprudence that had assigned land rights to Afro-descendant communities like those living on the Bebará. Winston denied the possibility of the man owning a private plot within a collective Black territory, and explained that Law 70 didn't allow him to mine as he pleased. "Let me help you a bit. Since 1993, there's no private property here. Your territory falls under the administrative control of the community council, which depends on *local* councils for its regulations. In your plot, no one can tell you to not cultivate yucca or maize. No one can take your property away from you, because it's ancestral and traditional. But when we made the request for the [collective land] title, it was for doing ecological activities, not for getting an excavator. So the decision on your case lies in the hands of the local community councils, which are the authorities here."

The meeting finished not long after Winston's speech. The matter was closed and the elder man had traveled for nothing. Law 70 had spoken.

But the way it had spoken was intriguing. Winston had been at the forefront of the regional process of land titling in the 1990s and knew all there was to know about Law 70. He was right that it did not concede the right to mine with excavators. But be that as it may, the bebareño communities' own performance of multicultural law also neglected this fact. Their riverbanks were replete with excavator mines, which were governed by the local community councils. In fact, Winston's dismissal of the elder's petition stemmed from a miner limit (but *not* a mining prohibition) on which the river's community councils had previously agreed. All in all, his defense plea of "ecological activities" seemed conspicuously pragmatic. Though he cited Afro-Colombian law and its ecological parameters to object to the senior's appeal to a "right to work," he overlooked these same parameters when he placed the decision power over excavators "in the hands of the local community councils," and, therewith, under the aegis of Law 70.

Seeking to fathom such unruly readings of ethno-cultural law, this chapter explores the convergence between Afro-Colombian legislation and gold mining. Social analyses have mostly approached this relationship as one of antagonism, describing multinational and "illegal" mines that wreak havoc on, and are protested against by, rights-seeking Black communities (Paschel 2016; Vélez-Torres 2016; Weitzner 2017). Here, however, I reflect on the political formations that emerge when the gold frontier and grassroots organizing are mutually constitutive—rather than at cross purposes. In Chocó's mining regions, Afro-descendant leaders appealed to their multicultural authority not so much to oppose excavators as to put them into phase with community council politics.

In presenting this nexus of wildcat mining and Afro-Colombian law, the chapter ties in to the broader agenda of this book's second part to uncover practices of bottom-up state-making in presumably stateless mining areas. That said, here I also make a more specific theoretical intervention. By favoring the goldfields over the bureaucracy as the ethnographic locus of multicultural lawmaking, I hope to answer to the "need," as identified by Viviane Weitzner (2017:1209), "to go beyond state-centric perspectives of lawmaking" and "to consider the perspectives of ancestral peoples and their lawmaking which question the very concept and locus of 'the state' as the central regulator." More concretely, I trace the empirical limits of the concept of "neoliberal multiculturalism," which in recent decades has been frequently employed to argue that cultural recognition is predicated upon "endorsement, implicit or otherwise, of the broader political project of neoliberalism" (Hale 2006:110). Although the notion of neoliberal multiculturalism explains persuasively what governing schemes pursue, it's less convincing, I find, in examining how these schemes unfold in contexts of strong political fragmentation—to which Colombia is no stranger. Accordingly, whereas "neoliberal" analyses say much about how policies entangle Indigenous and Afro-descendant populations within hegemonic projects of state disciplining, they say less about how populations reappropriate policies to construct political realities that destabilize these projects.

As shall become clear from the sections that follow, a case in point of such multicultural subversion is Chocó, where the consolidation of collective land rights has produced community council–based governance regimes of unlicensed extraction. To grasp such digressive cultural politics, I employ the term—following the book's title—"underground multiculturalism," which can be defined as a unique form of governance that, while deriving its legitimacy from ethno-cultural legislation, enjoys as its regulatory ambition the organization, taxation, and policing of mining activities that are in tension with official templates of law. As a way to give insight into such underground politics, the chapter mainly focuses on the Bebará River, where in the recent past the local gold economy was co-governed by community representatives and a regional fraction of the FARC. But first we need to ponder for a moment the overall organizational dynamics of community councils, which in Chocó's mining regions were guided less by neoliberal blueprints than by the gold-speckled alluvium.

Neoliberal Menaces and Menaces to Neoliberalism

Law 70 was drafted at the outset of Latin America's so-called multicultural turn. In the 1990s and 2000s, governments across the region began to actively endorse cultural rights of Indigenous and Afro-descendant populations, often under the ideological veneer of righting past wrongs (Greene 2007). A drastic shift away from previous ideologies of national homogeneity, the regionwide embrace of multiculturalism has been viewed by some students of Latin America as a result of the heightened exclusion that Indigenous peoples faced in the 1980s, when economic liberalization jeopardized their subsistence security, access to land, and sociocultural organization. This analysis, in turn, can be subdivided into "top-down" and "bottom-up" explanations, with some authors maintaining that governments adopted cultural reforms to solve their legitimacy crises (Ng'weno 2007; Van Cott 2000), and others seeing the reforms as having been propelled forward by Indigenous demands for more inclusive legislation (Brysk and Wise 1997; Yashar 1999).

But if in these readings multiculturalism is still foremost a counterreaction to neoliberal privatization, in recent decades a consensus has consolidated around the notion that cultural rights might also be servile to neoliberal statecraft (Gustafson 2002; Hale 2002; Muehlmann 2009; see also Introduction). Part of this argument holds that ethno-cultural policies stimulate communities to regulate themselves, acquitting the state apparatus from its moral responsibility to look after their well-being. Ostensibly, such administrative devolution should be analyzed not as a shorthand for increased grassroots autonomy, but as a stratagem of outsourced governance by which neoliberal governments expand their control over local populations. To adopt the wording of Charles Hale (2002), neoliberal multiculturalism may function as a "menace" to Afro/Indigenous politics, in that it enables national elites to distinguish between acceptable and unacceptable expressions of culture, and thus to endorse an essentialist multicultural subject that is no threat to private development.

During my time in Chocó, I too was sometimes tempted to think of the model of the community council as a "neoliberal" tool of state regulatory expansion. For instance, local politics was suffused with formal styles. Community councils relied on their own "board of directors" (*junta directiva*), an administrative body of around ten individuals who worked as "legal representatives," "vice-presidents," "secretaries," and "treasurers," all of whom were voted in during "popular elections" at "general assemblies." At these assemblies, as well as at regular meetings, bureaucratic prose abounded. Community members enjoyed the "right" to vote for or against a preset "agenda," junta leaders used their knowledge of multicultural reforms to win arguments, and audiences evaluated their leaders' actions in a vocabulary of "government," "democracy," and "corruption."

Community council organizing did much more than just mimic state jargon, though. Junta directiva members, often just ordinary residents without notably higher socioeconomic status, delivered with fervor on the responsibility of territorial management that Law 70 had devolved to them.[1] They mediated internal conflicts over land borders. They assigned tracts to individual families. They acted as gatekeepers to companies, NGOs, and public offices determined to realize projects in their territorial commons. And through their brokerage in requests for traditional mining reserves (see Chapter 7), they assisted the central government with mapping the subsoil and surveying subsistence miners. These various governing activities were carried out at multiple administrative levels, as community councils usually followed a somewhat bureaucratized two-tier structure. Their large territories—covering tens, if not hundreds, of thousands of hectares—were subdivided into "lower community councils" (*consejos comunitarios menores*), which were represented by their own "lower juntas directivas" (*juntas directivas menores*). The lower juntas reported to an overarching "upper junta directiva" (*junta directiva mayor*) that was in charge of the larger territory and community (*consejo comunitario mayor*) and served as the first point of contact for external governing bodies (state or nonstate).[2]

In tandem with the mediation of state governance, juntas directivas were also held accountable by their constituencies for welfare and service provisions. Chocoanos blamed the lack of medical centers, streetlights, and roads not only on local and national politicians, but also on their junta leadership, who, in their eyes, had failed to convert collective earnings into public works. On the banks of the Bebará River, community leaders were even expected to ensure public safety now that the FARC had left the territory. When, at one meeting, bebareño leaders discussed the rumor that several young males had been carrying firearms, the former complained about being abandoned by the national government, the police, and the army, yet also connected the safety problem to their own failure to enforce community regulations, especially their prohibition on carrying weapons.

All of which arguably adds weight to the aforementioned assertation that "multiculturalism . . . has the effect of . . . liberating the neoliberal government

from taking on certain forms of responsibility and . . . shifting this responsibility onto groups defined in cultural terms" (Muehlmann 2009:475). But
while Law 70 may have encouraged a closer alignment between localized
organizational forms and state disciplinary power, and possibly helps disguise
basic citizenship provisions as responsibilities of communal self-management,
the politics of Chocó's mining communities are much more than a hegemonic
"menace." In point of fact, in the presence of the new excavator mines, it was
community councils and their elected juntas directivas that predominantly
menaced formal governing rationalities.

This comment requires elaboration. In the end, by laying waste to collective lands and swelling the treasuries of armed groups, excavators may
appear, as other authors outline (Paschel 2016:194–195; Vélez-Torres
2016), as evidence of the contrary; that is, as an alarming intrusion into
Black-Colombian organizing. Most assuredly, to an extent they are. In different parts of Colombia, destructive mining activities have encountered
inspirational resistance from community leaders, who risk life-threatening
situations, inflicted by the armed groups feeding off gold, in defense of
their cultural traditions and biophysical environments. In some cases,
such resistance has led to remarkable political achievements; not the least in
Chocó, whose Atrato River was declared a *"sujeto de derechos"* (legal entity)
after an ensemble of grassroots organizations filed a lawsuit against state
entities for their permissive attitude toward the river's deterioration, particularly at the hands of miners.[3]

Yet in the areas of this research, extractive realities did not comply with
a neat juxtaposition of foes versus victims. Just as local households had started
economic relationships with the retrero newcomers, so too had the juntas directivas of community councils begun attending to the governance of the
new mines. The most significant feature of such governance was taxation. To
gain authorization to work in a collective land, retreros paid the junta directiva of the relevant community a small percentage of their net earnings. This
tax ranged from 2 to 8 percent and was due on top of the 12 to 18 percent owed
to the individual family who, on the basis of historical usage, was the customary owner of the specific swath of land where the miners had set up camp.
The excavator tax was by far the most significant income for community
councils and had helped build numerous communal buildings. Often these
were meeting halls, although there were also villages where earnings from
gold had paid for a church, a school classroom, children's playgrounds, paved

pathways, and boat brigades supplying medicines and doctors. However, the informal tax did not always translate into many "public works." In the out-of-the-way forests, miners could easily wash their sluice boxes behind the backs of community leaders. At the same time, stories circulated about junta members siphoning off community gold for personal gain (for a more detailed analysis of both sets of problems, see Chapter 5).

Apart from taxation, the juntas' mining governance involved a variously substantive form of land administration. This meant, primarily, that retreros were prohibited from working in places where they interfered with important socioeconomic activities (for example, they could be forbidden from working in farmlands or immediately upstream from the village). Community guidelines also dictated several environmental regulations. Besides a general prohibition on the use of mercury, miners were commonly expected to reforest their terrains with saplings, dig out tailing ponds (so that creeks would not clog up with mining debris), and refill with earth their abandoned pits (to prevent them from becoming hotbeds of malaria-spreading mosquitoes). Truth be told, these guidelines lacked strong policing, and their importance to community organization paled in comparison to the collection of gold taxes. Whereas a miner who failed in payment obligations could expect a tough conversation and the threat of suspension, those contaminating creeks or not planting trees rarely suffered repercussions.

Needless to say, these practices of taxation and spatial ordering clashed with official regulatory schemes. For starters, they sat uneasily with Afro-Colombian legislation. Although Law 70 describes Black Pacific communities as those living off "traditional production practices" (Congreso de Colombia 1993: Art. 1, 7), and excludes the mineral-holding subsoil from its definition of collective landownership (Art. 6), here there was a local governing system that targeted subsoil activities that looked anything but traditional. What's more, the juntas' governance connoted a serious transgression of mining law, since the extraction that was being governed lacked not just tradition but also mining titles.

And yet, such legal discordance notwithstanding, underground multiculturalism made continuous reference to state law. For one thing, juntas directivas legitimized their involvement in mining by invoking their territorial authority as vested in them by multicultural policy. In effect, to convince miners, landholding families, or myself of the fairness of their compensation schemes, leaders quoted concrete passages of Afro-Colombian law, specifying "their right to prior consultation,"[4] the "inalienable, inextinguishable, and nonnegotiable" judicial status of their lands,[5] and their own position as "the highest authority" within these.[6] For example, while discussing the refusal of a landowner to share his gold rents with the junta directiva of La Peña, the secretary of the latter told me: "He says it's his land and that there's no law that stipulates that he should pay us the percentage. But there actually is. The internal regulations of the community council mention the percentage and we are the highest authority within this territory."

For another thing, the environmental rules that junta representatives imposed on retreros were largely based on what the former reckoned to be the lawful guidelines for responsible mining. Therefore, miners' compliance with these regulations—especially the prohibition on mercury—mattered not just for the preservation of trees and rivers, but also for more political reasons: to increase the community council's odds of receiving a mining title, and to make the collective land a less likely target for operations by public forces. In other words, in their juggling with extractive legislation, the juntas attempted, to various degrees, to align their mining forests with state formality before such formality had been officially recognized, enacting a similar kind of legal accumulation as that of the retreros of the previous chapter.

Taken together, these two manifestations of statehood were indicative of a dissentious, or "vernacular" (Colloredo-Mansfeld 2007), kind of statecraft. With the juntas' underground multiculturalism, the state was molded into new forms, operating mainly in contradiction to centralized planning. To be sure, by claiming "legal" entitlement to gold, junta leaders consolidated the authority of the state as the righteous arbiter of mining governance. Yet this performance of statecraft was mostly on their own terms. They repurposed statutory languages, styles, and structures to make them comply with the regulation of an informal mining economy that, juridically speaking, was not theirs to regulate. And thus, by overstepping their legal mandate this way—by reconfiguring state categories—juntas directivas ended up producing multicultural territories that were more underground than hegemonic, more in sync with what lay beneath the earth than with neoliberal designs. Now, while such territory-making found resonance in all three places where I did fieldwork, it was on the banks of the Bebará River that cultural politics assumed a particularly dissident form. As the following section goes on to show, the bebareños' mining organization was strongly interwoven with the regulatory practices of the FARC, whose involvement with gold went far beyond the straightforward extortion of miners.

A Curious Case of Co-Governance

A tributary of the Atrato (Chocó's largest river), the Bebará encapsulates well what Veena Das and Deborah Poole (2004:8) have called the margins of the state: "sites of practice on which law and other state practices are colonized by other forms of regulation." State marginality, for instance, saturated the stories bebareños told about the preceding years of armed conflict. From the mid-1990s until the 2016 Havana Peace Deal, their river had fallen under the reign of the FARC's 34th Front. These years encompassed piecemeal displacement, night curfews, helicopter attacks by the Colombian army and, on one occasion, one of the villages on the river coming under fire from soldiers' bullets. Yet while the guerrillas had been gone for about a year when I did fieldwork in 2017, marginality was by no means a thing of the past. In our conversations, bebareños listed all the state services that they identified as righteous citizenship entitlements, but which to their dismay were absent in the depths of the rainforest. They mentioned that they had no roads; no terrestrial infrastructure that offered a rapid alternative to their slow boats. They had no sewage system and no potable water supply. They had no telephone connection and no internet. They had no secondary schools and no permanent teachers in their primary schools. They had no medical supplies nor personnel in their health clinics—the nearest hospitals were in Quibdó (four hours away by motorboat). They had no connection to the department's electrical grid and, since the late 1980s, no police officer stationed at their river. And of course, they had no legal mining. Despite having one of the most prolific excavator economies in Chocó, none of the retreros working along the river had a concession contract.

Even so, the Bebará was no stateless river, and this had a lot to do with Law 70. The banks of the Bebará were within the collective territory of COCOMACIA, at 685,000 hectares the largest community council in Colombia. Under the auspices of this mother organization, each of the river's four villages (El Llano, La Villa, La Peña, Pueblo Viejo) had an individual lower community council, represented by their respective lower junta directiva.[7] These four lower councils, in conjunction with three nearby villages/councils on the Atrato riverbank (Boca de Bebará, Boca de Agua Clara, and San Francisco de Tachigadó), were organized in a pan-riverine structure. Many community matters were discussed and decided on by the community leaders of the river at large, rather than by the individual lower juntas directivas or the upper junta of COCOMACIA.

Figure 7. The Bebará River. Photo by the author.

One of the organizational achievements of Bebará's leaders was a shared set of community rules, which were displayed on large plastic notices that adorned the walls of the villages' communal buildings. The level of legal detail was eye-catching. After an introductory statement that mentioned "ethno-territorial principles," "juridico-popular conscience," and "legal faculties established by Law 70," the notices charted out a solid thirty-two regulations that ranged from minor injunctions (no littering, no loose animals) to more serious rules (no selling of drugs, no physical maltreatment of children, no carrying or firing of weapons). The penalty for the breach of each prohibition was listed (mainly monetary fines and community work), while repeat infringements were punished with a "complaint to the competent organism."

What was also noteworthy about the code of conduct was that much of its content had been introduced by the FARC. During their stay at the river, the guerrillas had played an important role in setting up and assessing the local alliance of community councils. Besides the notices, this collaboration had spurred an unparalleled governance of the river's excavator mines—the owners of which were mostly chocoanos, and in several cases, bebareños. Governance stood out for various reasons. First of all, unlike elsewhere, juntas directivas' ecological demands had actually paid off. The riverbanks still boasted lush vegetation, because excavators had only been permitted in gold-fields roughly an hour's walk inland from the river. The shorelands, in contrast, had been safeguarded for future generations and could only be worked through farming or low-intensity forms of extraction. Moreover, in the inland goldfields, retreros by and large complied with their obligation to dig tailing ponds, and some had reforested their mined-out plots with saplings and subsistence crops. There was also a general ban on the use of mercury, which few miners dared to violate—at least publicly. As a matter of fact, several excavator owners impressed on me that it was because of their collective compliance with the environmental policies of their community councils, and because of the FARC's former commitment to enforce these policies, that in all those years they had not fallen victim to equipment-destroying police and army.

Yet arguably the most impressive feat of organization was the Asociación de Barequeros de Minería Artesanal del Medio Atrato (ASOBAMINARMEA). Under the supervision of the FARC's 34th Front, and in collaboration with their peers from the adjacent Bebaramá River, the Bebará councils had started the association (named after the Medio Atrato municipality where both rivers are situated) in 2009 to govern their *bareque*; the satellite form of mining whereby artisanal miners comb for gold within the slopes of excavator pits. From the mid-2000s onward, with the arrival of the first retreros in Bebará, the bareque had boosted the income of artisanal miners, who thanks to the excavators could reach deeper gold-bearing sands than before. But the bareque had also resulted in disorder, injury, and even death. Before ASOBAMINARMEA regulated the practice, barequeros had been trapped and sometimes killed by landslides (especially when working at night), while some retreros had given privileged access to their pits to befriended barequeros and denied entry to others. Furthermore, crowding in the pits had hindered the guerrillas in their endeavor to distinguish harmless villagers from infiltrated enemy elements.

ASOBAMINARMEA had been founded to remedy these ills. The association's rules restricted the bareque to specific days and times and to local miners registered with the association. They also stated that, on the days of bareque, excavator miners should remove their machines from the pit/bareque area. In addition, each community council had to assign one or more *líderes de bareque* to the association, who functioned as a type of bareque patrol, preventing people from entering at night and keeping an eye out for skirmishes and landslides (see Chapter 1). In the event of a disturbance (a fight, the sighting of a weapon), the líderes reported the relevant lawbreaker to their community council of origin, with the likely penalty of becoming temporally expelled from the pits. Further, both líderes and barequeros had to wear uniforms to facilitate the identification of those imposing the rules and those breaking them. Líderes dressed in green, while barequeros wore T-shirts whose colors signaled village affiliation, with some also having a unique identifying number on the back. As líder Moisés explained: "They wear uniforms so we can sanction them. If everyone is in uniform, we know which community is most disorderly. It's a form of control and discipline. The principal objectives of the association are control and vigilance, that people respect the norms, respect the hour of arrival and departure, and that all can benefit from the bareque in an equitable way."

Notably, the person on whom bebareños heaped most praise when discussing their sophisticated mine governance was not an association representative but Israel Zúñiga, a former FARC commander who in Bebará had been known by his nom de guerre "Benkos." When I interviewed Zúñiga in a Quibdó canteen, I asked him about his days as Benkos in Bebará.

"How should I describe your position within the FARC?"

"Companion of the community."

"I mean, commander or—"

"Companion of the community."

"When did you, the FARC, first arrive in Bebará?"

"We have always been part of the social structure, of the rehabilitation of the community. Their fight, their structure."

"So, how would you describe the relationship between the communities in Bebará and the FARC?"

"We are part of the community."

"How so?"

"We have always been part of the community. There is a common reading that we are some exterior factor, but we're not."

"So, a lot of bebareños belonged to the FARC?"

"Militias. Combatants. The FARC is more than a military entity. It's a sociopolitical project."

Most likely, he was mincing his words. It was December 2017, three months before the parliamentary elections, and Zúñiga was sixth on the list of candidates of the FARC (now a political party) for the Colombian Senate.[8] Yet to a certain extent, his carefully crafted sentences rang true. There was indeed little "exterior" to how the histories of the 34th Front and the community councils' project of extraction interweaved. Even during my fieldwork, in the proverbial post-conflict, the evidence of the matrimony was overwhelming. Now that the guerillas had left, one could arguably experience their historical involvement with the community councils more than ever.

Let me elaborate. During my stay in Bebará, the association's rules were still binding and moderately enforced. However, "control and discipline" was not what it used to be, as disobedient barequeros had started entering the mining pits before the designated times. Their disrespect for the schedule encouraged others to do the same, fearing that the mischievous early birds would catch all the gold. The situation eventually snowballed into whole villages boarding their boats to travel to the mines under cover of darkness. It was all too clear that in the FARC's absence, community leaders had great trouble keeping their barequeros in line. As Breiner, the legal representative of one local community council, argued at a village meeting: "We are lawless! Last Sunday people started their bareque at four in the morning! I told them: 'Mi familia, let's wait until the right hour,' but they hurried down to the mining pit and nearly knocked me over! We do not have the support of the state. The order comes straight from the council. But here, people only listen to the ones carrying the guns."

Who had started the chaos was a matter of debate. Most community leaders hurled their accusations beyond their village boundaries. All agreed, however, that the lack of respect for the bareque schedule was a serious matter. In the early morning, there were no association representatives checking for landslides. Also, by entering the mines early, the unscrupulous were profiting at the expense of the virtuous, as early arrival implied more time and more excavator-smoothed pit walls in which to find gold. In light of these worries, the matter was taken up at a pan-riverine meeting attended by the juntas directivas and the ASOBAMINARMEA leadership, as well as by Israel Zúñiga and his former head commander of the 34th Front. In dialogue with the two ex-combatants, the community leaders declared that further violation of the association's schedule would be penalized with the indefinite suspension of all excavator mining. In deciding on this general shutdown, the leaders and ex-guerrillas hoped not just to win the compliance of the barequeros, but also to motivate the retreros to do their part in not letting anyone near their pits before the right hour.

Figure 8. Bareque in Bebará. Photo by the author.

The threat didn't work. Although in the first bareque after the meeting
people did respect the schedule, from the second bareque onward chaos resumed. The barequeros entered the mines at night, the association's guards
did not stop their entry, the retreros did not banish them, and the community leaders did not push through any type of suspension. Pretty soon things
were, in their own disorderly way, back to normal. "It's the same as always,"
junta leader Sairi told me. "They always say they'll change it and then nothing happens. People here don't listen! I'll tell you something: Here the people
only listened when there were guerrillas."

Her opinion was widely shared. When confronted with self-governance,
bebareños acknowledged that it had been convenient to have the 34th Front
around, no matter how much they now enjoyed the nascent peace stemming
from the Havana accords. The most pressing case in point was the administration of the bareque. Nonetheless, I also heard people voice nostalgia for
the FARC when they reminisced that back then no youth dared to carry a
gun, no miner dirtied the water, no leader skipped a meeting, no villager
failed to carry out a junta-prescribed punishment, and no retrero had to fear
for his safety due to the threat of bandits. "They were the state here," said José
Luis, the legal representative of one community council. "They organized the

communities and defended our interests. You cannot deny this because you cannot deny the truth." Other leaders made similar comments: "Here, the guerrillas were the state"; "With the FARC gone, we are without governance." Indeed, without the combatants around, the jurisdiction of the juntas directivas seemed to be adrift. It was as if they had lost their military leverage.

This disintegration of multicultural authority following the FARC's departure, as well as the guerrillas' previous involvement in cultural politics, provide productive lenses to reveal how arguments of "neoliberal multiculturalism," though offering sharp explanations of the rationales of neoliberal rule, have less merit for understanding the practicalities of rule in contexts of fragmented state sovereignty. While "the neoliberal state" might increase its grip on peripheralized regions by delegating governance to multicultural subjects, it also inevitably opens itself up to the mimicries and counterfeits of the communities through whom it intends to govern—or, as in the case of Chocó, of armed actors who reappropriate Afro-Colombian law as an instrument for spatial control. In Bebará, as in the wider municipality of the Medio Atrato, it was not state technocrats but a coalition of FARC combatants and community councils who produced the symbolic and material conditions through which multicultural statehood—by means of Law 70—became territorialized. Thus, the statehood that had come about had more to do with the underground politics of the "margins" than with the bureaucratic rule of the "center." After all, community councils were key participants in an informal governance regime that regulated miners working outside the official legal framework: retreros operating without the proper permits, and barequeros whose excavator-dependent extraction was incompatible with formal mining law.[9] More strikingly yet, this community-based regime had developed out of, and depended for its effectiveness on, the rule of force of a "state-fighting" guerrilla group.

The confluence of community council organization with FARC governance should caution us not to confuse the reproduction of state power with the accomplishment of coercive regulatory regimes. One is not the other. In state margins like Chocó, neoliberal governing rationalities don't result in a unitary structure of political subjugation, but tend to generate what Rivke Jaffe (2013:737) calls a "hybrid form of statehood." Such statehood is "characterized by the prominence of multiple governmental actors" (737) and involves "techniques of governance [that] shape and are reinforced by populations that understand themselves as members of overlapping political communities" (736). Hybrid statehood is "neither hegemonic nor subaltern but a . . . mix of both," and meshes seemingly contradictory languages of public authority (736), as evidenced by the hybrid political formation of underground multiculturalism. In Bebará, specifically, articulations of multicultural and guerrilla sovereignty easily overlapped, the FARC felt an awful lot—to paraphrase José Luis—like the state, and Law 70 had no problem with getting tangled up in the outlawed business of gold mining.

Still, perhaps the most notable manifestation of hybrid statehood in Chocó's gold regions was the circulation of official-like mining documents. Consider again the Bebará River for a cogent example.

Make-Believe Documents

I squinted at the laminated card that Yulia (the same Yulia from Chapter 3) had handed me. One quarter of its front side showed a photograph of her face, looking grim and serious. It endowed the card with a formal solemnity, as did the rest of its personal data: a barcode, a social security number, and a registration serial of the Colombian tax authority. This wasn't the document I had expected to see when Yulia said she would show me her "new bareque ID." No, this wasn't the Mayor's Certificate (see Chapter 3) but an unofficial document belonging to the barequeros association of the Medio Atrato. Apart from Yulia's details, it carried the name and logo of both the association and the municipal administration. Whereas other barequeros had possessed these cards for years, Yulia was new to the river and had only recently registered with ASOBAMINARMEA. In pursuit of the ever-moving gold frontier, she had arrived to the Bebará a few months back, in the company of her niece Zuleidy, who like her aunt was just short of forty years old. The two women shared the house where the three of us were now sitting and chatting.

"What's it for?" I asked as I returned the card to Yulia.

Zuleidy answered for her. "The líderes de bareque use this so that they know you belong to this community."

"Do you always bring it with you?" I asked.

"Sometimes I forget it," Yulia responded, "but generally: yes. If you don't bring it, you're not allowed to work, because you cannot prove you're a barequero."

I turned to her niece, "And you, Zuleidy, do you have one?"

"No, I'm still illegal!" She burst into laughter.

"Meaning?" I asked, chuckling back at her.

"They can sanction me, kick me out of the bareque."

Because the card cost only five thousand pesos (1.50 USD), I asked Zuleidy why she risked suspension over such a small investment.

"Well, to be honest, I don't think they'll kick me out," she answered. "Here in the village, everyone knows who I am. I was already living here before I started to participate in the bareque."

"But you'll get into trouble in parts of the river where they don't know you," her aunt said. "What will you do if there's bareque in another village? You don't know anyone over there. And then they'll sanction you for not carrying the card."

After spending more time in Bebará, I realized that Zuleidy's relaxed attitude was far from uncommon. When heading out for the mines, most people left their association cards at home, confident that the líderes de bareque (their neighbors, friends, family) wouldn't kick them out of the mining pit. The barequeros had not always been so casual. I was told that when the FARC were still around, everyone always carried their miner cards. The 34th Front did punish failure to show ID, since they had promoted the provision of the cards as a means to implement the association's task of keeping intruders (e.g., state moles, paramilitary snitches) out of the region.

Though its usage was in decline, the ID card was captivating in several respects. First, while it appealed to bureaucratic symbolism (in being an ID card), the document had been endorsed by mining communities and guerrillas that identified themselves in opposition to the government; as the *pueblo*, the campesinos, and the miners abandoned by it. Second, the card fulfilled a surveillance function in an economy that was disregarded and combatted by the state apparatus. And third, despite all the former, the ID card was replete with state-referential data. This card was as formal as it was informal, as state as it was anti-state.

Both on and beyond the Bebará shores, there were many more of these "twilight" (Lund 2006) objects to be found. Juntas directivas continually issued official-looking documents when informing retreros and community members on mining-related matters. These could be humdrum papers of daily interaction: attendance lists circulating in meetings, or signed letters inviting retreros to discuss a new mining policy. Yet junta leaders also relied on more serious authorization documents, such as forms expressing their consent to a miner's presence, or usufructs proving a family's customary ownership of a piece of communal land (such documents had gained in popularity in the wake of border conflicts between neighboring families, set in motion by the arrival of excavator mining and the consequent increased value of land).

In producing all this paperwork, junta leaders emulated the state bureaucracy not only in form—employing writing as a deferential mode of communication—but also in content, in that their documents expressed no shortage of legal innuendo, community council logos, and personal and fiscal identification numbers. To give one poignant example: I once read an "approval form" that told miners that the junta directiva had "issued its approval" of their extractive operations, in view of the junta "being sheltered by Law 70 of 1993 and Decree 1745 of 1995." The paper furthermore stated that its recipient had complied with the requirement to submit to the junta an "Environmental Management Plan" (a term also employed in official formalization guidelines), as well as "documentation, authenticated by a public notary, that proves he is the owner of the mine." To validate the approval, the paper's bottom half provided a list of the junta directiva members, along with their respective signatures and social security numbers.

So, how should we read apocryphal documents like this one? What to think of their formal content and aesthetics, seeing as the mining they address lacks official accreditation? Anthropologist Yael Navaro-Yashin offers guidance. While understanding documents as "affectively charged phenomena," Navaro-Yashin (2007:81) contends that paper documentation allows the state to manifest itself in everyday encounters. She writes that "documents are among the primary paraphernalia of modern states and legal systems," and links their wide circulation to their "symbolism of permanence" (84). Put differently, documents "[carry] the image of proof, stability, and durability" and "within the Euro-American paradigm . . . are taken as references for truth and authenticity" (84). In illustration of this, Navaro-Yashin recounts how the "wannabe state" of the Turkish Republic of Northern Cyprus (TRNC)—which lacks UN recognition—enacts its contested statehood by mimicking the documentary practices of other states. In order to look like a state, it transacts "make-believe documents" that "not only represent specific identities and transactions, but also declare the legitimacy of the 'TRNC'" (87).

With Navaro-Yashin's analysis in mind, we may see juntas directivas' paperwork as serving at least a dual purpose, namely: communicating black-on-white "references of truth and authenticity" (Navaro-Yashin 2007:84) amid informal mining governance, on the one hand, and enacting legit "make-believe" identities in the absence of formal recognition, on the other. First, and perhaps most obviously, documents allowed the juntas' communication to "bear the symbolism of permanence" (Navaro-Yashin 2007:84). In mining forests loaded with rumor, deceit, and conflicting interpretations, computer-typed forms and hand-scribbled signatures helped to clarify and solidify agreements. I learned this all too well a few weeks before Christmas in La Peña. The junta directiva had commissioned its board member Giovanny to set up a football tournament around the annual holidays. To fund the logistics (balls, shirts, food), Giovanny had cooked up the idea of soliciting a castellano of gold from each of the local retreros. On arriving at the camp-sites, he did not simply ask for the gold. He had brought along a bundle of printed request letters that were adorned with the logo, name, and tax registration number of the community council, as well as three signatures of junta members above a short line where the respective miner could sign off their commitment. While these "legal" prints were eye-catching—in their objective of charging illegally mined gold—miners' reactions were even more so, as Giovanny struggled mightily to collect their signatures and social security numbers. After reading the form, paisa miner Rubén said: "No, no, no! I'm not going to sign that! Look, Giovanny, you're my friend, so let me explain it clearly: Here, we don't have fuel, we don't have a classifier, and our only excavator is half-broken. The way things are, I'll be happy to send two castellanos to my family at Christmas. Here, it says one castellano. I'm sorry, but I'm not getting involved with that."

Fascinated by the significance that both community leaders and miners bestowed on the letter, I asked Yelena, the junta's secretary who had drafted the form, why she and her colleagues insisted on these legal papers when dealing with informal gold transactions. Her reply was straightforward: "Because in the end we are the authority here and because they [the retreros] don't respect verbal agreements. Now, if they deny that there was an agreement, we can later always tell them: 'Look you said this and this, you've signed it.'"

As her answer suggests, the pacts and approvals of gold country obtained an "image of proof, stability, and durability" (Navaro-Yashin 2007:84) when being crystallized in documents; an image that was hard to capture by verbal conversation, whereby the veracity of agreements depended on present witnesses and their later goodwill. With this same reason in mind, customary landowners explained their need for junta-drafted usufructs over the lands they claimed, and the juntas their policy of letting gold-collection visits by individual leaders be verified with miner-signed receipts (indicating the exact amount of gold collected). Putting things in writing turned individual truths into social truths. Without papers and signatures, gold collectors could easily lie about the mines' productivity, and neighboring landowners could easily forget, purposely or not, about previous arrangements on land borders. Without papers, you had nothing to fall back on but people's word.

However, the agreements themselves were not the only conclusive truth that the leaders' paperwork solidified, bringing us to the second function of documents: performing the legitimacy of otherwise unlawful claims and identities. Documentary practices enabled the juntas directivas to enact their public authority. Although they were no "wannabe states," their extractive governance was definitely of a "make-believe" quality (Navaro-Yashin 2007), relying as it did on formal discourses and insignia. Such citation of formality, then, allowed leaders to confer a legal quality to their informal mining dealings. Via their textual and physical appeals to officialdom, "legal" forms sanctioned the juntas' contentious claim—articulated to miners and landholders, as well as among themselves—that the outlawed activity of excavator mining was a rightful concern of ethno-cultural politics. Through its community council emblems, signatures, and other official templates, paper-based communication on gold matters acquired a seal of legal authority, rendering such matters a legit part of community council administration.

Asked why they issued the documents, most leaders simply replied that important council business needed to be communicated through documents. Few leaders questioned whether mining should be excluded from such protocol because of its polemical legal status. To the contrary, although junta members and their documentary audiences were well aware that documents on unlicensed mining lacked broader judicial reckoning, they nevertheless "believed" the forms within the jurisdiction of the community council. For example, some retreros were unwilling to attend a community meeting because they had not received a written invitation. Others mentioned hand-signed council approvals to claim their entitlement to mine. Meanwhile, junta leaders appealed to these same approvals to remind retreros of their payment obligations.

Beyond validating the underground politics of juntas directivas, paper documentation also conveyed the legitimacy of the retreros themselves. In communication with state officials, the latter could show their letters of community approval as proof that their mining enjoyed local endorsement. Even if retreros were skeptical about the letters' official status, they still added them to their company folders as one more demonstration of accumulated legality. They explained that the forms, like any other legal-like document, might function as a better-than-nothing substitute for a formal mining permit in a future encounter with public forces intent on seizing their fuel or bombing their equipment. As retrero Everson set out: "Technically, the approval does nothing. It's just so we can show the army that we have the community's permission in case they catch us. There are communities where only the legal representative of the junta receives a miner's money [the community council tax], and where people call the police to have your machine burned. With the approval, you can tell the police you have the people's approval."

It is here where things had taken a wrong turn. On various occasions, I was told about an infamous judicial dispute. Apparently, to prove their legal status, a group of dredge miners had shown operational contracts to the National Mining Agency, signed by the former junta representatives of a local community council. Although the community in question had indeed held a mining title, the junta leaders had been in no position to transact these types of contracts, because they did not have the complementary environmental license needed for extraction. In the face of the unlawful contracts, the National Mining Agency retracted the council's mining title, a decision that convinced leaders from other communities to stop allocating signed permissions. Martín, the legal representative of a small community council, said: "We've stopped doing that. Right now, it's all by mouth. We cannot give permission to a mining company. We're the owners of the territory, not the subsoil. You know what happens? When they start burning machinery, if there's a permission signed by a legal representative, they put him in jail. So, we said: 'Let's just have a verbal agreement.'"

In other words, by being shown to public agents, junta-decreed approvals can end up working like surrogates for public documentation. But in being surrogates, they depend on the benevolent eyes of the state official reading them. And though some officials indeed interpret community documents as evidence of the legit status of informal mining (something Chapters 6 and 7 will address more fully), there is always the risk, as the case of the dredgers exemplifies, that documents will be read in a way that is counterproductive to their original purpose; as evidence of not junta-legitimized extraction, but illegal extraction corrupting legitimate juntas.

Conclusion

Instead of providing yet another case study of how multicultural jurisprudence helps reaffirm neoliberal hegemony, this chapter has zoomed in on bottom-up forms of state-building in Afro-Colombian territories. In doing so, it has identified the emergence of underground multiculturalism; that is to say, governing practices by community leaders who, on the basis of their authority as administrators of collective lands, assumed the responsibility (and benefits) of regulating the local extraction of gold. Although these cultural politics arose against a backdrop of neoliberal state planning and gained their authority from Afro-Colombian law, they connoted "forms of not-quite-neoliberal governmentality" (Anthias and Radcliffe 2015:261), insofar as their grounded dynamics were mostly determined by local social relations and the auriferous subsoils conditioning these relations. If anything, Chocó's underground multiculturalism mostly operated in opposition to the state regulatory framework: Its involvement in heavy extraction mismatched with the traditionalist and "subsoil-excluding" gist of ethnocultural law, its governed miner population was severely criminalized by extractive legislation, and—as in the exceptional case of the Bebará—its regulatory effectiveness could even depend on enjoying access to the military might of nonstate armed groups.

Suffice it to say that, in light of the former, the articulations of political life described here are neither absolutely formal nor informal, neither completely concurrent with nor antagonistic to neoliberal politics, and neither perfectly hegemonic nor emancipatory. By implementing formal-like organizational structures amid a police-persecuted activity, underground multiculturalism affirms and rejects statutory authority at the same time. By entangling nonstate groups in its operations, underground multiculturalism compromises community autonomy for armed governance, yet may also establish effective regulatory mechanisms for social order and environmental preservation where these have been unaccounted for by public institutions. And for sure, by endorsing excavator mining, underground multiculturalism participates in the destruction of rainforests, but also increases the short-term spending power of legally marginalized mining communities. In sum, rather than proposing a single answer regarding its revolutionary potential, the politics of the underground are as contingent as they are open-ended.

Yet while this chapter has studied these politics through the prism of bareque rules and documentary affects, what has still remained somewhat peripheral to the analysis are the daily interactions of conflict and conviviality that surrounded the juntas' governing of the excavator mines. In other words: How did the taxation and regulation of the secretive and outlawed mines take form on a day-to-day basis? How did junta directiva leaders have their multicultural authority recognized and rejected when governing these mines—especially in the absence of powerful institutions (state or guerilla) enforcing such authority? And which everyday challenges did leaders encounter from retreros and customary landholders? The next chapter zooms in on the village of La Peña to probe for fine-grained answers.

CHAPTER 5

Concealment, Conflict, Compromise

If they don't comply with our rules,
they will have to leave.

—*Giovanny (community leader)*

n my first visit to La Peña in early 2017, the junta directiva members of the community council told me they had inherited a debt-ridden administration. They had just been elected, having won the community vote from their predecessors following a campaign that stressed the corruption of the exiting leadership. They said they had demonstrated that the preceding president had bought three personal cars during his reign, while community input had been at an all-time low. As I spoke to more villagers over time, I discovered that the accusations against the ex-president enjoyed wide circulation. It was a public secret that communally taxed excavator money had disappeared into the pockets of the former president and his junta colleagues. The whole ordeal had made people lose faith in the community council, with many reckoning it to be an institution that was led more by the financial interests of the junta than those of the community.

The new leaders expressed a desire to move in another direction. No more corruption. No more unrestrained extraction. No more keeping gold and other secrets from the people. Several new regulations were to make this work. From then onward, two board representatives had to be present during gold collection as a mechanism of self-surveillance. Furthermore, all mechanized mining would be prohibited upriver from the village so that people could safely bathe and wash their clothes. Equally exciting was the excavator limit that would help to curb deforestation; retreros already present were permitted to stay, but for the time being no new miners were allowed in. The ones remaining, moreover, needed to complement their routine production percentages with the provision of additional wood and money (or gold) to accomplish the building of a tree nursery. In addition, they could no longer sprinkle mercury on their sluice boxes and were only authorized to use it in bateas and buckets in the final stage of washing. Ultimately, miners not complying with the new rules would have to leave the collective territory.

By the time I left Chocó eleven months later, much had happened. The La Peña junta directiva had begun building an economic future beyond mining, having reeled in externally sponsored community projects. Yet several unforeseen developments had hit the junta hard. Within the leadership, tensions had accumulated about personal benefits in one of the new community projects, resulting in the expulsion of a board member. Also, among both the junta and the community at large, a growing mistrust had arisen about the collecting of the excavator percentages. Leaders jockeyed for the position of collector, which came with financial compensation, while suspicions persisted among other villagers that the collectors were making good money from community gold. And while all this happened, the tree nursery had not happened. Miners were barely delivering the requested materials. Actually, they were doing their best not to pay the junta at all.

Leaning on fieldwork in La Peña, this chapter digs deeper into the quotidian effects of gold extraction on community organization. It follows the multiple ways that excavator mines get tangled up in the sociopolitics of community councils, weaving together an analysis of three intertwined characteristics of gold's micro-governance: concealment, conflict, and compromise. These themes enter the chapter in that very same sequence. The trilateral focus allows me to lay out the contentious dimensions of the everyday performance of multicultural law, as well as to outline how idealistic aspirations for change may get contaminated in the mundane messiness of resource politics. Claiming the legal right to govern wildcat mines comes with many caveats, and this the La Peña junta directiva discovered in no uncertain terms.

Tracking Down Gold

Community guidelines stipulated that excavator miners had to pay the La Peña community council 20 percent of their profits, which combined the percentages of the landholding family and the junta directiva. In an ideal situation, the retreros would call the junta's secretary before washing the gold-filled sacks of their classifiers and sluice boxes. This way, a junta representative could be present when gold was being weighed and distributed. In practice, though, miners rode roughshod over these calling arrangements. If they were to be believed, sediments were never washed and equipment was always faltering.

To keep clandestine washings in check, the community leadership conducted monitoring visits to the mines. The most common surveillant was Giovanny, a junta member in his mid-forties renowned for walking fast, talking equally fast, and getting along with everyone, including thrifty retreros. I often accompanied him. Our long forest walks were carried out at great speed, as Giovanny was always anxious about arriving too late, after a washing had taken place. Unluckily for him, his perseverance in heading out to the goldfields had stirred bad blood with other members of the board. Their annoyance stemmed from the fact that community regulations dictated that board members received, as compensation for the labor of mine surveillance, half a castellano of gold (2.3 grams) whenever they collected the community percentage. Although Giovanny's labor often bore no fruits—retreros only washed out their sluice boxes every few days—the walks did pay off for him, much to the frustration of his colleagues who felt these rewards should be reaped by all. Like Giovanny, most of them were working irregular jobs. Their income depended in part on being contracted as labor in community events and projects, financed by a public agency, NGO, or company. However, these opportunities were scarce, unlike Giovanny's walks to the excavator pits.

On one occasion, several discontented leaders had pressured Giovanny to stop his surveillance work. But in his absence, few had been willing to undertake the exhaustive journey to the mines. And so after two weeks of abstaining, Giovanny risked the wrath of his colleagues and took up his forest walks again. I went with him.

Things had changed in our absence. At the first mine encampment, it appeared that the owner, Roberto, had left his younger brother, Danino, in charge. With a strong Antioquia accent and little enthusiasm to elaborate, Danino said that no gold had been washed in the last two weeks. Giovanny asked him when his older brother would return. Danino did not know.

"But you do know that you should call our secretary when you start washing?" Giovanny asked, standing a few meters away from an excavator whose dipper was spoon-feeding bites of dirt to a rusty-red classifier.

"I only inform Roberto and Pablo. That's what Roberto told me to do. You can call Pablo yourself."

A colorful septuagenarian, Pablo was the *condueño* (customary land-owner) of the area where the three excavators of Roberto and Danino were digging. Giovanny knew him well. "Pablo doesn't call us. And there's a big difference between what he receives from you and what he gives to us."

"So, come here every day," Danino said. "I don't like to call. I call my mom, but no one else."

After a brief silence, I dared to comment. "Why don't you like to call?"

"Because I don't like it," the retrero snapped with undisguised contempt. "And I also don't like being interrogated."

Giovanny did not press him on his refusal to call, nor on his claim to have not found gold for two weeks. He accepted Danino's explanation that the mine would be washed the next day. Yet as we walked off from the classifier and outside hearing distance, he remarked: "Jes, these miners lie all the time. We're going to hold a meeting with all the dueños (excavator owners). And if they don't comply with our rules, they'll have to leave."

The rest of the day seemed a confirmation of Giovanny's observations about lying miners. The second mining camp on our route was run by Sergio, also a paisa. That day, its only occupants were a handful of rank-and-file workers, all seated at a makeshift picnic table. One of the men said that "to his knowledge," he and his coworkers hadn't produced any gold that week, because their one and only excavator had broken down. The explanation sounded unlikely to Giovanny, who, upon leaving the camp, told me under his breath that the clean sacks of Sergio's classifier and the reshaped appearance of his pit hinted at a recent washing. Thereafter, at a third mine, we caught a mining crew red-handed in the act of cleaning out their respective classifier. Giovanny took the opportunity to collect the junta's gold percentage and asked the men, to no avail, what they knew about any possible extraction at the nearby camp of Sergio.

While walking back from the forest to the village, it was the possible chicanery of Sergio's men—and not the proven chicanery of the third mine—that clouded Giovanny's humor and dominated his talking. His soft-spoken hypotheses turned into foul-mouthed complaints once we ran into an acquainted miner traveling in the opposite direction, who confirmed our hunch that Sergio's machinery had been operating all week. "Those swindlers tricked us!" Giovanny said, perhaps to me, perhaps to himself, as we resumed pacing the forest trail. "This junta complains that they want to go to the bush, but now I've not gone for fifteen days and now we don't control the territory anymore. We're harming ourselves, Jes!"

Back in the residential area of La Peña, we found Pablo (condueño of both Sergio's and Danino's mines) buying two friends beers in one of the village's taverns. He claimed ignorance about Sergio's bamboozlement. He said he hadn't gone to the woods in days, and "yes of course," he would have a heart-to-heart with the miner.

The next morning, Giovanny, Yelena (the junta's secretary), and I were out at first light to attend the washing that was supposed to take place at Danino's mine. Arriving at the camp, we spotted Pablo, another villager who functioned as his personal escort, and a bunch of miners huddling together in front of one of the camp's huts. As we drew closer, we realized that the men encircled a bucket that contained a gold-mercury amalgam. It was a déjà vu of the previous day: Washing had already happened! Pablo and Danino had not bothered to wait for the junta's collectors to arrive, nor had they informed them correctly about the hour of gold collection. We learned that the amalgam weighed ten castellanos, an awful little for the two weeks that Danino claimed to have worked without washing. To the junta directiva, ten castellanos equaled nothing; their tax only became effective if production topped twenty castellanos. The deceptive outcome had made Yelena lose all impetus to visit the other mines on our surveillance checklist. She decided to take the long walk back to La Peña with Pablo and his escort. Giovanny and I carried on to Sergio's camp, where we suspected Pablo had other secrets buried.

Unlike the day before, the camp was teeming with people, compelling Giovanny to bestow his investigative skills on whomever he saw fit. After an unsuccessful inquiry among various miners, a visiting spouse confirmed that Pablo had indeed been at the camp three days ago, turning to dust the condueño's claim of having stayed out of the woods. As soon as dueño Sergio appeared at the camp, his tree-cutting axe still in hand, Giovanny sat him down for questioning.

"Sergio, how much did Pablo receive this Saturday?"

"The thing is, I wasn't here on Saturday. I think Pablo sorted it out with Andrés." Andrés was Sergio's son-in-law and administrative right hand. Now a couple of trickeries the wiser, Giovanny was hesitant to buy into this justification.

"And Andrés didn't tell you anything?"

"No," the dueño said.

"But he's your administrator, right?"

"Can you imagine? I'm the boss of this mine. I must find myself an administrator who writes these things down for me."

On our way back to the village, we bumped into Andrés. "We gave your share to Pablo," the administrator said, unaware of all our previous runarounds. "Pablo told us he would deliver it to you. We made forty-six castellanos. You do the math with him."

The final two kilometers of our trip proceeded the same as the day before: an angry Giovanny racing back to the village to get redress from Pablo. "I can't believe it! This guy robbed 3.5 castellanos from us!" He spat out the words as if he couldn't stand their taste. "I'll talk to him! And if he doesn't have the money, we will stop the machines!"

In the village, Pablo was buying beers again, but now in a different tavern. Giovanny took him aside for a minute and then walked away. Pablo stayed behind, along with a befriended miner, myself, and our three bottles of beer. The washing mystery remained unsolved, at least to me. All Pablo gave me was the same answer as the day before: He did not know about any gold.

A few days later, Giovanny explained that the matter was settled. It had not been Pablo but Sergio who had wrongfully taken the community's gold, using it to pay for his excavator's diesel. But the junta had forgiven him. Giovanny never specified whether, and if so, how the miner had compensated for his secretive dealings. Inclined to let sleeping dogs lie, I never asked.

Concealing Gold

In an ethnographic article, Nancy Peluso (2018) observes how secrecy conditions social relations in a small-scale gold-mining region in West Kalimantan. She describes varied mining stakeholders who harbor different kinds of secrets: State officials negotiate bribes, buyers purchase gold by illegal means, and workers share inside information on the identities of mine owners. With these practices in mind, she argues that "Secrets about transactions, sites, and connections are components of everyday work and life in gold country, and are productive of a territoriality—a territorial belonging—by including mining subjects in the knowledge of them" (411).

The secretive territories that Peluso draws out for West Kalimantan map quite fittingly onto Chocó's mining villages, where much of the political economy of gold revolved around the production of secrets. As the cat-and-mouse game between Giovanny, Pablo, and the miners shows, knowing where gold ended up after extraction was sometimes just as difficult as establishing its whereabouts underground. In fact, these two "secrets" were intertwined: The ephemeral physicality of subterranean gold was constitutive of the secrecy that surrounded the metal above the soil. Let me clarify. Insofar as gold's location was a mystery to miners before and during extraction, their bullion varied strongly from one moment to the next. This variability, together with spatial isolation, permitted retreros to duck payment arrangements. After all, because their mines had no fixed returns, they could fabricate stories about unproductive washings and thus secure higher shares at the expense of juntas directivas. To not be kept in the dark about the exact number of extracted grams, it was pivotal for community leaders to be present at washing hours. Any miner tale told afterward might have been a lie masking the actual richness of the underground.

Yet in the ordinary business of mining governance, retreros were not the only ones holding secrets. With a resource as small, costly, and forbidden as gold dust, acts of concealment were all around, as were allegations about bribes, skims, and power abuses. Junta directiva members, for one, had to endure accusations of illicit enrichment, leveled against them by their communities or fellow board members. Landowning families, for another, were rumored to strike rogue alliances with miners to cheat the junta out of its gold percentage. And such alliances aside, the landowners—akin to the community leaders—also mistrusted the miners. To rule out retrero wrongdoing, families sent representatives to oversee the delicate hours of gold collecting. These representatives didn't escape gossip about bribery either, as in faraway mines they could easily funnel family gold into their own pockets. Luckily, miner-signed receipts helped to contain these excesses and to affirm the trustworthiness of the collectors. But there were also neighboring landholders to look out for, who, without the rightful landowners ever realizing, could charge miners for excavating subsoils that were not theirs to rent out.

Moreover, the secrecy surrounding gold was anything but restricted to the inner dealings of community councils. As already discussed in Chapter 2, miners needed to hide their illicit labor from the state bureaucracy. They concealed their activities by working in the depths of the jungle, the deafening decibels of their machines discernable only to long-distance walkers like Giovanny. Yet secrecy also pervaded the moments before and after excavation. Miners adopted stealth tactics to prevent fuel bins and equipment from being impounded by policy, army, or navy. They circumvented terrestrial and fluvial checkpoints by driving their fuel-packed pickups, bikes, and boats at

night. Some even demounted their equipment (e.g., dredges) ahead of transport to prevent them from being spotted by state troops.

Secrets also traveled in the other direction. On their journey to urban
gold-buying houses, miners and junta directiva treasurers hid their specks
in socks and underwear in anticipation of the quick hands of the police. Here-
after, the selling of gold likewise happened in shrouded ways. Insofar as the
origin of illegally mined minerals had to remain unknown to state agents,
buyers inscribed all gold as having legal provenance.

Naturally, in the interstices of centralized state rule, gold needed to stay
hidden from not only bureaucrats, but also thieves. Gossip about productive
mines had to be avoided at all costs. Community leaders and retreros who
talked too loudly or were too detailed about production volumes were
shushed. To further nip rumors in the bud, mine administrators were cagey
about the time and day of washing and were sometimes even reluctant to
share this information with their workforce. When a robbery did occur,
people speculated in whispers about the identities of the perpetrators, who
committed their crimes secretly, their faces covered by ski masks.

Far away from the goldfields, state figures, too, plotted their strategies in
secret. Who they would capture, what machinery they would blow up, and
when they would strike was all delicate intel that couldn't leave the bureaus
of law enforcement. UNIMIL, the Bogotá-stationed police unit tasked with
destroying illegal mines, did not reveal its planned logistics to local authorities, because, as its director explained, missions were regularly compromised
by leaks from corrupt officials: "We don't tell anyone when we go to Chocó,
because we don't want information to be filtered. We have leaks in the police, the army, among the mayors. All over the place. No sooner than we arrive to Chocó, they already know we're there."

Back in Chocó, community leaders and miners feared leaks of their cell
phones and wiretaps by government officials or looters. Because of this,
Giovanny and Yelena always used the euphemism of "activities" when calling each other about retrero washings. Mine administrator Tirso didn't even
talk about gold by phone. He had aspirations to run for mayor and worried
that one wrongly chosen telephone sentence could spur a police arrest that
would ruin his political career. And when Emiro (from Chapter 3) sent me
pictures of his mini-dredge via text chat—which he did several times—he insistently asked me to erase them afterward.

Amid this political climate of concealment, anthropologists who asked
too many questions could come across as interrogators. When meeting me

for the first time, some people denied, falsely, being or knowing miners. In a few cases, concerns about my identity lingered on. One day, Emiro said out of the blue: "Jes, I sometimes wonder if you're going to write bad stuff about us when you're back in the Netherlands."

I was taken aback by his comment. I had known him for six months and had befriended him and his wife, Sandra. We often shared dinner at their house. "Why do you wonder?" I asked.

"The thing is, we miners can never know for sure who you are. You say you're an anthropologist, but maybe you work for the CIA or a multinational. Who knows?"

"You still believe that?" I asked, slightly baffled.

"Sometimes I do."

Demanding Receipts

The secret that perhaps ignited the most moral condemnation in mining villages was that of junta leaders keeping community gold for themselves. Several times, leaders described to me their commitment to the community council as a sacrifice for their constituencies. This self-identification was impossible to disagree with. It was mightily inspiring to see the amount of time leaders invested in council matters without receiving a single peso, an investment that many made while living in harsh economic conditions. Nonetheless, it wasn't always easy to differentiate collective from individual agendas. When surveilling mines, organizing events, and managing projects, junta members received remunerations in the form of gold, cash, or having their families employed as labor. Although this compensation arrangement made up for the many unpaid hours that went into community tasks, its drawbacks were, first, that several community members criticized junta leaders for enriching themselves in faraway mines and nontransparent projects, and second, that leaders sometimes accused each other of eating too large a slice of the communal cake.

In La Peña, both accusations reached boiling point at the annual assembly of the community council. Anticipation in the village had been building up in the weeks preceding the assembly. Stories were circulating that leaders were earning good wages on their collection visits. More significant still, the junta directiva had suspended board member Ruth, who was alleged to have used money from a community event to cover personal expenses.

The theater of the assembly was the community hall, a cement-plastered building that was large enough to engulf two basketball courts, and whose corrugated-zinc roof muted all conversation when drummed at by rain showers (and rain showered lavishly in La Peña). People had shown up in great numbers, occupying several hundred plastic chairs that were spread over the length and width of the venue. The crowd faced the end of the hall, where the junta directiva was sitting, their ten chairs facing in the opposite direction. As they often did during these events, the leaders wore emerald-green polyester vests that showed the name and logo of the community council. In painful representation of her expelled status, Ruth sat vestless among the regular audience.

The meeting got under way with a profit-and-loss statement, presented by junta members Wilmer and Giovanny with the help of a flip chart. After guiding the audience through a brief revenue summary wherein mine taxes made up the largest share, the two men listed the community's expenditure posts. To the murmuring amusement of the people in attendance, the expenditures consumed more flip chart sheets than the preceding revenues. On reaching the junta's travel expenses, the crowd's murmuring increased in volume and morphed into a loud orchestra of private discussions once it became clear that the figures covered several sheets.

But the controversial bit was still to come: the wages earned from the collection visits to the excavator mines. To avoid the corruption accusations befalling previous leaderships, this junta directiva had embraced the principled policy of resolute "transparency" about all things gold.[1] Yet once the flip chart sheet on mining became visible, the transparent figures did not behave in the junta's favor, especially not in the unfortunately large time frame in which they were presented. Encapsulating almost a year of collection visits, the accumulated incomes comprised numbers with several zeros, with the sum behind main collector Giovanny's name dwarfing the other figures. The result was as inevitable as it was blunt: people talking, people shouting questions, people getting up from their chairs. In the face of the consternation, speaker Wilmer tried to overrule the audience, but to no effect. The louder he talked, the more his microphone's feedback mutilated his sentences. After seeing him losing his thrall over the crowd, junta member Yoser got up from his seat and snatched the microphone away from him to call for order.

"Please, people, please! Silence! This is a democracy! Let's talk with respect! Silence!"

It hardly affected the crowd's clamor. The mining salaries had created a cacophony writ large.

"Silence!" Yoser tried again, with a voice coming from the back of his lungs.

Noisy unintelligible complaints echoed back and forth between the hall's concrete walls.

"Silence!"

Spectators began to call for receipts signed by the miners, demanding proof that legitimated the leaders' earnings.

"Silence!"

A woman sitting at the front made an impromptu intervention. She asked the junta why her daughter had never received money for going to the mines.

"Silence!"

Yoser's plea was of no use. Not here. Not in the presence of this profit-and-loss statement.

The restlessness faded away during the succeeding presentation, in which Yoser listed the strengths and weaknesses of each junta member. Order was more fully restored when the president of the council announced the assembly's main topic: Ruth's suspension. A captivated audience listened silently to the president reading out a "public letter" that explained the decision, enacting, again, the junta's imperative of full public disclosure. "The junta directiva of the community council of La Peña, in the exercise of its function, aspiring to the normativity of the legislation of Black communities, and especially to what is stated in Chapter 4 and Chapter 7, has taken the majority decision to suspend Ruth. The reasons are, first, the abuse of her responsibilities, and second, the use of her position for personal benefit."

What followed was the chance for rebuttal. Visibly affected by the accusations, a proud-walking and stern-looking Ruth commenced a defense plea that stressed that the money she was accused of misappropriating had been rightfully earned by working in the community project. She said that the private company organizing the event had also paid other community leaders for their labor. "So if they suspend me for receiving money, they should suspend them as well." The speech gradually turned condemnatory as she ripped into her criticasters. "It's true, we don't have wages. We work from eight in the morning until nine in the evening without receiving a peso. But what happens in the mine?" She claimed the junta's collectors were earning well on their visits to the excavator pits, and calculated how much they subtracted from what was actually the community's gold. After this exposition, she ended her monologue with a surprise announcement. Since, as she reckoned, the junta had no right to suspend her, she would quit the leadership herself. "I renounce!" she proclaimed, before rushing back to her seat in the multitude.

People booed. People applauded. People shook and nodded their heads. People abandoned the hall. Different junta members stepped up to the microphone to make their objections, though most were drowned out by the blare of the crowd. Principal collector Giovanny, surprisingly enough, refrained from giving a speech and only rapped a few hardly discernable words: "I can show you all the receipts from when I went to the mines!" With his fingers, hand, and arm all fully stretched, he pointed in the direction of a retrero present at the meeting, as if to identify a witness who could confirm his claim.

During the session's remainder, the junta directiva invited people to express personal inquietudes. The majority of these focused on the "corruption" of the previous administration. Taking advantage of the presence in the hall of the community council's ex-president, several persons came forward to ask him where his junta had kept its retrero receipts, how they had made money from excavators and projects vanish into thin air, and why their financial records mentioned inexplicable expenditures. In making his defense, the ex-president gave a speech that underlined his good character and called out individuals who had benefited from his presidency as employees. The sympathy plea was cut short by unforgiving jeering in the hall. He was booed off stage, and to add insult to injury, received a trenchant comment from one attendant—known to never mince words—on leaving the venue. "The people don't want to listen to you! We don't want you here!"

The last speaker of the day was an older woman. "It's always the same," she said, while most seats were already abandoned. "I hope these excavators will soon be gone, so we may finally see the end of all this fighting."

In gold-producing Chocó, the treasuries of community councils were highly reliant on mining taxes and development projects. Praised were the leaders who, like those in San Miguel (Chapter 2) and Bebará (Chapter 4), transformed these revenue streams into collective benefits. buildings, infrastructure, work. Yet mines and projects also made leaders prone to better- and lesser-substantiated accusations of personal enrichment. Whereas earning good money doing communal work was in itself a reason for raised eyebrows—as Wilmer's flip chart presentation demonstrated—popular backlash multiplied when individual gains were made secretly: the bribes, the manipulated books, the pocketed gold. In the noisy community hall, both current leaders and the ex-president experienced this backlash in the flesh. Yet they were not alone in attracting criticism. Beyond La Peña, too, people indulged in fantasies about—and sometimes presented proof of—the skim-offs by former and contemporary juntas, which had allegedly brokered shady deals with retreros in out-of-the-way forests. Many of these fantasies targeted juntas that had governed the windfall gold profits of five to ten years earlier. What especially generated skepticism was why in all those years of excavator mining, specific administrations had produced hardly any public works. To make sense of this omission, people talked about "corruption."

Anthropological analyses show us that "good governance" buzzwords such as "corruption," "democracy," and "transparency" have strong performative dimensions, to the extent that they connote vernacularized political registers through which people understand citizenship and hold accountable state institutions (Gupta 1995; Hetherington 2011; Holston 2008; Nuijten 2003; Salman 2004). But in Chocó, these words also surfaced in conversations about the (in)correct administration of mining resources by previous and present juntas directivas: "At least this junta is not corrupt"; "This isn't how things should go in a democracy"; "They say there may be corruption again." These were notable moral evaluations, because they did not refer to civil servants, nor to a formal economy. Yet even if community leaders were not seen as bureaucrats, and did not self-identify as such, they did occupy a public office. They were elected through popular votes, organized strongly formalized meetings, and were expected to rake in public funds. More so, they held the responsibility to use these funds for the good of the people. It wasn't so strange, then, that leaders who failed in this responsibility were accused of corruption, which ultimately, in its conventional understanding, describes the "application of public property or license for private gain" (Tulchin and Espach 2000:4 in Hetherington 2011:49). Under conditions of muddled sovereignty, junta directiva leaders were one more set of actors to hold accountable for resource distribution, and—just like mayors, governors, and the Colombian president—were perceived as "corrupt" when abusing, and "democratic" when fulfilling, their public positions. There was little reason to keep the governance of mining outside of this moral framework. It happened out in the open. Gold showed up in community regulations, junta letters, signed receipts, and profit-and-loss statements. As a legit and overt aspect of community politics, it became deserving of similar ethical considerations as licit income streams.

Nuance is critical, though, for corruption discourse highlighted not just the alleged trickery of specific individuals, but also, less directly, the perverse regulatory expectations that Afro-Colombian community councils must live up to in structurally impoverished places. Juntas directivas are required to carry out in their own free time the immense task of administering vast tracts of land. Thus, if leaders confiscating communal money is an injustice, then the greater injustice is surely a political and economic context in which juntas receive insufficient public and private funds to do such demanding jobs; a context that, to restate a point made by juntas themselves, incentivizes leaders to spend, openly or secretly, what little community council money there is on individual expenses, at the assured risk of popular charges of malpractice. The complex morals of the situation become especially apparent when such charges are leveled at devoted people like Giovanny and Ruth, who—regardless of the false or justified nature of the indictments—spent uncountable hours of their unpaid time on community matters.

That all being the case, despite the rumored accusations against junta leaders—and despite similar accusations that leaders themselves gossiped about retreros like Sergio and condueños like Pablo—mining governance is as much about conflict as about compromise. The rest of the chapter picks up on this.

Seeking Compromise

Micro-conflicts like those in the assembly abounded in mining villages, borne out of competing interests over gold, land, work, money, or otherwise. Yet unlike the rift between Ruth and her former junta colleagues, most of the time people were hesitant to let disputes escalate into heated conflicts, recognizing that reconciliation yielded more satisfactory results. This inclination to compromise came especially to the forefront in the collecting of gold percentages. As illustrated earlier, junta directiva leaders had great trouble making retreros comply with payment rules in their spatially extensive commons. But it wasn't only topography (the isolated mines, the hidden physicality of subterranean gold) that explained their troubles. Unequal power relations were also at stake. Most money entering the community council derived from excavator mining. Against this financial backdrop, juntas directivas largely opted for "soft" measures against miner misbehavior, preferring to be cheated out of one or two washings over losing out on gold altogether.

In La Peña, leaders expressed a zero-tolerance policy regarding clandestine washings: Miners had to pay the rightful percentage or leave the territory. Nevertheless, each time Giovanny and others discovered they had been left in the dark about a washing, the respective lawbreaker got off easy. The miner promised better behavior and paid a minor compensation, but was never expelled from the collective land. Despite constant "last" warnings, extraction continued as normal and—as if no harsh words had been uttered—bamboozling started all over again. In one interview, I mentioned to Yelena, the junta's secretary, this discrepancy between the threat and the actual act of expelling miners. She admitted that she and her colleagues were in no position to banish the retreros. "It's not as if we can tell them to move. We don't have other incomes. That's the hard part. Here there are people who say we [the junta] are robbing money, but there is no money."

Another example of this lenience toward the retreros was the short-lived employment of Melvin. To address their problem of territorial blindness, the La Peña community leaders had hired Melvin, a friend of several of them, to be their eyes and ears in the faraway excavator pits. The idea was that he would live in a hut at one of the mines, where he would jot down in a notebook any activity worth mentioning—and washing activities in particular. He was chosen for the job because he was as principled as they came: a righteous evangelical of middle age who would never be corrupted by gold fever. Unfortunately, he was also a relentless blabbermouth. In his first week inside, he scared the mine's cook by talking to her about his absent sex life, and as a result, the miners barred him from the camp. The junta directiva then stationed Melvin at a second mine. Yet two weeks later, the mine's dueño informed the junta he no longer desired Melvin's presence because the chatty evangelical did not click with his workers. The leaders accepted, choosing to appease the dueño over sticking with their new strategy of remote governance. Less than a month after employing Melvin, they relieved him of his duties.

Like taxation, environmental management by Chocó's juntas also suffered from their economic dependence on mining. For instance, in La Peña, leaders expected retreros to supply wood and money for the construction of a tree nursery. The nursery would provide saplings to plant in the deforested mines and, so it was strategized, would buttress the community's effort to obtain a mining title. Again, the junta directiva presented the matter as a question of comply-or-leave. "I'm very sorry," leader Yoser told retrero Roberto during a surveillance visit, "but those who don't contribute to the nursery cannot mine here." But whenever Giovanny (the most dedicated junta collector) inquired about material contributions, miners changed topics, dodged questions, or laughed off his requests. Half a year after Yoser's warning to Roberto, Giovanny hadn't collected a single peso. Asked about this, Yoser admitted defeat—"Nothing happens with those miners"—and said he had started looking for other sources to fund the nursery.[2]

In social-scientific accounts of small-scale mining, conflict is a recurring motif. Competing interests over land and gold are described as stimulating myriad disputes and exclusions (Heemskerk et al. 2014; Luning 2014; Tschakert 2009). Similar accounts are written about Colombia, where gold diggers clash with landholders (Restrepo 2017), armed groups (Cohen 2014), bureaucrats (Siegel 2013), and multinationals (Vélez-Torres 2014). Yet along with this attention to conflict, the literature has said little about the relations of conviviality that render working in conflict-fraught goldfields an everyday possibility. A positive exception comes from Ton Salman and Marjo de Theije (2017:587), who note that latent conflicts in gold country rarely deteriorate into a "generalized all-against-all smacking and trashing." They maintain that disputes "are . . . channeled in *modi vivendi*, in ways to deal with these conflicts and turn them into practices that allow people to do and/or profit from the main motive to be there in the first place: to mine" (586). Stated otherwise: "Different players, even in competition, benefit from some predictability and (albeit tacit) rules . . . and from a certain acknowledgement of others' positions and legitimacy" (588).

Their argument of non-escalation chimes with the socioeconomics of excavator mining in Chocó. However much they felt their land rights entitled them to retrero gold, junta leaders like Giovanny often turned a blind eye to the scams of miners and individual landholders so as not to jeopardize productive arrangements. Landholding families, in turn, obliged retreros to reforest their territories, but were unlikely to make a fuss if their orders were ignored—especially if the retreros had proven profitable allies. And retreros, like landholders, might have conceived of the junta directiva as an unrighteous claimant to their mines, yet both parties were wise to let some gold specks flow into the communal fund, because the junta (as the legal representative of the territory) held considerable power to set police actions in motion.

This politics of compromise went beyond the distribution of excavator profits. Accepting your losses, swallowing your pride, and not pushing your luck imbued a wide array of extraction relationships. Dredge miners

complained that astute villagers charged unjustifiable percentages for working in rivers—which are property of the state—but they paid up anyway to
avoid tensions. The leaders of the *lower* community council harbored bad
feelings about the mining taxes that their *upper* junta imposed on them, but
they kept most complaints indoors, as they depended on the latter for the
mediation of outside projects and approval of excavator mines. The dueños
running these mines hated to pay guerrillas and paramilitaries extortion
money, but uttered these frustrations in low voices, as the brutality of the
armed groups was widely known. And the workers of dueños were annoyed
with the low pay they got for their hosing, cooking, and driving, but kept
their lips sealed to hold on to their jobs. In brief, even if simmering discords
were rife, mining stakeholders made sure that these did not develop into
irreconcilable feuds so as not to lose out on their gold winnings altogether.

To be sure, conflict aversion had other drivers than the enabling of extraction. In villages where everyone knew everyone, people also left matters
for what they were to appease neighbors and friends and family. For example, landowners could ask trespassing pump miners to leave their family plots,
but since they knew the latter—and their possible economic difficulties—they
did not always press them on the issue. In a somewhat different vein, people
who disapproved of mining sometimes needed to bite their tongues if local
power differentials demanded. Orlando, a senior university teacher, said that
he had always planned to spend his days of old age farming his family plot,
a long boat ride away from the city of Quibdó where he currently lived. However, he was unsure if this desired retirement was still possible. In his absence, excavator miners had laid siege to large swaths of his forest gardens.
"There are holes everywhere," he said in an interview in a Quibdó restaurant.
"It's so bad that when my son visited the land, he got malaria. Before, I wanted
to grow old and die in those lands. Now I don't know anymore."

He admitted that a few years earlier, in a situation of hardship, he too had
made money from the excavators' destruction by way of the condueño percentage: "I don't live there. I don't have family there. I couldn't prevent them
from getting in. In the conditions I was in, I accepted. I was in a wheelchair.
I was very sick then. Also, if I refused, because of their love for money, other
people would pressure me, because there is gold, bareque, and the percentage for the community council."

He was far from alone in accepting a flawed trade-off. In heterogenous
mining villages, principled desires and rules rarely inspired full acquiescence,
as they had to be negotiated in unequal encounters. When positioned at the

bottom end of a power relationship, community leaders and others often did not intensify their conflicts to actualize what they felt entitled to; rather, they settled for good-enough outcomes that made the most of imperfect situations.

Seeking Compromise (II): Settling the Hilltop

Juntas directivas occupied a peculiar position in all this. They established compromises not only when safeguarding their own gold income, but also, in being formal representatives of collective lands, when mediating in the mining conflicts of others. Such mediation included reminding retreros of their financial obligations to condueños, scolding dredge miners for dirtying waterways when this bothered local villagers, deciding on land borders in conflicts between families, and, as we see now, settling disputes between retreros who were not even members of the community council.

One morning, word reached the La Peña junta directiva of a turf war between two mining camps. Workers of paisa miner Sergio had threatened to kill workers of paisa miner Roberto. Worried about the possibility of bloodshed, community leaders Yoser and Giovanny, along with myself, set off to the mines to hold peace talks. On the walk up on the forest trail, we bumped into José, a paisa in his sixties who worked at Sergio's mine. José had defied the pattering rain to give his version of events before Roberto's workers could give theirs.

"I wanted to talk to you before they could. That man Pablo is an oligarch! He only lets Roberto work." As stated earlier, Pablo was the customary landowner of the tract where both mines were situated. He was not impartial in the feud. He sided with Roberto, who, unlike Sergio, had never deceived him, and who possessed three state-of-the-art excavators—Sergio worked with one thirdhand machine.

"But Pablo can say whatever he wants," the worker from Sergio's camp added, now walking alongside us. "For me, you have the power. And you know us. We've worked here for two years and always tell you when we're washing."

José continued his heartfelt plea until the antagonist mining camp came into view, which implored him to take a detour back to his own encampment. In hindsight, the decision seemed appropriate. Hostility reigned at Roberto's camp, and José was its main target. Three angry-faced men sat atop a mechanical worktable, which was sheltered against the rain by a black plastic canvas sustained on four wooden poles. The three workers of Roberto's ignored our "*buenos días.*" One of them engaged in attack mode. "Did you talk to José?! Do you know what he said to us? 'I'll go to Bogotá, so that no one can work.' You don't threaten like that! You can kill, but you don't humiliate!"

The men updated us about the recent events. They said that José had wanted to "send in the state"—hence the reference to Bogotá—and that another miner of Sergio's had threatened to shoot his gun. It was a conflict over water that had provoked such aggression. Roberto's workers had found themselves unable to wash their sluice boxes, because by doing so they would discharge tailings into a creek from which Sergio extracted water for his washing operation. The three workers argued that the creek was theirs to dirty and not Sergio's to keep clean, since it belonged to a plot that condueño Pablo had promised they could mine. They noted, moreover, that it made more sense for Sergio to get water from another, higher-placed creek, which was located closer to the classifier he used for washing. They reckoned that Sergio's decision to place his water pump at the lower, disputed waterway had less to do with operational logistics than with a vile strategy to prevent Roberto's camp from advancing in his direction. Apparently, the two mining crews had been working toward one another until they had gotten locked into a territorial stalemate, with only a small stretch of hill separating them.

Yoser, Giovanny, and I swapped the worktable for the hilltop. Dissimilar to its muddy surroundings, the hill was verdant with thickets of native bush, granting it the impression of an endangered ecosystem that had somehow managed to stand its ground amid the rage of the gold rush. But time was not on its side. On top of the hill, Roberto's men were chain-sawing the underbodies of the remaining trees, part preparing for future extraction, part marking off their territory vis-à-vis Sergio. Condueño Pablo watched their work from a safe distance, sitting on a fallen tree trunk next to mine administrator Danino, who ruled over the procedure in the absence of his brother Roberto.

"We don't decide anything here," Danino said to the community leaders, after getting up from the trunk. "The territory is yours. If you tell us to leave, we leave calmly. But no one should threaten to kill us."

"Who threatened you?" asked Yoser.

Danino offered a few names. "But we will not fight them. I don't want to kill nor be killed. I'm only interested in working."

From the opposite crest of the hilltop, Rubén, another man from Sergio's crew, climbed up to join in our circle. With both parties present, Yoser underscored the judicial purpose of this visit. "We came here to impose justice. You both know that you don't own this place. This *mister* here [Pablo] represents the territory and we came here as the authority. You are people who work here only because of the difficult situation in our country. Nothing more."

"Absolutely," Rubén affirmed. He directed his hand at me. "I always tell him: If there were something else, I wouldn't be here."

"So, the two of us want to mine," Danino said. "Then, don't make threats! Here, there's no need to draw a pistol. We all have families. Me, I still want to make four children. Where are you from?"

"Córdoba [a department on the Caribbean coast]," Rubén said.

"I'm from Segovia [a mining town in Antioquia]. You think that people from Segovia and Córdoba will come looking for us when we get killed? Where we are now, they will not even notice."

Rubén nodded his agreement. "We would only be a few more disappeared persons."

"So, let's work," Danino concluded.

In their willingness to let bygones be bygones, the two men agreed on a solution that would see Danino providing an excavator and fuel to move the pump of Rubén and his coworkers to the higher-up, nondisputed creek. The matter of who would mine the hilltop was less easily settled.

"We can cut the hill in half," Rubén said.

"Or who enters first," Danino quipped.

"Beh. You must admit, you have three good machines and we only have the one that always breaks down."

Hesitant smirks followed. A peace deal was pending, all to the delight of the moderating Yoser. "You see? Talk to each other. That's how you solve things." But to solve things, it was necessary to involve Rubén's superior, Sergio, in the talk. The two leaders, landowner Pablo, and I went out to look for him, and found him after a five-minute walk on his flank of the hill, at his pump next to the disputed water.

"You tell me, how are things?" the retrero asked Yoser, after shaking the hands of the whole mission. "We came here first and now they say it's theirs."

"You must reach a deal," the community leader answered. "Because if there are threats against people's physical integrity, we have to stop everything here. We will ask the army to accompany us and they will seize all equipment. And no one wants that to happen."

"Then let's go to the hill and divide the terrain," Sergio said.

Condueño Pablo then cut him short. "But that's not for you to decide. Am I right, Yoser?"

"Of course, we don't own the hill," Sergio answered on the leader's behalf. "But *don* Pablo, we only want to work. You've known me for two years. I've always treated you with respect."

Now it was Yoser's turn to admonish the dueño. "But each mine should only have one representative who talks to the others in such cases. We can't have all these people making threats."

"I'm the only boss of this mine," Sergio said through gritted teeth. "But I want to get back to work, so what is there to do?"

He got briefed about the suggestion of Danino helping him to move his pump. He didn't take it well. He had picked the far-off waterbody because the alternative creek—to which he would be exiled under the new arrangement—was unusable for pumping due to spillage from a previous washing operation by Danino's brother Roberto. Yet despite some unambiguous swear words, Sergio followed us to the hilltop, where the matter was quickly resolved. He accepted the relocation of the pump to the new creek on two conditions: He would be allowed to work his side of the hill, plus Danino would build a dam to raise the creek's water level to prevent Sergio's pump from clogging. The two men shook hands on it. The junta's mediation had been successful.

Looking back on the dispute, I see it as indicative of two important characteristics of mining socialities. First, it confirms once more that compromise was bliss in gold country. Rather than shooting guns, Danino and Sergio longed for a return to extractive normalcy. Danino was "only interested in working." Sergio, though unhappy with the relocation of his pump, eventually accepted his eviction. He knew he did not own the hill and simply wanted "to get back to work." It's this willingness to make amends that allowed miners to do the extractive work that had brought them to these faraway forests to begin with—where they "would only be a few more disappeared persons."

Second, the dispute highlights that outside the institutional trappings of bureaucracy, juntas directivas took up regulatory practices that fostered the imposition of justice and the de-escalation of conflict. When mining conflicts could not be solved by the involved parties alone, community leaders were called on to bring people to the negotiation table and establish middle ground. Most certainly, such mediation collapses rigid distinctions between what is lawful and what is not. Because even if the juntas targeted extraction practices that were considered "illegal" by state legislation, their interventions gathered much of their generative force from the symbolic authority of the state. At the end of the day, community leaders "had the power" to decide on mining matters, to paraphrase José, because they were recognized as land-holders under state law, and by virtue of this, could report people misbehaving in their legally sanctioned territory to armed troops (as Yoser's threat illustrated). Considering such legal access, it was a sound battle strategy to win the leaders over to your cause in order for compromise to be in your favor, which helps explain why the La Peña retreros—usually coarsely reluctant to inform the junta about their goings-on—were remarkably loose-lipped and reverential to Yoser and Giovanny during the conflict.

Conclusion

In the preceding sections, I have examined the everyday politics of commu-nity councils in Chocó's gold regions, where juntas directivas tasked them-selves with the governance of informal excavator mines. A significant share of such governance entailed the levying of taxes that, in accordance with cus-tomary law, the juntas shared with individual landholding families. Through the example of La Peña, I have shown that the relations between these three actors (juntas directivas, retreros, landholding families) were strongly disci-plined by concealment and conflict. Community leaders failed to exercise an effective surveillance over the distribution of retrero gold, which was dug up and washed in faraway forests. Due to such territorial blindness, leaders con-tinuously suspected—and not without reason—that excavator miners and landowners cheated them out of their gold percentages. At the same time, leaders themselves were sometimes rumored to use gold for personal gain. This, along with their (real or imagined) feeding off other communal revenues, had made some people skeptical of the institution of the community council.

Yet despite the back-and-forth allegations that spiraled around the local governance of gold, concealment and conflict coexisted with a complemen-tary determination among mining participants to not let tensions intensify to extreme proportions. Junta leaders and others settled their conflicts through pragmatic truces, in large part because the alternative—unbending loyalty to self-identified entitlements—yielded less favorable results. In conflict-ridden gold country, a certain tolerance of the deceits and half-truths of others was imperative to maintain economically productive relations, to continue operating a mine, or to make at least some profit from miners you couldn't stop from trespassing on your land.

These modi vivendi bring to mind Carolyn Nordstrom's (2000, 2007) work on shadow economies. Nordstrom shows that illicit economies, in lieu of formal contracts, impel their own moral regulatory systems, which are wedded to social principles and based on (largely nonviolent) relationships of interdependency and trust. But while Nordstrom identifies underground socialities and ethics in the "shadows" of state rule, this chapter has shown that state symbols may constantly weasel themselves into the social and moral fabric of a criminalized economy. In gold-producing Chocó, miners were supposed to comply with the informal rules of community leaders, because the latter enjoyed *legal* rights over the land. These leaders, for their part, risked being seen as slacking on their lawful mandate (as being "corrupt"), not so much when they collected illegal gold, but when they did so for personal benefit. And Yoser resorted to the threat of army intervention to broker peace between the mining camps of Sergio and Roberto. The next chapter will further interrogate this shifting terrain between legality and illegality. While zooming in on the governing activities of localized bureaucracy, it shows how mining stakeholders used their access to state agents not just to solve conflicts (as Yoser did), but also, possibly more radically, to sanction their participation in clandestine extraction activities.

PART III

Governing Miners

CHAPTER 6

Illegal, but Not Criminal

You're illegal, but let's make sure
you're not criminal.
—*Amed (municipal mining inspector)*

A s we got off our motorbike, we looked straight into four worried eyes that were sizing us up. The two men they belonged to were textbook examples of gold miners: ragged jeans, black rubber boots caked with brown-reddish mud, wretched T-shirts worn loosely over generous shoulders. They had ample reason to look worried. We had caught them in the act of illegal extraction. They stood stupefied in front of an excavator whose tracks were pulverizing recumbent timber, inching themselves toward the crest of greenery that formed the visual border between the strip of weedy rocks where we were standing and the unmined forest beyond—that is, between the extraction of the past and the extraction yet to come. What probably most worried the men, though, was us, the motorbike delegation catching them in the act. There was Amed, the uniformed official with a mean-looking ID card dangling around his neck. And there was me, the out-of-place white foreigner. In their eyes, I presume, we looked like officialdom. We looked like legal trouble.

The uniformed official offered the two men a prompt truce. "I'm the mining inspector for the municipality of Caliche. But don't worry. I'm not persecuting miners like the state does. Our mayor doesn't want to stop mining. Here, we understand that you have families and that this is your *rebusque* [livelihood]."[1]

Both chocoanos, the men introduced themselves as Gustavo and Óscar and said they had started excavating only this week. "We're actually working a motor-pump operation," Gustavo said. "The excavator is just to get us started, to clear the land. It's not ours."

"You should have stopped by the town hall," Amed instructed. "Now I don't know what the land looked like before you arrived. Many miners in our municipality work in a horrible way, and the state pressures our mayor to shut them down. The mayor told me: 'Amed, why am I paying you, if these miners keep on working like this?'"

Gustavo traded in his technology-based defense for one based on familiarity. "I'm a friend of Edwin's," he said, calling the mayor by his first name. "He already knows we're here."

This seemed to appease Amed. True to his office of mining inspector, he lectured the men on how to arrange tailing ponds, which tree species to use for reforestation, and what ecological disasters would ensue were the nearby stream to silt up with mine spillage. The two men listened, agreed, and promised to act on his advice. They indicated where they wanted to plant saplings and dig out ponds. "This is all very helpful," Gustavo said. "It's only when your work is disorderly that you get persecuted by the government."

Not all Amed's recommendations were of an environmentalist kind. "Did you inform the community council that you're here?" he inquired.

"We talked to the lower junta directiva," Óscar replied. "It's them we're paying."

"Talk to the upper junta," Amed said. "They're the ones who decide if you can work here. And do you already have the RUT [taxpayer identification number]?"

The miners nodded.

"That's good, but now you also need this form called the Mayor's Certificate if you want to sell your gold. Come visit me one of these days in the town hall, so I can confirm you're barequeros [miners working with hand tools]. You pay 18,500 pesos and then return some weeks later to pick up the paper."

"And with that paper we can sell?" Gustavo asked.

"Yes, as much as seven castellanos a month."

The news pleased the men. "You know, this is just what we needed," Óscar said. "That someone comes over to tell us how we can work legally."

"Well, what shall we tell them, Jes?" Amed cast a grin in my direction before commencing his lecture. "Look, with the state we have right now, you'll never be able to work legally. You're illegal, but let's make sure you're not criminal. That's what we're trying to do in our municipality, that you work formally."

At this and other moments I shared with him, Amed did not talk like "the state" that miners such as Gustavo and Óscar had come to dread for its punitive measures and criminalizing language. He talked like one more chocoano who knew everything about the difficulties of getting ahead. Likewise, his mining surveillance did not bear the markings of a castigatory judicial regime. He did not persecute Óscar and Gustavo, but authorized their operation, assessed their environmental commitments, advised them on formalization, and invited them to register as barequeros in exchange for a small tax. Amed didn't see himself as "the state." "I'm not persecuting you like the state does," he had stressed. And yet he was only in the position to authorize, assess, advise, register, and tax because he belonged to that same legal machinery with which he did not identify. Like any street-level bureaucrat, he personified the law. But his was a different kind of law. Thanks to Amed, miners who were "never . . . able to work legally" were nonetheless able to work "formally." Stated otherwise, miners who were illegalized by centralized legislation were authorized by Amed to work, as long as they conducted their labor in a formal-like way.

It's fractious state politics like this that lie at the core of this chapter. In it, I deviate from social analyses on Latin American mining that depict the state as a singular actor (e.g., Cohen 2014; Giraldo Ramírez 2013; Gudynas 2009; Perreault 2013; Siegel 2013) by calling attention to the multiple and disorderly workings of bureaucracy. To be more specific, I piece together the different ways that the social organization of gold mining is structured by, and structures, the regulatory schemes of the local state apparatus. To support this proposition, I start with an introduction to Colombia's decentralization process, and describe its unruly unfolding in Chocó, where municipal politicians paid for votes in both the elections of themselves and those of community councils. Subsequently, I make clear that local bureaucratic actors' interference in community politics was pivotal to the workings of "underground multiculturalism" (as described in Chapters 4 and 5), to the extent that the political backing of mayors and other officials empowered community leaders when enforcing mining regulations. Finally, I conclude with a section on the role that municipal offices and CODECHOCO (the regional environmental authority) played in miners' performances of make-believe legality.

Decentralization and Unruly Institutions

Colombia's adoption of multicultural legislation happened against a wider backdrop of public-sector reforms that meant to render the bureaucratic apparatus more efficient. This government shift in the late 1980s and early 1990s entailed neoliberal policies aimed at integrating the national economy more firmly into global markets, including through the liberalization of labor markets, the reduction of import tariffs, and the privatization of public companies (Orjuela Escobar 2001). On top of this, and inspired by the central government's faltering control over the countryside, reformers promoted a robust set of decentralization measures under the conviction that strengthening local institutions would motivate nonstate armed groups to enter formal politics and embrace the path toward pacification.[2] And thus in 1988, mayors—who during the preceding hundred years had been presidentially appointed—were for the first time elected by popular vote. Soon after, in 1991, a new constitution cemented such decentralization by extending elections to the appointment of governors, and increasing the administrative duties and spending power of municipal and departmental offices (Ballvé 2012).

But the reforms had unforeseen effects. They did not bring peripheral power relations into the thrall of centralized rule, but, contrarily, loosened the grip of national institutions on municipal and departmental ones. Decentralization not only emboldened left-wing guerrillas and right-wing paramilitaries to run their own candidates for office, as anticipated; it also, by expanding the jurisdiction and revenues of local (and manipulable) institutions, enabled these armed actors to more easily feed off public expenditures and institutionalize illicit activities (Eaton 2006). The result was a further blurring of the line between legal institutions and illegal actors, something that became all too clear in the governance of gold. Fiscal decentralization put mayors in the hot seat of the local mining economy, as they became allowed to retain 87 percent of mineral royalties. This newfound taxation power made mayors increasingly subject to criminal pressures and, more or less owing to this, spurred them to authorize illegal extraction, encourage fictitious gold declarations, and offer financial incentives to miners so as to have gold from elsewhere registered in their municipality (Giraldo Ramírez 2013).

Now, to make sense of such decentralization gone awry, many political analysts consider the governing activities of local institutions—and their divergence from centralized planning—as evidence of the destabilization or co-optation of the Colombian state.[3] For example, Giraldo Ramírez (2013) identifies a "relatively weak" state (53) that "does not control the gold economy" (46). Eaton (2006:533) writes that guerrillas and paramilitaries use decentralized resources to "destabilize the state" and construct "parallel states on the left and right." And García-Villegas and Revelo-Rebolledo (2010) argue that decentralization backfired because pervading "clientelism . . . captured the institutions . . . of the state" (66). Taking into account this book's preceding chapters on state-building from below, it should warrant no surprise that I don't concur with these narratives of state collapse. Unlike their "Weberian" ideal types of bureaucracy, which cast judgment on the (in)effective performance of bureaucracy and decide a priori what modern statehood is about—about "the state's monopoly on the use of force" (Eaton 2006:548), about "finding obedience to a mandate" (Giraldo Ramírez 2013:47), about "bureaucracy and state decisions . . . [obeying] principles of rationality and universality as previously established in law" (García-Villegas and Revelo-Rebolledo 2010:23)—I find it more analytically rewarding to look at what institutions mean to those who encounter them on a daily basis and, while looking in this direction, at the contingent ways that state governance comes into being through political formations that run counter to the formal legal framework.

I am certainly not the first to express a preference for a less formulistic and less legalist conceptualization of the state. A copious anthropological literature has repetitively made the case to view corruption, extrajudicial violence, and disorder as integral, rather than antagonistic, to state formation. Especially since Das and Poole made their famous plea to stop seeing the state as being less complete along its "margins," an ever-increasing number of authors have explored "how the practices and politics of life in these areas [shape] the political, regulatory, and disciplinary practices that constitute, somehow, that thing we call 'the state'" (Das and Poole 2004:3). A convincing example, in this regard, comes from Janet Roitman's (2004) work on the Chad Basin. Roitman shows how illicit trading and smuggling activities allow states to fill their coffers and pay government salaries. To grasp the political potentiality of such ambivalent statecraft, she proposes a distinction between "state regulatory authority" and "state power" (194). In other words, while activities in "the so-called informal economy" (203) might "undermine state regulatory authority" (221), they may nevertheless help reconstitute state power by "[contributing] to the viability of the state through the production of new rents and possibilities for redistribution" (216).

Along the same lines, several scholars have debunked the persistent idea that social turmoil in Colombia is an outcome of state absence, and have pointed to the historical relationship between violence in the "margins" and the politico-economic agendas of the "center" (Ramírez 2015; Sanford 2004; Serje 2013). In this tone of argument, Margarita Serje (2013) argues that scientific notions of statelessness resonate with the colonial narrative of Colombia as "a central area . . . surrounded by vast savage areas . . . thought of as not yet fully incorporated in either the national project or its economy" (96). She reminds us that for several centuries, the image of lowland regions as uncivilized provided the highland center with an ideological carte blanche for exploiting them. With this in mind, she warns of three disturbing effects that the "myth of state absence" generates: It instills the idea of a parallel Colombia whose precarity is disconnected from the center; it obscures the actions of state actors intervening in rural regions; and it legitimizes (para)military intrusions (111–112).[4]

Serje's arguments strike a chord with recent ethnographic studies on Colombia that explore how extralegal violence is interspersed with state-building. For the northwestern region of Urabá, Teo Ballvé (2012:611) contends that paramilitaries were "handmaidens" of the decentralization process, as their violent land grabs gave way to banana and oil palm plantations that were financed with public funds. This vexing collusion of dispossession and government money leads Ballvé to argue that "narco-driven economies of violence are not somehow anathema to projects of modern liberal statehood . . . but deeply tied to initiatives aimed at making spaces governable, expanding global trade, and attracting capital" (603).[5] Meanwhile, Aldo Civico (2012) describes how in Medellín in the early 2000s, paramilitary groups carried out neighborhood policing while counting on the collaboration of public agents. He sees paramilitaries as a "war machine acquired by the state" (80), and notes that "The intertwinement between the state and organized crime is not a sign of the weakness of the state but of the power of its presence" (89).

The following sections also point to a convergence between legal and extralegal politics. However, while many analyses of Colombia describe this convergence in terms of "state effects" produced through paramilitary and guerrilla violence, here I draw attention to a less dramatic manifestation of the "extralegal," namely the organizational activities of miners and juntas directivas. Indeed, whereas both the "cumulative" lawmaking of miners (Chapter 3) and the "underground" governance of juntas (Chapters 4 and 5) may contravene state regulatory authority—to recall Roitman's terminology—these are also forms of social organizing that are constitutive of state power, in that they provide local government actors with opportunities for taxation, territorial administration, and the enactment of public authority. Yet before plunging into the specificities of all this, let us first take a closer look at the unruly unfolding of decentralization in Chocó.

Unruly Institutions in Chocó

In accordance with wider patterns in Colombia, one unplanned outcome of the decentralization process for Chocó was a new dynamic of clientelism. Municipal elections highlight this best. In the gold regions of this research, mayoral hopefuls complemented their abstract campaign promises with person-to-person guarantees. To amass electoral support, they swayed voters by disbursing pre-election benefits (cash, bags of cements, corrugated sheets of zinc), or by promising to employ them upon being elected. Mayors were the gatekeepers of contracted work, and the municipal office was several times described to me as the "only company we have." This being the case, many people pledged their vote to a certain candidate in exchange for a chance to be part of this "company." Young adults aspired to employment at one of the construction projects the would-be mayor vowed to bring, restaurant owners expected their candidates to rely on their cooking at future events, and university laureates were the most vocal in demanding the electoral jackpot: a job in the town hall.[6]

Voting was betting. For the electorate, it was betting on different candidates—the morally admirable were not always the most likely to win— and election benefits—money up front versus the more lucrative, but less certain, option of a future job. But the biggest wager may have been running for office. Aspiring mayors needed to collect hundreds of millions of pesos to bankroll their political campaigns; money that was mostly shouldered by "investors," who ranged from well-off merchants through gold-rich miners to seasoned politicians.[7]

So what could be won with such high-stakes betting? One historical answer may come from gold. Winning the election means obtaining control over the mining economy. Other social researchers have documented that in Chocó, "Municipal administrations charge approximately USD 900 for the construction of the mine and a monthly fee of USD 250 while it is operating" (de Theije et al. 2014:139). No miner told me they were subject to taxes this high, but I did hear stories about a mayor demanding similar figures during the gold bonanza five to ten years before my research.

Apart from charging rents, mayors may have also earned on gold by way of royalties. In 2010, Salvatore Mancuso, an ex-commander of the Colombian AUC paramilitaries, informed a United States federal court about an ingenious money-laundering scheme. The AUC used drug money to buy gold on black markets, which they subsequently sold as locally mined bullion in municipalities under their influence. The royalties that the municipalities later received on the gold were split between the paramilitaries and the mayors (Tubb 2020:144). Mancuso's disclosure testifies once more to the difficulty of making an indeterminate underground submissive to regulatory control. For the invisibility of subsurface gold allows paramilitaries, mayors, and miners to fake its presence in places where it doesn't exist and to overstate the richness of their subsoils—and thereby fool the civil servants tasked with determining the legal origins of commercialized minerals.[8] Indeed, there is good reason to assume that similar underground simulations have happened in Chocó. In his book *Shifting Livelihoods*, anthropologist Daniel Tubb recounts a visit to the Alto Baudó, where he found no gold mines, even though for several years this municipality in Chocó was registered as Colombia's third-largest gold producer. Additionally, Tubb lists the registration figures for various chocoano municipalities and observes excessive alterations over relatively short time spans, coinciding with the terms of municipal politicians and hinting at royalty fraud (Tubb 2020:133–148).

And yet, while gold taxes may have once filled municipal coffers, and may, as Tubb (2014:384–385) has it, have encouraged campaign spending during the boom years of the early 2010s, it is unlikely that mining was of great influence in the later election rounds (2015, 2019, 2023) that surrounded this ethnography's time frame. One reason is that in the "post-boom" economy, opportunities for off-the-books taxation were much fewer. Another reason is that royalty fraud had become more difficult to carry out. Due to newly imposed selling limits, it was harder to register minerals as coming from legit activities (see Chapter 3). Also, perhaps more importantly, since 2012 mayors no longer had direct control over royalties and could only access these by proposing projects of public interest to regional administrative bodies. All of which seems to indicate that there were drivers other than just gold accounting for the high stakes in the municipal elections.

Fortunately, research collaborators (politicians, councilors, municipal employees, junta directiva leaders) spoke lucidly about these stakes. To them, it wasn't so much mining as access to public finances that explained why elections continued to spawn expensive campaigning. They said electoral investments were easily won back, with profit, by skimming off government funds. Having held important positions at the municipal and departmental level, Arturo was among those who explained things best: "So, the mayor owes a debt to the investor [in his campaign]. How will he pay him back? He gives him contracts. The investor gets a luxury contract to hire some company for a construction project. The company receives the money beforehand, so he can return it all to the mayor and the investor. Sometimes they don't carry out the project, sometimes only half of it, sometimes with poor quality. They inflate the numbers."

Investing in campaigns, winning elections, feasting on government money; there is much to say in favor of Arturo's analysis. On the one hand, there are the criminal investigations. Chocó counts many white elephants and uncompleted public works. On numerous occasions, elected representatives have been investigated and/or sentenced for appropriating funds destined for public infrastructure.[9] On the other hand, there is what local politicians explained. Whether aspiring for the position of mayor, municipal councilor, or departmental deputy, people who were running for office were frank about the under-the-table workings of voting. Some invited me (or business acquaintances I might have) to invest in their campaign in exchange for a long-term profit. Others admitted grudgingly that they would never win their election without the financial backing of shrewd businessmen.

Importantly, these votes-for-favors dynamics had also seeped into community councils. Mayors had begun investing money in the elections of juntas directivas to ensure that the community council was run by the same political color. In one illustrative case, a mayor had convoked his own junta directiva election, separate from the vote organized by the sitting junta leadership. This situation led to a political stalemate whereby both the party backing and the party opposing the mayor claimed victory in their own elections, urging the Office for Matters of Black Communities (part of the Ministry of the Interior) to intervene and call for a new vote. After this intervention, however, the two opposing factions once again held separate elections. I was invited to the mayor's election and attended what looked a lot like a raffle. At the event, which was hosted by the municipality's secretary of governance (the mayor's right hand), community council members were motivated to cast their vote for the only party present, in exchange for the possibility of winning kitchen utensils, food packages, washing machines, and other prizes.

Whereas my initial assumption had been that this politicization of community elections was related to the juntas' gold earnings, leaders and municipal employees explained that mayors' interest stemmed from a desire to control public projects carried out in the collective territory. One leader said: "[Mayors] do everything in their power to let their own party members win, so that they control the two powerful institutions of the municipality: the municipal administration and the community council. This way they can feed off community projects.... They now want to build a road that passes through our collective territory. And the mayor wants to manage everything: the finances, the personnel, the material. So, he needs to have the council on his side."

Such institutional meddling in grassroots affairs encountered criticism from the community council at large. Yet junta members getting into cahoots with the mayors perceived it as part of the game of politics. In Caliche, it was public knowledge that the junta directiva had achieved its electoral victory by outbidding the competing faction with the financial help of the municipal office. In interviews and conversations, the victorious junta members argued that this was simply how elections were won: "In a previous election, I opposed the idea of putting in money.... But then the mayor invested in the campaign of the others and they won. So, two months later, I regretted my decision. And now we did have the support of the mayor and we won."

Along with getting elected, teaming up with the mayor offered another advantage. And here gold did enter the picture. Effectively, although junta–mayor alliances might not have been primarily driven by gold, these partnerships were however imperative to the extractive governance of several juntas. The following two sections illuminate this point by focusing on the municipality of Caliche.

A Conflict over 0.5 Percent of Gold

The day after I first set foot in Caliche, I attended a meeting in which the newly elected junta directiva of the upper community council presented their mining agenda to a small room of retreros working in their collective land. Speaking in turns, the junta representatives were at pains to stress the importance of recuperating the forest ("Those acacias you're planting aren't helping us; try to combine them with guava and guama trees"), of preventing mercury pollution ("The state will not forgive you"), and of respecting the local mining authorities ("You need the permission of the Ministry, but also the permission of the mayor and the community council"). The larger part of the session, however, was devoted to a discussion of how the miners would compensate the community for their environmental damages. The junta let them choose between two schemes: a monthly fee of 3 million pesos or 3 percent of their net earnings. The miners univocally voted for the latter.

After voting, the community leaders sketched out what would happen with the 3 percent of collected gold. Half of it would flow directly to the junta directiva of the *upper* community council (the junta heading this meeting), while the other half would stay with the juntas of the subordinate *lower* councils (none of which were present in the meeting), in whose territories the retreros were working. From the upper junta's half, one third would go to the municipal administration (so, 0.5 percent of the total gold production). This payment, the leaders said, was needed to cover the logistics of the mayor's mining inspector, Amed, who would conduct visits that verified whether or not the retreros were complying with the community council's environmental mandate. Amed (also in attendance) wrapped up the meeting by impressing on the miners the importance of paying the new municipal tax: "The mayor is the only authority who can prohibit and authorize the work of miners in this municipality."

The arrangement caught the eye for several reasons. First, Amed's job as mining inspector fell under the rubric of UMATA, a municipal entity in Colombia whose formal task package entailed technical assistance in the fields of farming, livestock, fishing, and forestry, but not mining. Second, although Colombian mayors had the juridical responsibility to notify law enforcement about unregistered mines, they were not in the legal position, unlike Amed's claim, to "authorize the work of miners," let alone those working without mining titles. Third, and in view of the previous, Caliche's municipal government was in no position to claim a 0.5 percent tax on informal mining activities. In sum, Amed would be paid with informally mined gold, to do a job he wasn't supposed to be doing, for a state entity that had little to do with mineral extraction. But the deal was sealed. At the end of the meeting, the upper junta recorded the 3 percent rule in a document that was signed by themselves, the miners, and Amed.

A few weeks later, I visited Amed in the town hall to interview him about the mayor's mining regulation. He sat me down in his office cubicle and had me read a bundle of documents. Some of the paperwork (a miner census, a field report, a decree prohibiting illegal mining) had been drafted for the

annual control of the Procuraduría (the government agency that investigates and sanctions public functionaries). Yet other documents seemed
unlikely to have been written for this purpose. Amed walked me through a
text on his computer that contained a six-point ethical code telling excavator miners to not use mercury, to reforest, to fill in tailing ponds, to not
mine near rivers, to let workers rest at weekends, and to not spill sediments
into waterbodies. After he told me that all local retreros had signed the list
with their names and ID numbers, I asked, considering the prohibited status of their labor, why UMATA bothered to pursue such environmental
surveillance.

"Look, according to the law these mines are illegal, but here a lot of people
live off mining," Amed answered. "So, the mayor wants to keep this economy in his municipality. He looks for the legal means to protect these miners, so people can send their children to study, to have money. I visit the
miners so they do things the right way. Sustainable mining. But basically, I'm
visiting delinquents."

In the months following this conversation, I found out that these visits
rarely happened. Getting to the mines required traversing long dirt roads,
but the town hall's one and only motorbike had been defunct for years. Over
time, though, I learned that Amed's job was about much more than just environmental assessment. I learned this through the community council's new
taxation arrangement.

The "1.5 + 1.5" percentage rule had stirred bad blood in Caliche. Leaders
of the lower juntas directivas complained they had not been consulted by the
upper junta about the policy. They had only heard about it via the retreros
who worked in their territories. An even bigger concern was that the terms
settled behind their backs were not in their favor. The lower juntas had lost
half a percent, as under a previous arrangement they had been authorized to
impose a 2 percent tax. To me the difference felt negligible, particularly in
these times of retired retreros and mined-out lands. However, the lower leaders
set me straight. It was especially in the post-boom times, they argued, that
every grain of gold was welcome. Besides, with the variable productivity of
the unknowable underground, a profitable washing was always imminent,
and therefore so was a profitable 0.5 percent. And then, of course, there was
what felt right. The mayor and UMATA, the lower leaders agreed, had their
own sources of income and had no jurisdiction over retrero gold.

It was the leaders of the lower community council of Santa Teresa who
most vehemently objected to the percentage decrease. They were known to

be part of the political opposition to the mayor and the upper junta. They had endorsed the competing party in the upper community council vote, and had championed a different mayoral candidate during the municipal elections. Now, it seemed, they would not accept a third defeat, as they insistently declined to pay UMATA its half-percent share. Luckily for them, Camilo—the only retrero remaining in Santa Teresa and himself a chocoano—reasoned it was indeed the lower (and not the upper) board that held the legitimate claim to his mine. As such, he paid the full 3 percent to the Santa Teresa board, which thereafter divided the percentage two-to-one in its own favor.

"What they did was illegal," one of the Santa Teresa leaders said in a group interview about the upper junta's new tax scheme. "We're not ignorant of what Law 70 says. The lower council is the owner of this territory and we decide what we charge." A second leader called attention to another legal incongruity. "Because of the environmental damages, we should pay UMATA? That's illegal. Those are functionaries of the municipality. If we want a visit from UMATA, they have the obligation to give it to us."

A whole different notion of ownership surfaced in conversations with the upper representatives. "The lower junta doesn't have the juridical authority," the upper junta's treasurer said. "Law 70 says that the upper council rules over the lower council. So, only the upper junta has juridical authority over mining."

To both sets of community leaders, the question of who had the right to Camilo's informally mined gold was first and foremost answered by multicultural legislation. Yet state law popped up in the conflict not only by citation, but also through the rule of force. Since neither the Santa Teresa junta nor Camilo was willing to budge an inch, the upper leaders eventually called on the help of the town hall. Upon their request, the mayor drafted an "order of suspension" for Camilo, which municipal mining inspector Amed handed over to him at his encampment. The order was unforgiving. In case of noncompliance with the new UMATA "environmental tax," the mayor would ask the local police to seize Camilo's mine equipment.[10]

The measure effected immediate change. The day after receiving the mayor's document, Camilo phoned the legal representative of the upper junta and invited him over to get his due compensation. Straight after the call, the upper treasurer and secretary went out on motorbike to Camilo's mine to collect the gold, yet without previously informing the lower leaders—who only took heed of the matter when the two-man mission stopped by their village afterward to pay them their 1.5 (and not 2) percent of gold. To the Santa Teresa junta, the whole ordeal signaled a breach of authority. They sent out a "resolution" to their superiors, stating that the territories belonged to the lower council and that "we would appreciate it if you show us which law says that the municipality is in charge of administering this activity, and that we must pay them a percentage of our production."

Strikingly, the collection visit had also aggrieved the upper leaders. Unwilling to immerse himself deeper in the dispute, Camilo had refused to simply hand over to the treasurer and secretary their half. Instead, he had insisted on giving them the full 3 percent, burdening them with the unenviable task of paying the Santa Teresa leadership. With Camilo refusing to divide the percentage himself, the upper junta once more threatened with a shutdown. However, this time things cooled down quickly. Camilo and the upper leaders reached a settlement that kept both parties happy and did away with the troublesome Santa Teresa board: Camilo would relocate his mining camp to a land that fell under the reign of a different lower junta, one that showed no opposition to the new percentage agreement.

The "Muscle" of Local Bureaucracy

The tug-of-war over Camilo's gold shows how the effectiveness of juntas directivas' extractive governance hinged on local bureaucrats' capacity to suspend the mines. When miners did not live up to community rules (e.g., when they didn't pay up), junta members threatened to ask the municipal administration, the local police, or the regional environmental authority CODECHOCO to cease mining activities. Although all these entities were legally obliged to police unlicensed mines, in practice they left such work to national defense forces, unless extraction interfered with local interests. In La Peña, for instance, the municipal police only made a fuss about mining devices when these dirtied the water that inhabitants used for bathing and washing clothes. In Bebará, the mayor had on one occasion commanded a total halt to excavator operations, not because he had recently got wind of their illegal status, but because he wished to encourage retreros to comply with an order from local community councils—summoning them to get certain documents in service of a formalization procedure. And in Caliche, Amed distributed suspension threats while wearing an UMATA jacket and municipal ID card, but only when miners disrespected the upper junta's regulations.

Chocoano mining was thus subject to what we might call, with Snyder (2006), a "joint extraction" regime, in which the distinction between "the state" and "the community" wasn't always clear; or rather, in which the former functioned as the muscle of the latter's governing. This situation produced a haphazard dance with legality, because here there was a local state machinery that tolerated, and indirectly regulated, a mining economy that was supposed to be its antonym: "informal," "illegal," "criminal." Yet nonlegal mines and legal identities locked hands in another significant way. The claim by community leaders that their rent percentages were a lawful expression of their multicultural authority worked, peculiarly enough, because it could bank on the illegality of extraction. Like Camilo, most retreros perceived the juntas' taxation not as a genuine enactment of land rights but as a misuse of power. Nevertheless, they always followed community rules to some extent, knowing that the juntas, as formally recognized landholders and community leaders, enjoyed considerable clout to launch police missions against unlicensed mines.

Naturally, the community leaders' appeal to the brute force of the law did not always result in desired outcomes. Akin to other actors in gold country (see Chapter 5), they, too, sometimes had to compromise in order not to estrange important allies or cashflows. This became very clear in the aftermath of Camilo's departure from Santa Teresa. In response to the relocation, the president of the Santa Teresa council, in alliance with displeased counterparts from other lower juntas, had stood up against their seniors. The dissident presidents were planning on going public with the upper junta's ill-conceived mine taxation, and had threatened to inform a regional radio station and the Ministry of the Interior (which deals with the enforcement of Afro-Colombian legislation).

To avoid a political backlash, the Caliche upper junta eventually permitted the junior leaders to collect their gold independently, as well as to decide on whatever percentage they wished to levy. Actually, not long after, the upper leadership also changed its own collection policy. Like elsewhere in Chocó, they confronted a retrero population consisting of lousy rent payers. But unfortunately, they did not rely on effective mechanisms to enforce their taxation. They had not managed to accomplish a strict surveillance regime—à la La Peña (see Chapter 5)—because the mines were widely dispersed and far from the municipal capital, where most leaders lived. Moreover, due to the dispute about the percentage agreement, they no longer depended on a trustworthy network of local collectors.

Confronted with this illegibility of the terrain, the Caliche leaders opted for an alternative strategy. They briefed local retreros about Agreement 214, established between the Ministry of Mines and Energy and Chocó's environmental institution, CODECHOCO. According to this new agreement, so the junta announced to the retreros, small-scale miners were able to enter a formalization process for which they had to fulfill two conditions: compliance with the state's environmental rules, and registration with the respective community council where they were working. For such registration, the Caliche junta directiva would charge the miners 2 million pesos as initial payment, after which the latter would pay the same figure each succeeding month. The leaders warned the miners that Caliche's mayor could only endorse extraction that complied with Agreement 214. Purportedly, he would order the police to discontinue all operations that remained unregistered with the community council.

In truth, Agreement 214 dealt not with formalization guarantees or community inscription, but with a program of mercury eradication. Nevertheless, the junta directiva had instructed municipal inspector Amed to visit the two most recalcitrant rent payers and present them with a letter cautioning that "those not complying with the formalization process shall suffer the consequences." Amed allowed me to join him—and had me chip in on the rental cost of a motorbike.

The visit was a failure. The first miner was nowhere to be found. We missed him at his house and spent the whole morning, without success, riding through the woods in search of his mine. In the afternoon, we did locate the second miner, Camilo, at his campsite, standing with his working crew beside a broken-down excavator. We dismounted our motorbike about ten meters away from the men, who did their utmost to ignore us. Camilo said nothing. His workers said nothing. We said nothing. It was awkward. It was well known that Camilo had not taken Amed's previous threat of suspension lightly. Now, with him occasionally scowling at us, it was clear he had not forgotten.

An eternal minute later, Amed beckoned him to come over. "Señor Camilo, please do me the favor."

After shuffling slowly in our direction, Camilo shook our hands, mine more enthusiastically. Amed bet on a joke to break the ice. "Look at you all sweaty, only because you're staring at an engine."

"We're working," the miner fired back.

"Señor Camilo, the upper junta has told me you're not paying. They've sent me over so you can register."

"I have no problem with registering, but there's no money. Right now, we're *trasteando* [moving between pits]."

He did not pay the registration fee, not then and not ever. Nor did any of the other excavator miners. And so two weeks after Amed's motor trip, with no miner willing to pay up, the mayor signed one more resolution, telling the police to close down all illegal mines within the municipality. The resolution— which both community leaders and retreros had in their possession— mentioned two direct motives for the police order: a "shut-down request" from the community council, emanating from the miners' refusal to commit themselves to the aforementioned anti-mercury agreement; and the arrival of a CODECHOCO letter at the town hall, signed five months (!) earlier and citing a 2008 resolution that demanded all mines without an environmental license to be suspended.

In summary: Again, Caliche's mayor stepped in to assist the upper junta with their collection problems. And again, the environment was cited as the catalyst for the interference, now via a mercury-prevention policy and a decade-old resolution. This time, however, the threat of shutdown proved ineffective in strong-arming the miners. Even after the resolution, none of them showed up at the community building to pay the 2 million pesos. Moreover, despite this collective noncompliance, no local policeman entered the mining pits. The suspension was called off and it wasn't clear to me why. Junta leaders differed in their explanations. Some argued that a complete shutdown would have been harmful to the income of the community council. Others said the police had been unwilling to obey the mayor's command, anticipating a popular backlash. As for the police sergeant, he denied having received any order. And Amed? He didn't know any specifics. He was off work "sick" in the run-up to the police mission to avoid having any part in it, fearing that the retreros would proverbially shoot the messenger, as Camilo had done before. What was crystal clear, though, was that the miners had emerged victorious from the situation. They picked up their business as usual and continued to pay the upper junta when they could, or pleased. Whoever had not been willing to enforce the suspension warning (the junta, the police, the municipal office), the flexing of the mayor's muscle had not borne fruit this time.

Cumulative Legality (II)

It was, however, not just the underground politics of community leaders, but also the "cumulative" lawmaking of miners that had a bearing on the governing activities of public institutions. Gold forged unlikely alliances.

Although local state entities participated in mining as the institutional muscle for leaders' suspension warnings, these same entities also offered the miners (the recipients of the warnings) opportunities to accumulate, mimic, and claim their lawfulness. In confronting enduring illegality, miners relied on improvisational authorizations from local bureaucrats to legitimize their mine activities; or, inclusively, to render these activities visible as nonextractive (and licit) affairs. This chapter's introduction already discussed one form of such extractive whitewashing, namely that of municipal employees issuing the Mayor's Certificate, intended for manual operators, to mechanized miners. Yet the role of state actors in accumulating legality exceeded the mere provision of selling papers.

The Deal Between Jackson and the Mayor

Jackson had established a name for himself. There were the stories of wealth. With various degrees of admiration, people from different parts of Chocó could narrate that he owned multiple cars and a fancy apartment in Medellín, the fruit of his former mining imperium that consisted of around a dozen excavator mines. There were also the stories of redistribution. Villagers living in the vicinity of Jackson's mines heaped praise on him for helping out with money, jobs, and construction materials. They also remembered how he, a native of Chocó, had financed churches, paths, roads, and electrical grids in various corners of their department, all for the good of communities.

These were the stories.

Personally, I had come to know Jackson as a man bursting with pride. He was proud when recalling, for the umpteenth time, that he had brought roads and electrical light to the dark depths of the rainforest. He was proud when reciting the history of his self-made career. Having started out as an adolescent panner, he had become one of the region's most illustrious miners. He was proud whenever he bought me drinks or lunch, no matter how much I insisted on having it otherwise. And he was proud when he refuted the violent threats of the criminal gangs that profited from the righteous labor of him and fellow retreros.

No doubt, Jackson's pride sat uneasily with how his work was seen from state offices in Bogotá. He despised those "shameful" politicians who were attacking him and his fellow retreros. He invoked examples of the public works he had built to buttress his claim that miners like himself had done more for Chocó than whichever Colombian president. Above all, he reckoned it to be a travesty of justice that the Santos government was blowing up miners' equipment. In our first interview, he said he had never personally experienced a destruction operation, but could imagine what it would feel like. "If they burn my property, they would have to kill me the same day, because I don't know what I would do. For me, it's the same as someone killing your mother in front of your eyes. Or your father. Because these machines are our subsistence."

It was not as though Jackson could easily afford such property destruction. His glory days were in the past. For reasons that I never completely deciphered, he had only two mines left in operation, both in partnership with others. After I had visited him repeatedly at one of the two mines, he invited me on a road trip to see what the other looked like. It was there that I realized how he intended to circumvent the police.

Even before our arrival, I sensed that something was off with the mine. Three minutes after we passed the small town of "Ríobravo," Jackson drove his pickup truck off the asphalted road and parked it a stone's throw from the river. "We're here," he said.

"Here" hardly seemed the place to conduct prohibited extraction. Here there was no dense foliage to camouflage the vibrant colors of excavators. Here the distance from the well-traveled road was far too short to muffle the excavators' growling. And here mine runoff would flow straight toward the town, less than a kilometer downriver. But here it was. On getting out of the car, we encountered two excavators working the riverside. One of them dug up rocks and gravel from the shore and loosened them on a classifier device (used to wash gold-bearing sediment) that stood on a half-stranded metal raft. The classifier was positioned in such a way that the outflowing stones and dirt ended up on the riverbank. There, they were picked up by the second excavator, which drove the sediment to a storage point some fifty meters away, alongside a one-meter-high stone dam that directed the river away from the land lying behind it.

Jackson led me on board a large raft where he sat me down in a plastic chair. In contrast to the classifier raft, this one was totally afloat and was kept in place by thick steel cables, which connected its ends to two metal poles on the shore. He poured me several glasses of agua de panela from a cooler, sufficient to live on for the rest of the week. In between sips, I asked him if the stone dam was of his doing. He answered affirmatively. He explained that the mayor of Ríobravo had asked him and a socio to canalize the river, whose water flow and shoreline had been severely disfigured by stone banks left behind by previous mines. To whip the river back into shape, the socios had one excavator removing stone banks from the shoreline, while the other machine used the stones won from this movement to build a retaining wall farther downriver. The two excavators were working upstream, canalizing the river a few meters a day. Work was already paying off. "Whenever it rained, the water reached the town," Jackson said. "Thanks to our wall, it doesn't enter there anymore."

He and his partner did not charge a single peso for the work. But nor did they work for free. In tandem with fixing environmental damages, the two men were digging up gold. In the end, the sediment that they removed from the shoreline—and that helped them build the retaining wall—slipped through the sloughs of a mining classifier. Jackson explained that the mayor allowed the two socios to keep whatever precious metal was caught in this passage. The deal was that the miners got municipal authorization for their extraction, while the mayor got a canalized river without having to pay the construction costs.

"Who came up with the plan?" I asked.

"The mayor. He liked our work in another river here in Chocó. There we did the same thing: canalize the river. And he had this idea for canalization, so he contacted us."

"And do you produce enough gold to make it rentable?"

"No, all these sediments have already been worked," he said. "Higher up [the river] I think there's still gold."

"So, would you not like to mine higher up?"

"No, over there we're illegal. Here, we're legal."

I was skeptical about this. "But in both cases, you don't have a mining title."

"True, but at least here we're protected when there are *operativos*. Because the mayor and CODECHOCO support us and tell them not to come burning over here."

"CODECHOCO?"

"Right now, the mayor is trying to get us a CODECHOCO permit for the exploitation of stones. A contract for two years."

Before we left, Jackson told me to take pictures of his mine. I grabbed my phone and snapped whatever I could snap. Most miners did not like me taking photos, wary as they were to have their faces end up in who knows what type of document. Anonymity is king in the realm of the illegal. But not for

Jackson. He was proud; proud of his mine and proud of his canalization work. What's more, he claimed to be safe here. He did not need the richest of sub-soils, nor the remotest patch of jungle, to keep him protected from police helicopters. He had something better: the approval of the local bureaucracy, affording him and his socio—or so he reckoned—a safe and easy-to-reach worksite with long-term production stability. Of course, this was a different kind of state approval. The two socios were sanctioned not by official mining titles, but by an unruly mayor and soon, maybe, CODECHOCO. And all this under the pretext of a landscaping job. As far as substitutive legality went, Jackson, his socio, and the mayor had taken its accumulation to the extreme. Presumably, the miners no longer needed to make their extraction infrastructure invisible to the national police. They could hide in the open. Their scheme performatively transformed an illicit mine into a legit business that had nothing to do with gold. Reverse alchemy—or something like that.

Two days later, a public message on social media mentioned the destruction of an illegal mine near Ríobravo. An accompanying photo showed a metal raft burning fiercely, with orange and yellow flames shooting from it. It looked like the raft on which we had drunk agua de panela. Another photo showed a plume of black smoke rising from an excavator. It looked like Jackson's machine. My suspicions were confirmed when I read the message in full and found Jackson's name among those of other miners who had been arrested for committing environmental crimes.

I tried to call Jackson. I was worried about him. He had equated machinery destruction with seeing "someone killing your mother in front of your eyes." But frankly, I was also worried about his assessment of me. I thought about the pictures I had taken and about the many times miners had suspected me of working for the government.

He did not answer. A befriended barequero from Ríobravo did. He said he had witnessed the police action in person. He had even recorded a video of it, something he felt regretful about in retrospect, because it may have made him come across as a government agent. His words were far from comforting. I called Jackson again. No response.

After five weeks of occasional calling and texting, he picked up his phone. Suddenly, my worrying felt misplaced. He sounded cheerful, asking when we would see each other again. Not long after, we met up in his hometown, far away from Ríobravo. As he had been sentenced to domiciliary arrest, it was the only reasonable place to catch up. At his house, he said with his trademark confidence that he would prove his innocence at an upcoming hearing.

He was preparing "a thick dossier," chock-full of photos of his community works, his reforestation, his chamber of commerce inscription, his paid taxes. "I'm a legal miner!" he exclaimed, as though I were the judge ruling over his case. "That judge said: 'You have sold more than 1 million [pesos] in gold, so you're illegal.' But the judge doesn't know how I work and all the things that I've built. It's a good thing I always take photos before I enter a territory. So they can see how tidy I leave the land afterward."

I did not share his confidence. Had he not also claimed legality in Ríobravo? I didn't say this, but I did pose another hard-to-ask question. "In Ríobravo, you said the mayor would prevent police operations. Why didn't he?"

"The mayor . . ." Jackson paused for a few seconds to think. "The mayor has to tell these people of the state that he knew I was mining. Why does he say he didn't know? That was the whole deal! You think I'm burning diesel for free?"

Later, as we walked through his town, we ran into an excavator working on the river shore. I signaled to Jackson the similarity with the Ríobravo operation. To my surprise, he said that also this excavator was his. "I'm building a dam for the mayor here, so that the water doesn't damage the esplanade." Another town, another mayor, another dam. Still, there was no classifier this time. When I pointed this out, Jackson shook his head. "I'm only doing this to keep myself busy. They told me that I'm not allowed to mine until at least after the hearing."

The Quibdó Dredge

Talking to research collaborators and skimming news media, I occasionally came across anecdotes of municipalities building retaining walls to protect residential areas from river floods. When I learned about these projects, I couldn't help but fantasize about some secret deal that these walls might camouflage. Gold and Ríobravo were never far from my mind.

One project in late 2017 particularly stood out. Next to the main square of Chocó's capital, Quibdó, on the far shore of the Atrato River curling alongside the square, a "dragon" of two stories high was dredging the riverbed. The slanted and paved riverbank at its rear suggested that this was one more canalization project. It was something of an oddity, though. To newspaper pens and popular tongues alike, mining dredges were considered one of Chocó's biggest environmental enemies. Yet this one was performing at full capacity in the figurative heart of the province, disturbing the same river that had been famously allocated political rights by the Constitutional Court one year earlier to protect it from vehicles such as this one.

My interest was further piqued when a local state official told me the canalizing dredge was a cover-up for extraction. As part of his job, he had carried out an assessment visit to the machine, during which he had observed all sorts of mining tools. Partly on his insistence, I subsequently contacted an employee at CODECHOCO, which as the regional environmental authority gave canalization works the green light. This employee maintained that the dredge was simply building a retaining wall that had been commissioned by the mayor. Mining was not an option, he said, since CODECHOCO had permitted the work and were actively monitoring its activities to ensure no gold would be dug up.

Questions beckoned, though. Why was a mining dredge being used for a landscaping job? How (im)perfect was CODECHOCO's surveillance—taking into account the other official's observation about mine equipment? And how could the environmental authority be so sure that no gold was being extracted? Whatever sludge this machine was sucking up, it had to be glittering with gold dust. Situated in plain sight of the city, this patch of river shore had surely been left unmined by others.

I wasn't alone in my curiosity. Research collaborators in Quibdó and elsewhere fantasized with me. As I talked to them, the canalization work started to sound increasingly like a Jackson-type arrangement. Some people laughed at my doubts about the matter. They were adamant that this was mining and that the local bureaucracy was involved. A retrero mentioned that his cousin worked at CODECHOCO and was making good money from the dredge's gold. A state-employed engineer asserted that from a technical perspective the canalization job made no sense at all: "If he wants to do a good prevention job, why does he not build a retaining wall of concrete or wood?" And a junta directiva leader said the dredge was owned by a friend who had boasted to him that the Atrato was loaded with treasure: "Last week, they dug up three arrobas [forty-one kilograms]!" This same community leader also knew Jackson and had heard about the fate that had befallen him. "The problem in Ríobravo was that Jackson lacked the permission of CODECHOCO. That's why it did not work there and why it does work in Quibdó."

Granted, whatever extractive "truths" I heard about the dredge, they were only hearsay. I did not personally speak to the dredge owner or the cousin working at CODECHOCO, nor had I witnessed any gold being washed.

Figure 9. Navigating past the Quibdó dredge. Photo by the author.

Nonetheless, due to the cumulative weight of these testimonies, on top of other accusations of malpractice leveled at both CODECHOCO[11] and Quibdó's then-governing municipal office,[12] it may be short-sighted, as interlocutors argued, to not give some credence to the idea that this was a smokescreen for unlicensed extraction. In view of the abovementioned gold earnings of mayors (informal taxation, royalty fraud), it's quite plausible that the Ríobravo scheme existed elsewhere in Chocó.[13] By contracting miners to build retaining walls and clean rivers, mayors may reduce their own landscaping expenses (as in Ríobravo) or inflate their paychecks (as in the possible cover-up in Quibdó). Furthermore, when an investigative body detects these schemes, the municipal office can easily deny awareness of the gold being washed, shifting blame to unscrupulous miners who conducted their extractive crimes covertly. Of course, as it concerns an underground economy, the argument remains tentative and it's anyone's guess—including mine—what the breadth of these canalization schemes is.

The CODECHOCO Banner

But there was arguably a more conclusive case in which CODECHOCO met miners' need for make-believe legality. At the beginning of fieldwork, I partook in several CODECHOCO field trips, which were part of a project that incentivized miners to adopt "cleaner production techniques." A four-man technical mission had been assigned to do the groundwork, although usually it was just field coordinator Nelson who showed up. During the field trips, he—and occasionally one or more co-workers—visited several excavator mines, whose administrators he advised on reforestation, landscaping, water canalization, and not using mercury. The project, thus, neatly resembled what anthropologists have called the state's "legibility effect" (Trouillot 2001:132, see also Scott 1998:80), to the extent that its standardized environmental criteria contributed to "the production of both a language and a knowledge for governance" (Trouillot 2001:126).

However, the project did much more than just align disorderly mines with orderly state grids and protocols. To begin with, there were Nelson's trivial acts of political recalcitrance. Like any lower-echelon bureaucrat, he belonged as much to local worlds as to the law. He detested the destruction of excavators as much as anyone else, and gave the retreros he supervised tips on where to hide their machines in the event of a police crackdown. Additionally, the ingenious Nelson had the miners pay for our motor transportation to and from their mines, explaining to them that such sponsorship showed proof of their commitment to the project.

Yet the field visits also subverted official planning in more significant ways. For one, CODECHOCO assessed the same unlicensed retreros whom it was also supposed to prosecute. More significant still was the fact that, in trying to motivate these miners to partake in the project, Nelson repeatedly told them that the backing of the regional environmental office would protect them against having their equipment demolished by law-enforcement groups. While this promise was, legally speaking, a dubious one, several retreros in the project gave it a lot of credence. One of them even asked Nelson to provide them with a CODECHOCO banner, which, as a sort of additional piece of cumulative legality, could convince public forces to leave their excavators untouched.

After taking it upstairs to his superiors, Nelson complied with the request and promised an official banner to the most committed project participants. In conformity with his vision that CODECHOCO's backing was essential to avoid police harassment, he regularly presented the banner—to miners and myself—as an actual legal object that allowed retreros to work without fear. Such discourse was particularly manifest in a conversation we had while we were lost in an extraction-scarred landscape, in search of a mining pit. Wading through calf-deep pools and waist-high weeds, Nelson ranted: "We are walking and walking, without knowing how to get there! They should pick me up at their mining camps. Now I'm searching for them, while they should be looking for me! If I give them some device that says 'CODECHOCO,' they can tell the police: 'Why are you burning me? I participate in this project.' All the time they talk about being formal and getting the banner. But if they want it, they should show me that they're serious miners. I cannot just give a banner to anyone. I'm a functionary of the state."

Disbelieving Nelson's theory of police-deterring banners, I asked: "But they lack concession contracts. Why do you feel that the police will pay attention to the banners?"

"Because no miner in a CODECHOCO project has ever been burned. And now there's an official agreement between CODECHOCO and the Ministry of Mines. It's a window for formalization that authorizes us to work with miners who don't have a title."

"But really? Does the agreement state that you can work with miners without a title?"

"I haven't read it. But CODECHOCO has authorized me to work with these miners. And if they authorize me, it means that they can endorse the miners."

A few months later, I learned that the respective agreement made no mention of such endorsement, but more modestly aspired to "unite technical, administrative, and financial forces" between the ministry and CODECHOCO as part of a wider plan to eradicate mercury (Ministerio de Minas y Energía 2017). In fact, in a later interview, a higher-ranked CODECHOCO employee denied Nelson's assertion that their office enjoyed the political leverage to fend off police operations. He even acknowledged that his institution was prohibited from assessing title-less retreros. "As far as I know, we cannot officially work with them. No state entity can use public resources for an illegal activity. That's why it's so difficult to work in such a project. Because in Chocó, all mining is illegal."

Yet regardless of what should have officially happened in the project, once it was finished, an official-looking banner was indeed erected at the pit of the most project-dedicated miner. By displaying the logos of CODECHOCO, the municipality, and the departmental government, the banner physically imprinted the authority of the state on a mine that was operating without the required credentials. Nelson had extended the ontology of state formality to the voids of formal rule.

Conclusion

Here I have been tracing the unruly forms of political life that flourish when informal mining and formal politics amalgamate. To this end, I have examined two distinct ways in which the sociopolitics of an "underground" economy tied into the regulatory practices of local public servants. First, juntas directivas relied on their connection to the state bureaucracy to obtain acquiescence from excavator miners to their rules. When the miners flouted community law, juntas called in the assistance of mayors, CODECHOCO, and local police to get the respective lawbreaker in line. In Caliche, the mayor was especially quick to act on community leaders' complaints about indocile miners, not in the least because he had funded the leaders' electoral campaign and had a small financial interest in their gold taxes. Second, miners depended for their makeshift legal performances on de facto authorization by state actors. The latter sanctioned illegal operations by granting miners legal objects (selling certificates, banners, environmental licenses), or by promoting canalization projects that functioned as smokescreens for mining infrastructure—washing illicit gold clean, both physically and figuratively.

Together, these two types of formal/informal entanglements illustrate that "the state" regulating gold was not a single force of government. The operations of the Colombian legal apparatus ran at different velocities and worked according to conflicting ideas. While national government representatives tended to envision wildcat mines as an illegal menace, in the forests of Chocó gold frequently crossed the lines of the legal and the extralegal, fostering unlikely collaborations that enabled community leaders to enforce regulations, miners to enjoy access to variously convincing legal mechanisms, and the local bureaucracy to raise its tax base (royalties, informal taxes), build its infrastructure (canalization works), and perform its public authority and environmental ordering practices (the visits by CODECHOCO and UMATA). It is these "hybrid" (Jaffe 2013) collaborations that are overlooked in mining watchers' theorizing about "illegal" and "stateless" gold frontiers. Above all, it is such collaborations that underwrite the analytical need to conceive of the state not as an external monolith that intervenes (or not) in miner society, but as an ever-shifting amalgam of multifarious power interests and localized practices—including the interests and practices of small-scale mining participants. In point of fact, the influence of miners and community leaders reached further than local government; sometimes, as I will now demonstrate, their underground social organization penetrated the aboveground realm of centralized bureaucracy.

CHAPTER 7

═══════

The Good, the Bad, and the Permitted

You can improve, but only to a
certain degree.
—*Vicente (assessor of the National Mining Agency)*

They arrived, much too late, but they arrived: the representatives of the national government, a small aircraft of bureaucrats flown in from Bogotá to discuss mining matters. Their discussants, a dozen community leaders, had been waiting for over an hour in the conference room. Every two months, the leaders and the officials met here as part of the *mesa minera*, a discussion platform that sought to smooth the stagnated formalization of Chocó's countless gold miners. Because time was ticking—the officials' return flight was only a few hours away—the meeting quickly kicked off. Chocó's secretary of Economic Development and Natural Resources offered a few introductory words: "We know that we must continue making an effort to achieve a type of mining that is both responsible and *well done.*" It must have sounded like music to the ears of the just-seated Ministry of Mines and Energy officials. *Minería bien hecha* (well-done mining) was their catchphrase for describing the legal mining industry.

After the secretary's introduction, the community leaders took the floor. One after another, they shot their words directly at Carlos Cante, the vice-minister of Mines.[1] Their list of problems was long. There was no money to pay for mining titles and no chocoano miners working legally. There was no compassion among defense forces, who used explosives to crush miners'

equipment to a pulp and, despite the mesa minera, were doing so indiscrim-
inately. And there was no "differentiated" ethno-cultural politics that provided Afro-Colombians with legal protection against multinational titling.
There was no nothing: The mesa was half a decade old and the leaders had
nothing to show for it in their home villages—inspiring one leader to propose doubling the meetings' frequency. The last speaker specifically bemoaned
the gold-selling cap that the government had imposed to combat illicit extraction. "Every day there's a new rule that goes against the development of
our communities. Although we're only barequeros (manual-based miners),
the government insists that we can't sell our metals without certain documents." His eyes watered. His voice quivered. "This is a lot of regulation for
people who aren't used to it!"

In a rebuttal, the vice-minister countered the leaders' dissatisfaction by
listing the achievements of the mesa minera. He presented numbers of
awarded concession contracts, retracted forest areas, labor subcontracts, and
traditional mining reserves; all products of the mesa, all boosting the formalization of Chocó. Additionally, he stipulated his disagreement with the community leaders' contentions. The need for meeting more frequently? "There
are other departments to visit than just Chocó." The nonexistence of "differentiated" political treatment? "To the contrary, we've tried to do things differently. This is the only department where we do periodical visits to discuss
formalization." And the selling maximum? The barequeros, the vice-minister
saw, were not harmed but protected by the cap, which prevented gold buyers
from registering illegal bullion in the names of unaware chocoanos. "We have
said this for a while: They are using our barequeros to launder the gold that is
extracted irregularly. . . . Many community councils have even given permission, while knowing that this is illicit and illegal exploitation!"

In their sporadic encounters with government heavyweights, mining and
community leaders were not afraid to speak truth to power. In the end, the
livelihoods of their people were at stake. In emotional pleas, they drew legislators' attention to their quotidian hardships: the police interference, the selling restrictions, the impossibility of getting mining titles, the living with
illegality, day after day. But when power spoke back to leaders, it did so in a
programmatic language that left little room for miner tears. Central state representatives talked about laws, numbers, contracts, formalization protocols,
conflict variables, and collected and missed taxes. They talked in moral op-
positions, speaking of good, "well-doing" companies that deserved titles and
bad, "illegal" wildcatters who deserved punishment. Yet the language of

neoliberal government did more than just demonize small-scale operators. State emissaries also identified a segment of them as vulnerable citizens who, though working mostly outside formal channels, were worthy of institutional protection. Vice-minister Cante, respectively, talked about the special treatment that Chocó received in the form of the mesa minera, about the need to protect its barequeros from malevolent gold buyers, and about formalization achievements that helped out traditional mining communities.

This chapter seeks to make sense of this puzzling language of simultaneous punishment and protection. In social research on mining, formalization has been repeatedly championed as a remedy to the socioeconomic precariousness of small-scale operators (e.g., Güiza and Aristizábal 2013; Hilson et al. 2017; Siegel and Veiga 2009). Less has been written on what formalization programs do when being implemented. Rather than making one more plea to legalize miners, I ask about the political potentiality of actually existing formalization initiatives—and especially those that, like the Colombian ones under scrutiny, are implemented in a legal context of corporate partisanship.

While contemplating this question, I hope to foreground two things. The first is that Colombian formalization can only be analyzed by paying attention to miners' own pressures for reform. Small-scale mining actors did not only exert influence on municipal governance (as shown in Chapter 6); they also made themselves knowable to centralized bureaucracy, and set the stage for formal governing interventions, by organizing protests, participating in public meetings, and administering their mines in conformity with state criteria. The second thing I highlight is that the legislative changes that such bottom-up mobilization brought about often failed to live up to the expectations that miners had from bureaucracy. When formalization happened, it lacked the transformative potential that miners had envisioned when mobilizing for change. This was in part owing to the regulatory difficulties of bringing government programs to fruition. Yet it was also due to the way the programs had been designed from the outset, which allowed them to overlook power differentials. As such, I maintain that miners who became legally recognized under Colombian neoliberal extractivism were "permitted" political subjects (Hale 2005), whose recognition did less to jeopardize than validate the corporate concession regime. While conventional anthropological readings of Latin American neoliberalism see political inclusion as being contingent on "integration into the market" (Postero 2007:16), this chapter homes in on small-scale miners who seem to acquire formalization—become "permitted"—by proving not so much their contribution to capital accumulation as their harmlessness to it. Now, to initiate my inquiry into the chasm between government vision and miners' desires, let me start by recounting the Bogotá-based interview that manifested this chasm most clearly.

Tunnel Vision

I was asked to wait in a meeting room with white walls, a white ceiling, a white air-conditioning unit, and, well, a white whiteboard. No flowers, no pictures, no paintings; no effort at adornment. The room was situated somewhere in the bowels of a labyrinthine building of the Ministry of Defense. The building had protocol. Lots of it. To get to where I was, I had undergone an ID check and metal detector scan, and had been assigned a lieutenant as personal escort who had zigzagged me through several empty hallways that formed the passage from metal detector to colorless room.

I didn't mind the wait. I reasoned my interviewee, "Rodrigo," was a busy man. He had postponed our interview and then squeezed me in between two appointments for a meeting that could last half an hour, tops. He was in charge of coordinating the Ministry of Defense's strategies against "illegal" mining. His agenda was a full one.

Two besuited men entered the room. The first was Rodrigo, who introduced the second as "*el doctor* Saúl," invoking the honorific address that in Colombia is used for persons with high educational and social status. Saúl appeared to be director of the ministry's Office of Infrastructure and Public Security. In that position, he was Rodrigo's superior. A confident talker, Saúl said he didn't understand why I had spent nearly a year listening to miners. "With all due respect, you cannot just include their opinions. You also need the vision of the state to have the whole picture of the problem."

Rodrigo interrupted the small talk and implored me to make haste, at which point I turned on my audio recorder and asked the two men which regions and miners have priority when it comes to actions such as equipment destruction.

"There are many variables," Rodrigo answered from the other side of the table. "We have illicit extraction, criminal structures, damages to the ecosystem. On the basis of these variables, we determine what strategy to follow; whether or not it's necessary to launch destruction operations or just carry out detentions." He used the example of the Quito River in Chocó, whose unmatched ruination made it a key site for defense missions.

"So, the more variables, the higher the possibility of a police operation?"

"No," Rodrigo and Saúl declared almost in one voice. The latter, sitting on my side of the table, took over. "In this activity, there are various links and each one is affected by a number of variables, right?"

I wasn't sure what he meant. I nodded "yes."

"One part of the variables is the machinery, another part are the gold merchants, the people laundering the gold, the people extorting. There are a number of elements that come into play and the summation of these generates a statutory reaction."

Trying to move the conversation away from criminal "elements," I bet on a cumbersome act of language mirroring. "One important *variable* in my study was that many people mine because they lack economic alternatives."

Saúl nodded enthusiastically. "Absolutely, absolutely! That's why we need an inter-institutional agenda. Not just the stick, but also offering life options. The problem, what we've seen, is that people don't have the intention."

"What do you mean?"

"Look, if I tell you: You cannot perform your activity because you are obeying absolutely nothing that the law demands, and therefore I'll bring you an agricultural project so you can grow your pepper crops. A miner says: [Saúl changed to a whining voice] 'No, I don't want it. With a kilo of peppers, I earn only one million pesos per month, but with four, five, six castellanos [of gold], I make two million.'"

"Are you talking specifically about Chocó?"

"About everywhere. You know the cowboy movies, right? Gold is a curse. The moment they take it out, they want more, more, more. What you see in the communities of Chocó is that, before people guarantee the education for their children, before their food, before they buy a house, a dignified house as it should be, unfortunately in many cases they end up drinking away what they've earned. And then they start drinking away the earnings again, leaving ten *muchachitos* [little kids] with oversized bellies in the same conditions as when they started."

The stereotypes startled me. I mentioned that many miners feel there is no way to legalize their activities.

"That validation is viable," Saúl said, "but only from their perspective about what formalization should be. The miner says: 'I formalize because I decide what formalization is.' The miner doesn't say: 'The process of formalization establishes this and you have to obey to formalize.'"

Rodrigo now interceded: "They want formalization without the environmental rigor."

"Without the environmental rigor!" Saúl underlined. He offered a diatribe
against what he saw as miners' political opportunism: "We tell them: 'You
have a mini-dredge, you are a small-scale miner.' And they say: 'No, I'm not;
I'm a traditional miner.' Why? Because traditional miners don't have to follow mining legislation. And they don't want to pay taxes or follow environmental norms. They want to ignore the whole process and do it their way.
But their way is not the law! It's a problem of interpretation, their interpretation of the law, to their advantage."

"It's not even interpretation," Rodrigo said. "The law is very clear!"

His superior agreed. "The law applies to all."

I played this truth back at them. "As for the gap between what the law
says and what happens in practice, I've heard miners in Chocó criticizing the
public forces for targeting them as criminals, while not receiving their protection against extortion."

Saúl saw things differently. "They don't like that we call them criminals,
that [again changing to a whining voice] 'we put everyone in the same bag.'
So, denounce! If they denounce, there will be a state action against the extortioners, demonstrating that they are obligating miners to conduct these
activities."

"For example," Rodrigo added, "while there are communities immersed
in this activity, there are others against it. They're very explicit: men of the
state, act! And this is exactly what we're doing. . . . Many regions were very
complex, but the indicators have improved a lot."

"Yet many people don't want you to destroy these machines," I countered.
"Some even own machines themselves."

Saúl shook his head. "Their ethic is always to earn, earn, earn."

"Also look at it from a geographical point of view, an eco-centric point of
view," Rodrigo said, as if to underscore the fairness of punitive intervention.
"The environment is not an ecosystem that is only their patrimony; it's the
patrimony of all Colombians, including the whole of humanity; which they
are degrading!"

"Destroying," the other official corrected.

"Destroying! So, our job does not respond to the desire of only the communities, because this belongs to all Colombians."

During that half an hour tops, Rodrigo and Saúl saw from their Bogotá
office a chocoano forest that was unlike the one I had grown familiar with.

They saw a place of "variables," "criminal structures," "links," "elements," and "indicators"; a technocrat's forest, if you will, shorn of power discrepancies. This came particularly to the forefront in Rodrigo's seemingly impartial ("geographical"; "eco-centric") plea for the environment. By objectifying the forest into a universal patrimony belonging to all Colombians, to all humankind even, he emptied Chocó's mining geographies of their specific human histories and, in doing so, was able to delegitimize local claims to resources. Yet the two men also stripped the forest bare of power by way of another universal criterion: *the* law. In claiming that "The law applies to all," Saúl delineated the problem of mining informality, not as one of unequal access to extraction rights, nor of the impunity of criminal groups, but as emanating from the deficient character of miners themselves, unwilling as they were to denounce their extortioners and obey formal criteria.

Sure enough, talking in the presumably neutral tropes of nature, law, and individual decision-making, Rodrigo and Saúl sucked all politics out of mining regions that were saturated with it. They did not see differentiated access to the subsoil; they saw miners flouting universally valid formalization rules. They did not see the legislative dead ends that these rules produce; they saw irresponsible cowboys who spend their riches lavishly. They did not see centuries of structural violence nor the quotidian anxieties of present-day poverty; they saw, with stigmatizing eyes, chocoanos refusing pepper crops because these only pay "one million pesos per month." And no, they did not see the complex social life of mining towns, where conflict coexists with compromise, nature lovers partake in environmental degradation, and today's adversaries may be tomorrow's allies; what they seemed to see was a binary opposition of victims telling the "men of the state [to] act" versus conspiring communities who only want to "earn, earn, earn."

What, then, to make of such tunnel vision? Anthropological analyses of governance might help. In his book *Seeing Like a State*, James Scott (1998) insists that modern states rely on simplified designs of reality to make society legible. Administrative tools like maps, cadasters, and surveys provide state governments with templates to control and "improve" their populations. The standardized knowledge that is harnessed from these instruments functions like an "administrative grid" for the distribution of resources, rights, and privileges (24). However, as state officials concentrate on only those aspects of reality deemed relevant for governing purposes, they miss out on what Scott terms *mētis*—localized knowledge "that can come only from practical experience" (6)—and, as a consequence, fail in their attempt to establish effective control.

Another strand of research, sympathetic to Michel Foucault's ideas on governmentality, treats regulatory blindness as servile to the reproduction of the political status quo. Such scholarship consolidates around the notion that regulators tend to look away from issues of societal inequality, instead casting governed peoples as capacity-lacking subjects in need of technical solutions. When translating social suffering into an intelligible field of policy intervention, "experts . . . exclude the structure of political–economic relations from their diagnoses and prescriptions," for "They focus more on the capacities of the poor than on the practices through which one social group impoverishes another" (Li 2007:7). The art of governance, in other words, functions like what James Ferguson calls an "anti-politics machine." Policymakers and development practitioners "squash political challenges to the system" by "reposing political questions of land, resources, jobs, or wages as technical 'problems'" (Ferguson 1990:181). Furthermore, they propose their technical solutions in the emancipatory vocabularies of "development" (Ferguson 1990), "environmental protection" (Doane 2012; Ojeda 2012), "democracy," and the "free market" (Sawyer 2004). This confers a sense of objectivity and inevitability to their governing and, correspondingly, helps disqualify their critics.

These arguments gain traction when we study the previous decades of Colombian mining governance. Saúl and Rodrigo were far from alone in understanding the problems surrounding gold as stemming from miners' personal aptitudes. To explain away the political detriment of small domestic miners, Colombian policymakers routinely underscored the threats they posed to the incontestable truths of democracy and peace (by funding criminals), the environment (by using mercury and felling trees), and private sector development (by not paying taxes and squatting on the concessions of large-scale miners). Either by defect or default—or perhaps, either by an administrative failure to effectively "see" miners through state simplifications (à la Scott), or by willfully looking away from them so as to depoliticize inequality (à la Li and Ferguson)—this framing of miners as dangerous rested on a "tunnel vision" (Scott 1998:11) that ruthlessly disregarded grounded politico-economic complexities. When certain central state representatives recurred to generic notions like "illegal mining" and "a criminal activity,"[2] they were silent on the distinction between those carrying guns and those carrying washing pans, and with that, on the extortion the former inflicted on the latter. When the same representatives stressed the degradation of the universal patrimony that is the Chocó rainforest,[3] they were silent on the structural poverty that impelled the rainforest's inhabitants to embark on destroying it, as well as on the exhaustion and pollution of soils and waterways that accompanied government-condoned industrial mines. And when a National Mining Agency president complained about informal miners "stealing state resources," while signaling them as a threat to mining corporations,[4] she was silent on miners' incessant attempts at formalizing, on the red tape thwarting these attempts, and on the multiplier effects that small-scale mining, unlike corporate mines, tends to generate.[5]

Even so, in Colombia and elsewhere, the "vision of the state" (using Saúl's words) is rarely one of sheer repression and restriction. Rather than just excluding, disciplining, and criminalizing people, policymakers frequently aspire to include, reward, and formalize, manifesting an obstinate "will to improve" the target populations they claim to rule over (Li 2007). Not infrequently, this productive dimension of governance is the result of the mobilization of governed populations themselves, who actively challenge and expand the parameters of formal democracy through practices that may or may not be legal (Anand 2017; Das 2011; Holston 2008).

In Colombia, too, stringent measures against "illegal" mining in the 2010s existed side by side with government emissaries advocating and enforcing the legalization of traditional miners. Even a hard-liner like Saúl was not impervious to "an inter-institutional agenda." "Not just the stick," he preached, "but also offering life options." What's more, formalization processes that materialized in that decade were not simply a matter of the centralized bureaucracy imposing its will on peripheral territories; instead, these processes coalesced around the demands of small-scale mining associations. Miners undermined, negotiated, and invigorated legislation by way of their protests in the streets, their blockades of highways, and their discussions and dissent in meetings with public functionaries. In Colombia, *mētis* (Scott 1998) forced itself upon the state apparatus.

One grassroots interference that especially impacted formal policy happened in 2013, four years before my field research. After the Ministry of Defense issued a decree that allowed for the incarceration of miners and the destruction of their machinery, mining associations decided that a line had been crossed. They struck. Big time. Thousands of miners blocked roads, shouted slogans, and stopped commerce across the country. Forty-eight days of protest had to pass before representatives of the government and CONALMINERCOL (the national confederation of small-scale miner associations) reached a four-point agreement: (1) the Ministry of Mines and Energy would adopt legislation clarifying distinctions between different mining scales, as well as between "informal" and "illegal" mining; (2) property destruction would be limited to cases supported by judiciary investigation; (3) the Ministry of the Environment would provide guides to assist miners with formalizing; and (4) the Ministry of Mines and Energy would institutionalize "reserves" for traditional miners. In the aftermath of the agreement, mesas mineras were set up in different regions, enabling mining leaders and politicians to evaluate the extent to which the settled terms were fulfilled.

But it's one thing to become seen by a legal regime and a whole different thing to overhaul it. If anything, the years following the strike were indicative of the "switch points" that sociologist Nikolas Rose (1999:192) cautions against, as in the reactionary moments in which "an opening turns into a closure," when ruling systems absorb criticism and undo it from its radical edges (see also Li 2007). No institutional revolution took off after 2013. Titling procedures remained costly, reforms lacked the revolutionary fervor that mining leaders desired, and grassroots-driven legalization initiatives failed to reach fruition, either because they became stranded in the "regulatory pragmatics" of everyday bureaucracy (Hetherington 2020:11), or because they did not comply with the larger policy framework. Meanwhile, formalization largely consisted of not-so-radical capacitation programs, geared toward the prevention of mercury use (see Chapter 6) or the promotion of farming as a substitute for mining.[6] And on the punitive side, police missions continued with unprecedented force, partly encouraged by the mining multinationals whose operational stability was compromised by informal mining.[7] At the same time, selling gold became circumscribed to a production maximum, and criminal investigations increasingly targeted the commercialization of gold.

In the following, I will render the issues raised here more tangible by illustrating, for one thing, how formalization interventions were made possible by the social mobilization of mining stakeholders, and for another, how these interventions, once executed, tended to transform miners' hopes into deception, as on-the-ground realities were incongruous with top-down regulatory capacities and concerns.

Breaking Out from the Underground

The role that community council leaders played in state-making was not limited to configuring "underground" legalities in out-of-the-way goldfields; their governance also paved the way for formal government initiatives. By administering mining through state-like designs, the juntas directivas made it simpler for external powerholders to "see" (Scott 1998) local mines and recognize their lawful potential. To understand this better, let us head back to the Bebará River. There, localized organizing practices propelled forward official regulatory schemes in the form of, on one hand, community-produced documents that served the local town hall for identification purposes, and on the other, informal (yet formal-like) mining organization that helped get under way a development project of the Ministry of the Environment.

The ID Card and the Register

As discussed in Chapter 4, I came across a torrent of community documents during fieldwork. Probably the most remarkable of these was the laminated ID card of the ASOBAMINARMEA barequeros association. Even though the card was adorned with formal data, it allowed local community councils to regulate an informal mining economy, and had previously helped the FARC's 34th Front to keep enemy forces at bay. But the peculiarity of the ID card went further. A few years back, the document had also been employed by the local bureaucracy. Talking to community leaders, I learned that a previous municipal administration of the Medio Atrato (where the Bebará was situated) had certified miners' membership in ASOBAMINARMEA as official proof of their status as subsistence miners. In keeping with this policy, the then-mayor had signed the association's ID cards so that the barequeros could use them to sell their manually mined (and therefore legal) gold to buyers in town, as well as to prove their permitted barequero status vis-à-vis the navy, which in the Bebará–Quibdó fluvial passage checked whether miners were carrying illegal minerals. "The gold leaves a mine that has no title," association leader Moisés explained. "But the barequero is a legal miner. So that's why the card is important. When public forces identify you, they won't take away your gram of gold."

The current mayor, however, was unwilling to sign the cards. Consequently, the barequeros had stopped using them to sell and transport gold,

much to the dismay of association leaders like Moisés: "They [the municipal government] harm the barequeros! Without the signature, the card
does not have the validity that is required to sell [gold]. But signing it only
benefits the mayor. We're only reducing his workload. If we don't organize
the barequeros, the law obliges him to provide them with a certificate that
says they're legal. But a card is easier to carry in your pocket than a
certificate."

Moisés's ideas were not shared by the Medio Atrato's secretary of governance, who as the mayor's right-hand man was the municipal official responsible for registering the barequeros. In an interview, he argued that
ASOBAMINARMEA's card had no legal value. He preferred to validate miners by way of the official document, the Mayor's Certificate, enacting, in his
own words, "the certification coming from the normativity of the National
Mining Agency." Nevertheless, the secretary did require the assistance of
ASOBAMINARMEA for administering this official line of certification. To
ensure that applicants for the Mayor's Certificate really were barequeros from
the Medio Atrato, he used a register that had been created some years previously by the barequeros association for the distribution of its ID cards. In fact,
at a meeting with junta directiva leaders belonging to ASOBAMINARMEA,
the secretary of governance complained that their census was outdated.
Because the association's—and therefore the municipality's—obsolete records
failed to mention all currently active miners, the secretary was unable to as-
certain if miner applicants were indeed local barequeros. In the face of such
administrative myopia, he called on the junta representatives present at the
meeting to provide him with an up-to-date census.

> I want to remind all the community councils, all the juntas, that the
> certification of barequeros expires in December. Since I don't have a
> workforce, nor secretaries, I work with the register. . . . And I
> encountered a little problem, because many people [applicants]
> come here and tell me: "They have not certified us, we are not in the
> census." Let me repeat what I've said before: Conduct another
> census, so that the people can work with their certification! . . . I
> want this information to be disseminated widely, because this is
> your responsibility. People request their certificates personally. But
> we need a census to check the list. The community councils should
> send a register to the municipal administration on which it can base
> its certification.

Though the speech did not generate its desired effect—the juntas directivas did not conduct a new census—it is most effective in illuminating how the overt politics of state bureaucrats and the underground politics of community councils were not strictly separate domains. The Medio Atrato municipal administration, like the preceding administration, resorted to the community councils' association and its documents (its miners' register and ID cards) when faced with the arduous task of territorial governance. In this way, documents that had been produced outside the formal economy eventually became closely implicated with actual government interventions. Having said that, the power that the FARC-assessed communities wielded over the legal apparatus went beyond the municipal level. Their underground multiculturalism also impinged on centralized state planning in the form of a pilot program for formalization.

The Pilot Program

By the time I did fieldwork there in late 2017, the Bebará River had been just selected, along with the neighboring Bebaramá River, for an imminent formalization project. This project was led by the Ministry of the Environment and supported by the United Nations Industrial Development Organization (UNIDO), the Office of the United Nations High Commissioner for Human Rights (OHCHR), and the Canadian NGO CIRDI. For bebareño junta members, excavator miners, and barequeros alike, this "pilot program of formalization," as it was popularly known, was a source of great joy. It was supposedly thanks to the forthcoming pilot that police and army clampdowns did not go near the Bebará River, and that the bebareños would soon enjoy their own mining titles and receive refined equipment to prospect and extract more efficiently.

Equally enjoyable was that this was *their* project. In a mining department that was so often criminalized, they were the chosen ones. Bebareños proudly explained that they had been selected for the program because of their sustainable excavator economy, and because local community leaders and the FARC had managed to convince their government to acknowledge this. The notion that such brokerage had been quintessential was cemented by the leaders and FARC mediators themselves. At a pan-riverine meeting, former guerrilla frontman Israel Zúñiga claimed that his organization had managed "to propel the theme of the pilot program" amid the peace negotiations in

Havana. And at that same meeting, community leader Winston stated that the Bebará and Bebaramá had been "prioritized for the pilot" due to local leaders' negotiation efforts in the department's mesa minera.

However, the spokespersons of the Ministry of the Environment and involved UN offices whom I interviewed mentioned other project drivers. These had less to do with grassroots organizing than with reestablishing government control in a post-conflict zone. They made no mention of extracting gold more efficiently (the topic on community leaders' minds), nor did they foreground titles or the cessation of police missions (the perks that local retreros associated with the pilot). Instead, they laid out the project in three key lines: "clean mining," "the empowerment of community councils," and "alternative development"—or, as the ministry's spokesperson put it: "alternative forms of entrepreneurship that support the communities in focusing on a direction outside mining."

Still, even after these "institutional" interviews, there was good reason to believe that the bebareños were right about this being at least partly a community initiative. First of all, Miguel Sánchez, coordinator of OHCHR's Quibdó office—who, as several stakeholders said, had been instrumental in pushing the project forward—confirmed to me the local theory that the formalization pilot had originated in the mesa minera and the Havana negotiations. Sánchez had attended a meeting of victim organizations in Havana, during which the FARC had raised the issue of the formalization of Medio Atrato miners. From there, he had passed the idea on to the minister of the Environment and UNIDO.

Second, the institutional stakeholders reiterated the local assertion that the decision to hold the project in the Medio Atrato was inspired by the communities' high-standard production practices. The stakeholders had conducted field visits to the region to verify whether extraction was really as environmentally friendly as community leaders indicated. According to Miguel Sánchez, the two rivers had been chosen as the zone of intervention because of both the region's "post-conflict" regulatory vacuum and its "different" way of mining. "These are riverbanks where the mining associations said they worked in a different way. . . . But we have to prove that. . . . We arrived with CIRDI and we saw some interesting practices that caught our attention. Indeed, it appeared to be true. . . . So let's say, we chose the region because it's a riverbank that conducts mining, that wants to be formalized, that is part of the mesa minera, and that is in a region where there was influence of the FARC."[8]

In brief, although the pilot program's outline seemed rather familiar with neoliberal doctrine—its objectives being community empowerment and ecological entrepreneurship; its operations being delegated to civil society—it was nevertheless a project that had partly arisen from the ground upward. The community councils of the Bebará and Bebaramá, together with their FARC assessors, had not passively waited for regulation to be imposed on them. They had attracted the eyes of bureaucracy, first, by organizing their excavator mines in accordance with formal criteria, and second, by convincing their legislators of such de facto formality. In other words, by staging mining law in a sufficiently convincing way, they had allowed for the emergence of the pilot program and, concomitantly, for the possibility of state centralization.

Nevertheless, besides exposing the far reach of underground politics, the pilot program also testified to the sluggishness of political change. On visiting Chocó in August 2019, two years to the day after I first arrived at Bebará, local leaders explained that the development program was dying a slow death. For months they had heard nothing from the government and UN agencies, and they had fallen out with the NGO CIRDI—the external stakeholder that most actively visited them—over its involvement in the project. Worse still, political rifts within the communities' leadership had deepened, as leaders disagreed on who was in charge of what remained of the formalization process. When I subsequently talked to UN officials in Bogotá, I was told that the project had been delayed because of the change of national government (August 2018), implying a reprioritization of funds. The Medio Atrato pilot was on standby and would commence once the communities had acquired their mining titles.

But as of January 2023, another three and half years later, still no title had been allocated. Apparently, not long after my 2019 visit, the ministry withdrew its participation from the project out of fear that its true beneficiaries were ex-guerrillas, rather than local communities. UNIDO eventually decided to realize a mining technology project in another region of Chocó, seeing as the ongoing illegality of the Medio Atrato mines made it impossible to find international donor money. To exacerbate matters, police missions had finally reached the Bebará shore in late 2022, bombing the excavators of a retrero who had been at the forefront of the formalization project. All in all, the pilot program had turned out to be a terrible deception.

To some degree, the deception was borne out of unforeseen regulatory difficulties (the CIRDI fallout, the change of government, local power struggles). But as community leaders emphasized, the cause for failure was also more structural. Despite its emphasis on legalization, the pilot program had done little to address the communities' problems of resource access, nor had it arguably had the means to do so. Legislation demanded mining titles, and these continued to be too complicated to get, even with the institutional support of the UN and the Ministry of the Environment.[9] In this regard, the project was quite illustrative of the "anti-politics" (Ferguson 1990) of Colombian mining governance, whereby regulatory responses to bottom-up demands did not address the focal point of these demands: meaningful legal access to gold. The sections below help drive this point home.

Formalizing Traditional Miners

In addition to local development projects such as the Medio Atrato one, there were also exceptions on the national level to the political climate of small-scale miner informality. Two exceptions, to be exact, as in the years following the 2013 miners' strike succeeding ministries of mines championed two formalization strategies with more flesh on their bones than sheer capacitation. The first strategy was subcontracting, the regulation of which had actually begun ahead of the miners' strike. With subcontracting, mining companies were encouraged to establish production contracts with local miners, permitting the latter to work in corporate concessions. These industry–community alliances mostly emerged in tunnel-mining regions, outside Chocó, where most multinationals were, and still are, active. The alliances, though, were poorly viewed by small-scale miners and their associations. They accused the multinationals of drawing up predatory contracts, allowing the companies, among others, to retain large amounts of small-scale miners' bullion, to restrict miners' working space to small and unproductive deposits, and to force miners to sell their ore to company-owned processing plants, which paid bottom prices and circumvented traditional selling networks (see also Kaufmann and Côte 2021; *La Silla Vacía* 2012).[10]

The second strategy suggests a less exploitative form of formalizing than multinational outsourcing and was more pronounced during my field research in Chocó. For these two reasons, it deserves to be analyzed in more detail. In accordance with the agreement that ended the 2013 miners' strike, the Vice-Ministry of Mines complied with its mandate to create a formalization mechanism for traditional mining communities. By means of resolution 546 of 2017, it institutionalized the ARE (shorthand for *Área de Reserva Especial para Comunidades Mineras*). Concretely, AREs were zones where miners were permitted to conduct subsistence extraction activities. They were *not* mining titles. Rather, miners pertaining to an ARE entered into a formalization process that could transform their traditional reserve into a genuine title—or so it read on paper.

In order to become eligible for an ARE, a mining community needed to send an official request to the National Mining Agency, mentioning the names and working techniques of all applicants. If the request complied with the agency's administrative requisites, a mining engineer flew in from Bogotá to verify whether the applicants were indeed traditional miners working with traditional methods within the requested "polygon." The engineer for the field visits to Chocó in 2017 was "Vicente." I joined him during one such assessment visit to the village of "El Platino."

The afternoon before the field trip, Vicente set out the rules of the game to the aspiring miners in the building of the local community council in the municipal capital. He described the objective of his stay as "the verification of traditionality." To accomplish this, he would visit all thirty-one applicants at their placer mines in the coming two and a half days, after which he would submit a report to the agency's "people in Bogotá," who then evaluated the miners' application by "looking at it juridically and technically." Although to miners and community leaders—and also to the present anthropologist—two and a half days seemed too short a period for this monumental task of tradition assessment, Vicente claimed it was enough. He assured the audience that being recognized under the ARE was determined not only by his inspection of the mines, but also by two documents: a photocopy of the miner's national ID card and a letter, signed by the mayor, affirming their historical occupation as a miner. Vicente explained that traditional miners were persons "who have carried out mining activities since before 2001," and who "have social and economic characteristics." Clarifying what he meant by the latter, he said: "I'm not going to look at excavators. You know that this is prohibited without a title. I'm here to see traditional work."

And so the following morning, Vicente paid a tuk-tuk driver to take himself, a community council leader, and me from the municipal capital to El Platino. The first mine was one of many. A diesel-powered pump channeled water via a rubber tube to an adjacent muddy pit, where a bronze-colored earth wall, twice the height of an adult person, was set to be hosed away. Once Vicente had georeferenced the mine's longitude and latitude with a GPS device, he shot off a one-page survey at the owner of the mine, the seventy-four-year-old Ignacio.

"What would you call this system?"

"Artisanal mining."

"But what type of artisanal mining?"

"Here, we say artisanal mining."

"But is it called an *elevadora*?[11] Or what is it?"

"Yes, an elevadora."

"How many persons work here?"

Willy, another pump miner who accompanied us as a guide, intervened. "You cannot say how many. This always fluctuates. One day people work with Ignacio and the next day with José."

"But right now?" the mining engineer insisted.

"Now there are three persons," Didier, whose mine we would visit next, answered.

"Three," Ignacio confirmed.

"How long have you been working here?"

"Here?" Ignacio looked at the other two pump miners. "One year? Two years?"

"You know, we always move around," Willy said. "If this place doesn't catch, you go to the next."

"How much is the production per week?" Vicente continued.

"It varies," Willy once more replied on Ignacio's behalf. "With mining, you don't have a fixed income."

"But tell me an average."

"Well, in that case, just write down one castellano [4.6 grams]," Ignacio said.

"Per week?"

"Per week."

"And for how long have you worked as a miner?"

"I don't know." Ignacio mumbled some numbers to himself before he decisively replied: "Write down thirty-two years."

"But we have been mining here since being in the bellies of our mothers," Willy added. "We are miners because of our grandfathers and—"

"No, no!" Vicente interrupted. "The 'bellies,' no! I don't know how many times they've already told me this. 'From the belly, from the cradle,' the only thing I haven't heard is that you mine from the moment of conception."

We all laughed. Vicente once more delineated the tradition he was after. "I didn't come here for the work of your fathers, or your grandfathers. No! I came here for the work you are practicing. . . . I came here to see if you are traditional or not. And the current concept of traditional mining talks about persons who conduct mining since the year 2001 and whose principal activity is mining."

Once he had wrapped up the Q&A, Vicente told Ignacio he needed a photo of him at work. Accordingly, the older man, along with two adolescent helpers, pretended to work. One of the boys hosed the front, the other removed gravel, and Ignacio threw away some cobbles sideways, in the meantime freezing his gaze on Vicente, who, for his part, froze Ignacio's "traditionality" into his digital camera.

The entire routine of geocoding, questioning, and taking photos was an impeccable demonstration of what Scott (1998) describes as "seeing like a state," in that it attested to an evident mismatch between formal ordering mechanisms and the localized knowledge they mean to standardize. By walking in the faraway mines of Chocó, by looking at them from up close and transforming them into GPS coordinates, survey data, and photo files, Vicente extended the "administrative grid" (Scott 1998:24) of the state apparatus. But when he asked miners about gold averages, personnel numbers, and the history of geographically fixed mines—the intelligible data translatable across cases—miners hinted at the indeterminacy of their production, the fluctuation of their workforces, and the nomadism of their extraction. And when Vicente pushed for answers, as he did with Ignacio, he got hesitant replies that were formulated in the subjunctive and the hypothetical: "if the mine gives"; "sometimes you make"; "well, in that case, just write down one castellano."

Yet it was not just the act of measuring that caused friction, but also the content of what was being measured. The cadastral knowledge that Vicente hoped to produce—the eventual ARE—was an affirmation of traditionality. Now, the miners of El Platino perceived their cultural history in collective terms. When Vicente, or I on other occasions, asked them about their mining traditions, they commented on their family backgrounds and the history of the region. Vicente, however, did not want to talk about bellies and fathers and grandfathers. Tradition, according to him and "the current concept," started in 2001 and was to be individually assessed. In abstracting tradition this way, in segregating it into an individual characteristic based on sixteen years of labor, Vicente isolated miners from their forefathers and contemporary social lives. As such, his questions proved hard to get one's head around, let alone answer.

In all fairness, Vicente's take on tradition was also lost on me. Listening to his questions, I struggled to grasp with which evaluation criteria ARE applicants had to comply. The part about being a miner since 2001 was clear. But how could Vicente verify such historical continuity on the basis of this questionnaire? And then there was the benchmark of miners' "social and economic characteristics." These characteristics presumably entailed not working with excavators. But surely, I figured, there had to be more; surely there had to be some type of equipment by which Vicente drew the technological line of traditional extraction.

A couple of mines later, there were answers. We had arrived at what another miner had described as his water pump mine. During the respective interview, Vicente called the miner's attention to a bulky, cube-shaped pumping engine, lying unused in the distance and clearly belonging to an excavator operation.

"What type of engine is that?"

"A diesel."

"But that one doesn't enter the ARE."

"You know, when you have worked for a while you have to go deeper, because a pump is no longer enough for subsistence," the miner explained.

"But the ARE is for traditional mining and not for heavy equipment," Vicente said. "If we accept excavators, you people will be out of work in no time because they destroy everything. Of course, after the ARE you're allowed to improve. With a good proposal for a concession contract, the agency may accept excavators. I'm not saying you shouldn't improve. You can improve, but only to a certain degree."

Upon leaving the mine, I hitched on to Vicente to ask why excavators did "not enter the ARE."

"Because they have an advanced economic level," he said. "And the ARE is for communities with certain necessities. At the agency we prefer to work with the communities."

After he mentioned other low-tech devices that were permitted in the reserve (pans, pumps, mini-dredges), I asked: "But then what's the biggest machinery that is allowed in the ARE?"

"You cannot see it like it that. I just know when someone is a traditional miner."

I felt I was getting nowhere. The technological yardstick of the mining reserve remained unclear. "So, if you've been working for thirty years with excavators, the agency may define you as a traditional miner?"

"No, the excavator cannot enter here. Because if we accept excavator miners, they will enter with thirty machines and leave nothing for the people. . . . It breaks social and economic traditions. That's what we're trying to prevent from happening. The problem of Chocó is that the people have accepted the excavators. It's a complete lack of knowledge. People want everything now and in the long run there'll be nothing left for them."

Vicente's ARE miner seemed to be primarily a miner of dependence; an individual of low economic means who needed the state for protection against outsiders trampling on their economic customs. But here we were, traversing a brutally scavenged forest. For Vicente, too, it had to be impossible to ignore the rocky slopes, caterpillar tracks, rusted tools, and turquoise pools that retreros had left behind. If traditional territories implied no excavators, he seemed in the wrong place to designate a mining reserve. "But do you think there have never been excavators here?" I asked.

"Of course there have been, but you can tell that these men are traditional miners."

"What do you mean?"

"Well, we can never know for sure if they've worked continually since 2001. So, what do we do? First, we visit the site to see if there has been mining. Second: the community. They should be part of a community. Sometimes there is no social connection, people don't know each other. If we see this, we reject the application."

He used me as an example. "I know you're not part of this community. You look like a student, not a miner. Also, you don't have the same skin color."

"But I imagine it can be difficult to tell in just a few days whether or not people are a community."

Vicente agreed. "You depend on what they tell you. That's why I'm constantly asking questions. . . . But because of experience, I know. For example, you saw the president of the community council yesterday? He looks different from these men. You can tell he's not a miner, just by looking at his hands." He paused for a few contemplative seconds, and then said: "Sure, it's all very subjective. But that's why there is the report of the mayor. He confirms they are artisanal miners."

The two and a half days I walked with Vicente confirmed that the confined vision of centralized bureaucracy revealed itself not only when miners were being criminalized, but also when they were subject to regulation that was actually constitutive of formalization. At mine after mine, Vicente decided on the veracity of sixteen years of traditional work with a few structured questions. Just like that, in the proverbial blink of eye, he made Chocó's ever-changing and ever-mobile mines conterminous with the isolationist truths of formal paperwork. No doubt, this was "seeing like a state" par excellence: a bureaucratic appraisal of tradition that was insulated from historical nuance and contemporary context. But while in Scott's account statutory knowledge emanates from the technopolitical vision of a panoptical center, the vision of Vicente was above all—in his own words—"very subjective." In separating the authentics from the frauds, he endorsed a notion of tradition that rested on an essentialist ideal of community, one that was rooted in economic hardship and demarcated from people demonstrating signs of a nonextractive career (e.g., who didn't have miner hands). Of course, the miners were told about this ideal from the get-go and were happy to play along. Walking with Vicente, I witnessed them recreating the subsistence tradition that the National Mining Agency was after, as they claimed to actively work in areas where weedy rocks suggested prolonged abandonment, complemented the answers of less talkative companions, and denied their professional careers or involvement with excavators.

Fortunately, Vicente proved willing to let the best stories stick. When encountering sites that had been devoured by excavators, he encouraged miners to show him more artisanal working spots. And when discovering that an applicant worked in education, he recommended putting the mine in the name of a relative. Better still, his colleagues from the agency in Bogotá appeared equally cooperative. Only two months after the visit, the community got its ARE approved, all applicants included. All things considered, the fast and uncomplicated approval of the reserve stands in tension with all the shouting of "criminals" mentioned in earlier chapters. So why this small opening in a political context of continuous closures? What might be *served* by the ARE and its celebration of the subsistence miner? These are questions that the next section ponders.

Permitted Miners

Whether focused on Colombia or elsewhere, social studies of mining have repeatedly argued that reforms of economic liberalization—designed to lure in mining corporations—deny small-scale miners opportunities for formalization.[12] I share with these studies their preoccupation with discriminatory property regimes. Nonetheless, I also believe that their somewhat binary reading of mining (in)formalization—in which small operators are excluded at the expense of companies—may evoke the image of a uniform small-scale mining sector and, therefore, has less potential for studying cases whereby the sector is differentially incorporated into formal policy. One of these cases is Colombia, where in the past decade, at the height of small-scale miner criminalization, a small window of formalization opened up by way of the ARE. By early 2022, the National Mining Agency listed no fewer than 103 designated AREs across Colombia (of which eight were in Chocó),[13] all prompting legalization processes for miners for whom these were previously out of reach. Peculiarly—and unlike the cases of Tanzania (Fisher 2008) and the Philippines (Verbrugge 2015), where limited formalization efforts excluded the most vulnerable within mining populations—the Colombian ARE was drafted for subsistence miners and inaccessible to those relying on heavier machinery. Even if legislation was agnostic about which techniques constituted "traditional mining,"[14] the National Mining Agency targeted the AREs at the smallest of operators. In fact, although engineers like Vicente might have been prepared to include pump and mini-dredge miners in reserves, the official reading of the agency was that the ARE's "exploitation prerogative" applied only to those working without mechanized equipment (Agencia Nacional de Minería 2018).[15]

In viewing subsistence methods, opposed to economic production, to be a requisite for state recognition, the ARE may at first glance seem antagonistic to what I previously characterized, for 2010s Colombia, as an extractivist model of industrialized production (see Chapter 1). Here, the impoverished and the traditional were rewarded, while those with better possibilities for accumulation (e.g., excavator miners) remained politically sidetracked. For this same reason, the ARE also sits uneasily with the usual critique of the Colombian legal framework of those years as one that treated "local miners . . . as occupiers of . . . resources instead of legitimate historical users or marginal subjects in need of policy intervention" (Álvarez 2016:57). With the ARE, being "marginal" and "historical" were actually the qualities by which miners acquired legal inclusion. Meanwhile, in constituting to some extent a legislative reaction to miners' own desires for change (the 2013 strike), the ARE did appear to acknowledge their "need of policy intervention."[16]

The argument that Colombian mining governance was (or is) exclusive to vulnerable citizens is an echo of the conventional story about neoliberalism.

Time and again, social and political analysts have shown that unfettered privatization hollows out the content of national citizenship, drawing attention to neoliberal policies that trim down the rights of marginalized peoples and strip them of protections against the havoc wrought by industrial development (Arias and Goldstein 2010; Dagnino 2003; Escobar 2008; Rojas 2009).[17] Several authors have additionally made the case that neoliberal reforms, apart from abandoning the poor, have also begun "punishing the poor" (Wacquant 2009) for their newfound precarities. This argument holds that neoliberalism replaces welfare programs with punitive measures, which not only worsen social insecurity, but also remove the accountability of insecurity from the state apparatus and place it upon the impoverished themselves (Gledhill 2005; Wacquant 2009). Needless to say, Colombia's regulatory landscape of recent decades fit this narrative excellently. For here, economically deprived miners were held responsible for their own social dislocation by official discourses that described informality as a question of individual will (or malice).

But even if the description of neoliberal neglect is impossible to refute, we need another conceptual framework to fathom some of neoliberalism's unexpected outcomes in Latin America. Because along with cementing the vulnerability of poor people, neoliberal planners have at times also recognized vulnerability as a precondition for political participation, especially when challenges to financial markets loom large. In this regard, as you may remember from Chapter 4, Charles Hale offers a particularly provocative argument. Hale opposes the conventional proposition that multicultural reforms are counterintuitive to neoliberal capitalism. He sees these reforms as compatible with "neoliberalism's cultural project," which has the objective "to harness and redirect the abundant political energy of cultural rights activism, rather than directly to oppose it" (2002:498). According to Hale, Latin American governments' endorsement of an apolitical Indigenous subject—the *indio permitido*, a term he borrows from Silvia Rivera Cusicanqui—allows for a "strategic deployment of resources" (498), "separating acceptable demands for cultural rights from inappropriate ones, recognising the former and foreclosing the latter, and thereby creating a means to 'manage' multiculturalism while removing its radical or threatening edge" (507).

On a somewhat different note, Austin Zeiderman (2013) moves beyond the idea that Colombian politics entails the heightened insecurity of vulnerable citizens. He shows that in Bogotá, people's access to public services is circumscribed by demonstrating conditions of vulnerability and becoming "recognizable as lives at risk" (83). In order to evaluate citizens' degree of being at risk—and entitlement to public benefits—state officials rely on "systems of verification to separate authentic from inauthentic claims and to adjudicate between deserving and undeserving claimants" (77). Thus, as with Hale's politics of permittance, *bogotanos*' recognition of vulnerability depends on a limited expression of political agency. To be acknowledged as deserving of rights, claimants "are expected to be passive" and should refrain from "too actively [engaging] the state," for such would render them susceptible to being a *vivo*; a cultural category used to describe a "manipulative, opportunistic" person (82).

Along the same lines, the access to formalization programs of Colombian miners in the 2010s was premised on being identified as vulnerable. In ARE assessment visits, miners needed to prove they were subsistence workers so as to be included within mining reserves. They were asked about their pensions, professional careers, and previous dealings with excavators. Such questions allowed the National Mining Agency to differentiate the subsistent from the nonsubsistent, and to rule out applicants with an economic mobility contradictory to the identity of the "traditional" miner. Now, one obvious political effect of this performative assessment was the reification of state functionaries as benevolent protectors of those in need. But there may have been another politics at work, more in the sense meant by Charles Hale. This is because the act of allocating AREs, like *any* other act of formalizing, reaffirms the identity of the state apparatus as the sovereign ruler over the national territory, and therewith, the supreme authority to decide which forms of politico-economic life are to thrive within it. Put more simply, and falling back on Hale, distinguishing between deserving and undeserving subjects permits formal legislation to performatively define the contours of legit economic conduct (i.e., traditional extraction), and, by extension, to shut the door to claims deemed too economically radical.

It's this inherently exclusionary quality of institutional recognition that implores us to observe the mining reserves with critical eyes. For if anything, the ARE promoted a formalization scheme of legality *lite* that diverged not an awful lot from Colombia's preceding extractive politics. At least three factors contributed to such lite-ness. First, there was the issue of space: The AREs occupied a relatively small amount of subsoil. The agency-assigned polygons were often much smaller than the areas requested by communities. This discrepancy derived in part from the agency's policy of only assigning areas where miners were contemporarily at work, ignoring their geographical mobility over time. Yet it also stemmed from the spatial restrictions that the reserves faced from multinational titles and other legal categories (e.g., forest reserves). Most notably, Colombian legislation dictated that the mining reserves could be allocated only "without harming mining titles already in force" (Congreso de Colombia 2001: Art. 31).

Second, the reserves incorporated only manual forms of extraction. They legally sanctioned miners with "certain economic necessities," as Vicente put it, but yielded no formal benefits for those who owned "untraditional" machinery. Although well-meaning agency officials like Vicente de facto condoned low-tech tools such as water pumps (in placer mines) or explosives (in tunnel mines), those working with such equipment within a reserve enjoyed no legal protection against police detention, seeing as the Colombian mining code prohibited all nonmanual extraction in the absence of a mining title—which, again, the ARE was not.[18] Therefore, spokespersons of mining associations generally discussed the reserves with me in a pessimistic tone. The president of CONALMINERCOL, the national small-scale mining confederation, said: "The National Mining Agency only accepts certain ways of working. But today in Colombia it's simply impossible to mine with a pick and a shovel. . . . In alluvial mining you need to make a cut of five to six meters deep and thirty to forty meters long. That is not that simple. You're not going to do that with a pick and a shovel. That's not mining, that's slavery!"

Third, even if the ARE came with the promise of a future mining concession, titling continued to be a highly complicated process. ARE miners had to submit a Work and Construction Plan (PTO), requiring them to pay for expensive geological studies that their rudimentary tools were unlikely to cover; more so because once miners had been awarded the reserve, they were expected to pay royalties and provide their workers with social benefits.[19] If ARE grantees did not present a PTO within two years' time, or if they did not fulfill their new financial obligations, the National Mining Agency could revoke the reserve. If, on the other hand, miners succeeded in acquiring a title through the PTO, they had six months to carry out the Environmental Impact Assessment necessary for an environmental license. In the meantime, they were still legally circumscribed to work with hand-based equipment. Mining leader Franklin belonged to one of the communities that had actually managed to acquire a mining title. Despite this, he reckoned that working with excavators was all but a certainty, because of the high costs of the environmental license: "The ARE has fallen short. Why? Because the requisites and processes of formalization remain equally difficult. Within the ARE, they don't allow you to work with mechanized equipment. But an environmental license costs 200 to 300 million pesos [50,000–70,000 USD]. So to pay this, they basically oblige you to look for outside financiers."

I know of three municipalities where "traditional" mining communities did eventually receive both a mining title and an environmental license. Franklin belonged to one of them. Nonetheless, his concern about external assistance was not a moot point. In all three successful cases, the communities had relied on fortuitous financial assistance from Oro Legal, a USAID-funded development project for small-scale miners.[20]

Bundling together the here-mentioned restrictions of space, production, and procedure, we may read the ARE as a dressed-down set of extraction rights that, although eating away some marginal sections of the subsoil, did not interfere much with the status quo of industrial-scale extraction. In effect, the ARE was likely less a challenge than a confirmation of this status quo. Its endorsement helped establish a legible concession regime in which traditional mining was axiomatic with manual extraction within reserves, which—in being reserves—were limited in size and did not much disturb the accumulation of extractive capital. Put differently, ARE miners were minimally mechanized workers who laid little claim on the subsoil, and seemed unlikely to make larger claims in the future, insofar as their economic assets were no match for the demanding requirements of concessions and environmental licenses; at least, as Franklin noted, if they would fulfill these requirements without the help of external financiers (mining firms or, in the case of the lucky few, development projects).

All of which leads me to conceive of ARE miners—in a play on Rivera Cusicanqui and Hale—as *mineros permitidos*. By "permitted miners," we can think of mining subjects who are formalized not for their contributions to capital, but rather for their minimal obstruction to it. In 2010s Colombia, such miners were ARE recipients, but they could also very well be manual operators who were permitted to sell gold despite not having a title, subsistence miners in Bebará who were recognized as war victims in need of a development project, and, most assuredly, tunnel miners in the Andes who were subcontracted by multinationals under terms of the latter's choosing.[21] In other words, by *mineros permitidos*, I refer to small-scale miners who were comparatively harmless to the narrative of "well-done mining"—i.e., mining that was amicable with private markets, public safety, and corporate environmentalism—given that their labor was confined to reserves, subcontracted employment for multinationals, manual-based methods, and post-FARC development programs. It follows, then, that policymakers rationalized these miners' legal recognition not so much through conventional neoliberal arguments of economic maximization as through pragmatic arguments of tolerance that, ironically enough, emphasized miners' *lack* of economic agency. Unlike "criminal" miners who supposedly capitalized on their informality, permitted small-scale miners were deemed vulnerable subjects in need of state assistance.[22] They were not viewed as sharing the malevolent intentions of the "criminals." By all means, permitted miners were willing miners. They *wanted* to formalize, to work sustainably, profitably, and legally, and to receive the support of government and corporations to do all this. Former president Santos summed them up quite well: "We are not demonizing the small-scale miners who have the will to formalize and to do well-done mining. Them we want to help. Small-scale mining, subsistence mining, is one thing, and the illicit extraction of minerals, what we call criminal mining, is a very different thing" (Presidencia de la República 2015b).

This brings us to the counterimage of the permitted miners: the presumed tricksters who presented themselves as small-scale operators but who were actually "criminal" resource exploiters. Ostensibly, these were the miners who decimated forests, financed the war, avoided taxes, and threatened international investment. In different variations, dichotomies of "small-scale/illicit" and "willing/criminal" popped up constantly in government statements, like in this one, wherein ex-president Santos pledged a twofold strategy to combat informality: "On the one hand, a frontal war against the mafias who pretend to hide their illicit acts behind the mask of small-scale mining and, on the other hand, the support to small miners who can and want to make use of formalization politics to regularize their activity" (Presidencia de la República 2015a). The "illicit" and "criminal" ends of these moral dichotomies almost invariably invoked cunning mafias thieving from the subsoil, whereas "willing" miners appeared primarily as subsistence workers.[23] As Silvana Habib, former president of the National Mining Agency, put it: "We should shut down the mines of those looting the riches from our subsoil. . . . Formalizing those who have historically done artisanal and traditional mining is the way to be inclusive with the ones who want to do things right, help the country, and grow as entrepreneurs" (*El Espectador* 2016).[24]

It requires, however, a big imaginative leap to designate as "inclusive" the formalization that Habib and Santos envisioned. At first hearing, their point to support "the ones who want to do things right" seems well taken, revealing a healthy aspiration to only assist mines that are not implicated with environmental and criminal harms. There is no denying these are relevant concerns. Yet their assertions of being "inclusive" and showing "support" sound rather opportunistic when put in dialogue with all the miner stigmatization that suffused their government's policies and public statements, as laid bare in this book, or when juxtaposed with their own smoothing over of the environmental suffering occasioned by "well-doing" Canadian and South African corporations. At its worst, their claim to inclusiveness sounds like neoliberal window dressing. At its best, it delivers a message of toleration: small-scale miners can "grow as entrepreneurs," as long as they comply with a brazenly pro-corporate regulatory model, and, on that basis, do not stand in the way of industrial enterprise. When read this second way, the inclusiveness of Santos, Habib, and several other central government figures becomes something of an echo of what Vicente told the El Platino miners: "You can improve, but only to a certain degree."

Of course, in the mouths of the public officials and mining company representatives pleading for permissible growth, it is all for the protection of small-scale miners themselves. If they were to believe, restrictive formalization prevents miners from losing "social and economic traditions," paraphrasing Vicente, or allows them to "help the country," quoting Habib.[25] The natural corollary of such policy appraisal is that, while the permitted miner might be willing, their willingness should correspond to a desire for guidance by state agencies and companies; it is not to be confused with demonstrating an economic agency autonomous from formal channels. If the economic intentions of the permitted miner are not amenable to the *legality lite* of official formalization—to panning, to subcontracted work for corporations, to subsistence work in small reserves—they run the risk of no longer being considered "traditional," and of no longer being permitted.

Consider this snippet from a conversation in the Bogotá office of the National Mining Agency. I mentioned to Vicente and two of his senior employees that artisanal miners in Chocó deemed their production maximum unfair, as it prevented them from selling all their gold whenever they had a few lucky strikes. The comment fell flat. "With their maximum, they can make two million pesos per month," one of the senior officials remarked. "That's much more than many people make in Bogotá. They only don't like the maximum because they want to sell illegally."

Vicente agreed. "They like to be illegal."

After I had asked "Why do you think so?" the senior official who had spoken earlier said: "Because they don't want to pay taxes. They always feel special in Chocó. They say they are special and need special laws. To me, they're like all other miners. They must obey the law. They earn much more than people in some neighborhoods here. They want to mine illegally so they don't pay taxes and can drink away all of the money they make."

Permitted miners are expected to "obey the law." When working in poverty, they should receive the help to "do things right," in the words of Habib. But when their extractive aspirations become too "radical" (in Hale's terms), or "*vivo*" (in Zeiderman's), and no longer conform to restrictive legal principles, they can see their tradition being called into question and be framed as undeserving subjects of rights at best, criminals at worst. Mining leader Franklin knew this all too well. I give him the last word: "In Colombia, you can only realize traditional mining when it's manual. So when they talk of traditional miners who have [mechanical] equipment, it's not traditional to the government. It becomes 'illegal mining.' They make no exceptions! Everything that is mechanized is illicit extraction. It's not traditional nor ancestral."

Conclusion

This chapter has fleshed out the discursive and regulatory contours of the centralized mining governance I encountered in field and desk research, approaching it as a neoliberal modality of rule that suffered from tunnel vision. When discussing widespread informality, policymakers tended to channel attention away from questions of inequality and toward the supposedly dangerous and incapable bodies of miners. Their rhetoric undergirded a formal legal framework that, while welcoming the "well-doing" corporate industry, addressed the presence of informalized small-scale miners through castigatory measures.

With that said, there was more to these politics than sheer criminalization. However much they insist on "punishing the poor" (Wacquant 2009), neoliberal governments—in Colombia and elsewhere—are likely to endorse some moderate recognition of the rights of peripheralized populations (whether through extractive, multicultural, or victim legislation, or otherwise) when faced with crises of legitimacy and/or conspicuous social protest. In this vein, the Colombian legitimacy crisis that was the 2013 miners' strike gave impetus to ensuing negotiations (i.e., mesas mineras) between government officials and mining leaders. Such negotiations helped actualize several formalization initiatives, ranging from the locally enforced Medio Atrato pilot program to nationally enforced mining reserves and capacity programs.

And yet, even if these efforts were touted by policymakers as realistic panaceas for informality problems, they did not drain the legal quagmire in which Colombian miners had been drowning since the 2001 mining code. Reforms left unaddressed the vexing issue of unequal access to titles, while confining legalization to small reserves, subsistence extraction, and workers subcontracted by multinationals. As a matter of fact, by advocating the narrow definition of the "traditional" miner, formalization discourses reaffirmed the inauthentic traditionality of miners left unlegalized—those who exceeded the parameters of tolerated spaces and technologies, and those who refused to be ensnared in exploitative subcontracts by companies working on their ancestral lands. Thus, purposely or not, small-scale mining formalization can actually have the perverse effect of sustaining the "large-scale" status quo, inasmuch as it may incorporate grassroots formalization discourses into a concession regime that leaves most minerals in the hands of corporations.

To summarize, the case of Colombian mining confirms the oft-reiterated observation that the privatization of resource regimes sidelines vulnerable populations who are deemed obstacles to financial markets (Rojas 2009; Sawyer 2004). Nevertheless, Colombia also shines a new light on how neoliberal extractivism might unfold, as private sector development coexisted with the legal recognition of the least capitalized within the small-scale mining population. Arguably, as mining engineer Vicente argued, the plus side of such politics is a certain caution to legalize the forest-killing sections of a wildcat economy. Yet as mining leaders such as Franklin pointed out, there is also a menace in such politics, especially when, as in the case presented here, it exists in tandem with the endorsement of (forest-killing) large-scale extractive ventures. Indeed, "permitted" formality can enable governments to extend their regulatory framework, while leaving intact its corporate underpinnings.

Conclusion

Living in the Afterlife of Extraction

You tell me: What will we live off
when there are no more excavators?

—*Flor (barequera)*

n the late 2000s, one of Colombia's most impoverished departments, Chocó, became gripped by a gold rush. Pushed by rocketing gold prices and pulled by tales of rich subsoils, outside excavator and dredge miners came, saw, and eventually conquered great quantities of gold from the alluvium. It was a mining boom that went as quickly as it came. With their hopes set on a "post-conflict" Colombia, national government officials began to view informal gold frontiers such as Chocó's as the antithesis of the desired future of development, which revolved around foreign mine investment, neoliberal conservation ethics, and the absence of gold-taxing guerrillas and paramilitaries. From the early 2010s onward, they increasingly problematized Chocó's miners as forest destroyers, henchmen for criminals, and unproductive occupants of the national subsoil. In tandem, they ordered police and army helicopters to dynamite the illegally operating excavators and dredges to smithereens. As a result, many of the new miners called it a day. They left in their wake forest landscapes that were peeled of trees, shorn of crops, and robbed of grains of gold.

This book has told the story of this extractive afterlife. It has shown how a diverse cast of mining characters negotiated livelihoods in a legal climate that was rigged against them, and, more specifically, how this climate fueled underground sociopolitical practices that refuted popular tropes of mining lawlessness. To a great extent, I have looked at such underground politics through the prism of abandonment. Asked about their legal troubles, miners described themselves as purposely "abandoned" by their policymakers. This was a multifaceted experience. Being abandoned was the experience, for one, of being unprotected by the police and army against criminals, and, for another, of being stripped of citizenship—of personhood even—when seeing these same public forces destroying one's mine equipment (along with one's savings and plans for the future). Being abandoned was the experience of being left behind by government promises of formality; of tirelessly submitting paperwork and never receiving a title, or of giving up trying and working "until they let us." And being abandoned was the experience of hearing politicians denouncing mining as the culprit of Chocó's poverty and crime—denunciations against which miners defended themselves by recounting their economic contributions, or proposing that the true cause of local deprivation was a larger-than-life history of government neglect and racism, a history that lingered on in the present.

Curiously enough, the political vocabulary of abandonment wasn't only spoken by the retreros suffering equipment destruction, but also by the subsistence operators whom the government recognized as the victims of the gold rush—and whom the draconian measures against illegal mining were supposed to protect. Even if restrictions on selling gold and transporting fuel affected the big players the most, they also made it harder for smaller miners to work however they pleased. Moreover, local communities suffered the government's punitive policies in another way, for they had readily participated in the mining boom by charging the newcomers rents, working in their mines, panning for gold in their cuts, and replicating their methods. Such engagement had allowed them to increase their financial autonomy, provide for family and friends, and consume goods and services associated with a good life. State policies had put an end to these freedoms, urging many people to opt for nonmining livelihoods or shift back to smaller and less lucrative extraction.

This return to the artisanal mines resists easy moral evaluations. Certainly, when witnessing the ecological pathologies of excavators, it's tempting to sing the praises of their demise and to endorse artisanal mining as a sustainable alternative to their destruction—a temptation that many news outlets, legislators, and development practitioners indeed have trouble resisting. In this book, however, I have set out that such praises do not necessarily correspond to how many chocoanos viewed their extraction. Panners, guacheros, and water pump miners hailed the autonomy, comradery, and ancestrality of artisanal mining, but they also saw it as a strenuous way to make ends meet. That is, they loved the freedom of the pits and streams, but also spoke of draining working days, the risk of injury and death, and the more recent hardship of scouring for gold in scraped-out surface layers.

Their grievances were not indifferent to the negatives of the gold rush. On the contrary, their newfound precarity was undisputable evidence that the boom years had brought unequal benefits to those visiting and those staying behind. Now that most excavator mines were gone, a collective realization had sunk in that the migrants had taken most of the gold, whereas chocoanos were left with the same old worn-out economies—but now relying on less minerals, wood, crops, and fish. Yet even in extraction's afterlife, many held positive attitudes about the retreros. In effect, people who suffered the afterlife most palpably—those who had relied on land rents, bareque, and indirect turnovers in commerce and motor taxis—blamed the current economic impasse not so much on the excavators as on the state politics that were grinding the machines to a halt. Correspondingly, their preferred solution to the impasse was not a return to subsistence extraction, nor a conversion to farming, but a comeback of the retreros and a government that allowed this to happen. Gold was now too deep to dig up manually, and the gains on crops too insufficient to dedicate oneself fully to forest gardens. For lots of mining-town residents, the desired future was in excavators.

In view of this, Chocó's mining participants—and especially its excavator miners—were torn between desiring more and less of the state. On the one hand, they despised their "evil state" for making them work in hiding like criminals; in other words, for making them flee their pits at the sound of whirring helicopter blades, sell gold under the table for unfavorable prices, and transport their supplies at night to avoid defense checkpoints. On the other hand, miners longed for the state, and diagnosed its absence, when invoking the almost mythical mining titles they would never receive, when recounting how tin-eared legislators had no idea of their honest labor, and when claiming their entitlement to police protection from machete-slapping bandits and pocket-looting armed groups. By calling out the state's absence, research collaborators articulated the moral claim that politics could and should be otherwise.

They were not alone in situating their mines outside of the state. Regarding both Chocó and other small-scale mining regions, remarkably similar notions of statelessness have been uttered by politicians warning about the heinous crimes of extraction, by development practitioners warning about social and environmental decay, and by social scientists warning about the same. Here I have suggested that these theories of state absence, although saying a lot about the politics that are missing, are silent on the potent affectivities that state power generates in variously peripheralized resource frontiers. For this reason, I have explored state legality less as an objective political fact that indexes compliance with formal protocol—i.e., a stable status that is either present or absent—than as an unsettled everyday performance through which residents of mining regions stake claims on each other and the bureaucracy, and, in so doing, enact ostensibly unlawful activities as morally legit.

Even if retreros, artisanal miners, and junta directiva leaders repeatedly railed against the state's absence, they were never idle bystanders in the cultural production of statehood. By appropriating legal discourses, accumulating documents, governing gold mines, and planting the trees they thought the government wanted them to plant, they were constructing from the ground up a formalization regime that had yet to emerge top-down. Of course, from a formal juridical perspective, these configurations of law did not reduce the gravity of the extractive crimes being committed. Most miners and community leaders were well aware. Even so, the miners calculated that a limited expression of legality could better their odds in a pending police operation, while the leaders knew that their lawful land rights afforded them a practical leverage to carry out their mining governance.

What's more, such underground politics sometimes also broke out into the open. However much in tension with official legislation, the legal performances by miners and community leaders partly arose from, and gave rise to, the governing schemes of the state apparatus. Junta leaders' governance relied for its regulatory success on the "muscle" of local state actors, who—far from expressing a zealous devotion to formal doctrine—exerted their capacity to police unlicensed mines chiefly when community norms were being breached. And in a similar convergence of gold and law, miners too depended for their legitimacy on state "accomplices." In providing certificates for gold selling, banners against police actions, and alibis for the presence of extractive machinery (in the form of canalization works), local bureaucrats helped miners cope with an inhospitable legal framework and rendered informality slightly less informal.

All this reveals, of course, that this ethnography offers not simply one more example of the conventional critical narrative about liberal governance, in which centralized rulers thrust themselves upon local populations and act against their interests.[1] Although this narrative certainly resurfaces in several of the book's scenes,[2] I have primarily tried to shift attention to the political agency of governed populations themselves. That is to say, I have sought to visualize how miners and their surrounding communities make possible the expansion of state power by anticipating, and responding to, the public institutions that fail to accurately "see" them (Scott 1998). Analytically speaking, this has not always made it easy to detect where state power starts and ends. But this is exactly the point. States are unfinished and multifarious projects. They unfold in everyday lifeworlds by virtue of their inconsistencies (Abrams 1988), semantic ambiguities (Das 2004), regulatory compromises (Li 1999), and public/private assemblages (Jaffe 2013)—all of which holds especially true for marginalized places like Chocó, where "the state is continually both experienced and undone through the illegibility of its own practices, documents, and words" (Das and Poole 2004:10). Indeed, just as chocoano mining navigated the interstitial space between the legal and the extralegal, so too did its practitioners continually straddle the ontological lines between state and community, government and grassroots, and official and customary law. If anything, their bottom-up statecraft didn't stop at local bureaucracy; at times, it even laid the groundwork for state centralization. As mining and community leaders convoked meetings, set up protests, and organized their informal mines in accordance with formal designs, they ended up penetrating the vision of central state representatives. And every so often, they managed to convince the latter to visit their mines, formalize their labor, and push for new legislation.

All in all, to cast informal economies such as gold mining as suffering from state absence is to overlook all of the above; it is to overlook how chocoanos constantly entangle state law in their extraction, be it miners committing themselves to the rigor of formalization, community leaders acting on multicultural jurisdiction, local bureaucrats endorsing underground activities, or all of them joining together in protest marches to demand legislative change.

A Messy Picture

The picture that this book leaves behind is a messy one, and deliberately so.[3] You will find no monolithic power-mongering state, no precise benchmark of where cultural tradition ends and destruction begins, no unwavering grassroots embrace of the economies of old, no perfectly adversarial nor amicable relationship between landholders and frontiersmen, nor a clear-cut distinction between the two. At the same time, while the analysis has presented damning evidence of injustices that seem hard to pardon—the ruination of the jungle, the legal persecution of impoverished miners, the armed extortion by criminal groups—it has also kept an eye open for the normative rationales underlying the killing of trees, for the rusty and jumbled works of the state machinery, and for the praise that communities may heap on the organizational expertise of the same guerrillas whose violence they suffer.

Perhaps such nuance and contingency doesn't make for an easy political read. Perhaps the skeptical reader will find that stereotypes about informalized miners are better countered with a more orderly narrative about power; one of evil versus good, of dominators and resisters, of intrusive capitalists locking horns with noncapitalist production modes. Perhaps. Yet the "witches' brew of situated processes and relations" (Li 2007:271) of resource frontiers hardly ever conspires to such binary logic. Looking from up close, as we've done here, we see not only organizational forms that unsettle persistent clichés of frontier lawlessness, but also the undeniable messiness—not, mind you, lawlessness—of gold country, where opinions and rules exist along with their own exceptions, and social relations rarely settle for stable form, as they move along with the opportunities set in place by the mines.

Indeed, looking from up close at the goldfields means staring messiness in the face. Artisanal operators aspire to higher gold yields, but not if the labor required infringes too much on their autonomy. Pump miners badmouth their work when digging for nothing, yet love it, unconditionally, the moment an unproductive pit turns productive. Landholding families desire the comeback of the same excavators who made them ecologically bankrupt. Their neighbors may be more critical about the pillage of the forest, but might also favor extractive pragmatics over environmental idealism when opportunities for bareque arrive. Excavator miners, while being applauded by themselves and others for their economic contributions, do their utmost to evade paying their dues to the community, which, in turn, is headed by a junta directiva whose governing concurrently affords them acclaim for self-sacrificial leadership and accusations of illegitimate enrichment. And though all these local players are involved in various conflicts over gold, they are almost always ready to make amends. Fighting is bad for business.

Looking from up close, the inconsistencies of state governance also stream into view. We encounter small miners being excluded from a legal framework that favors transnational companies, yet also find this corporatist framework opening itself up to the smallest of the small-scale. We encounter bureaucrats shifting blame to other bureaucrats for the non-policing of unlicensed mines. We encounter, in one unpoliced river, a history of FARC combatants

enforcing the multicultural laws of the same state apparatus they were fighting. And in the midst of it all, we encounter miners and community leaders
declaring the simultaneous absence and presence of the state. We encounter them claiming their "legality" and bemoaning their "illegality" in the
same sentence. We encounter them fleeing the law—hiding in the forest,
running away from helicopters—but desiring the law when bandits appear.
We encounter them seeing their situation as "hopeless," but still entertain-
ing a glimmer of political hope when dutifully planting seedlings, or opening company folders filled with legal documents.

It's not easy to tell where this messy story is heading. During my time in
Chocó in 2017, many people expressed fears of a gloomy future. Not a small
number foresaw that without the excavators Chocó's population would starve
of hunger, flock to the cities in the Colombian interior, or start thieving and
killing. "You tell me: What will we live off when there are no more excavators?" barequera Flor asked me, without seemingly expecting much of an answer. Her fellow miner Lucho had even suggested (as you may recall from
Chapter 1) that "Chocó is one of the departments that will disappear."

On my return in August 2019, there were even fewer active excavator
mines. Many of the retreros I knew were no longer around. People gave the
same reasons for the ongoing decline as they had two years before: The departed miners had become too fed up with the bandits robbing them of their
gold, too bothered by the mined-out subsoils robbing them of their fuel, and
most of all, too fearful of the policemen robbing them of their mines. Effectively, while the president had changed—Juan Manuel Santos was out, Iván
Duque was in—the scale of police operations had not. On April 8, 2019 (four
months before my return), the town of Tadó had made national news head-
lines after one of the last local excavators was destroyed and an angry crowd
took to the streets. Amid the confusion, a few protesters set fire to an army
truck that had accompanied the destruction delegation. "What would you
do?" a young man asked me after bringing up the burned-out truck. "I'm not
defending it, but that excavator belonged to a family. You can't just destroy
something like that and expect people not to be angry!"

Not all excavators had stopped revving. Gerson was still trying his luck.
When I spoke to him two years earlier, he had cast the planting of saplings as
a possible way to remain friendly with the police. Now he dismissed that strategy as ingenuous: "Honestly, they don't care about it. Here they are burning us
down all the time. *Pum. Pum. Pum.*" His decision to keep on mining was
based on a lack of alternatives. He fantasized about quitting, but for that he

Figure 10. Burnt-out excavator. Photo by the author.

needed retirement capital, and with that, putting it in his own words, "the luck of the earth."

The other two excavator dueños I spoke to expressed similar desires to get out—along with similar hopes of stumbling on a pot of gold. Their words imbued in me a sense of continuity. All three of them had articulated the same desires and hopes two years before. Nonetheless, here they still held out, risking their luck as always. (One of them had even had his two excavators bombed in a recent police mission, prompting him to solicit a hefty loan at a gold buyer to fix up one of the vehicles.) Yet it was not only these remaining retreros, and their persistent desires for change, that seemed only slightly affected by the passage of time. Much of what I had come to know as Chocó's mining life proceeded as usual. Great numbers of artisanal miners carried on their work. Although the subsoil had not suddenly become more productive, neither had its surface deposits been much more depleted in the absence of the earth-scouring excavators. Thus, Tagachí (Chapter 1) was still dragging his motorized water pump from one prohibited lot to the next, most workers in Darwinson's tunnel (Chapter 1) were still venturing into the underground (though he himself now supplemented his income with laying roofs in town), and Emiro (Chapter 3) was still diving for gold, but now with a bigger dredge and a more powerful motor.

Subsequent visits in 2022 and 2023 did not paint a radically different picture. Gerson continued combing the landscape for gold, as did Tagachí, as did Emiro. Lucho had even found work in a new excavator mine, regardless of the ongoing police actions. Arguably because of the persistence of these and other miners—and because of the persistence of public sector salaries and remittances to supply rural households with cash incomes—the daily economics of mining villages also seemed not too different from 2017, excavators or no excavators. Yes, shop owners mentioned the decline of excavators to rationalize the adversities of their businesses, and yes, motor-taxi drivers lamented that there was no one to drive around anymore. But these complaints had already been uttered five to six years previously, and now people still opened new restaurants or reached deep into their pockets to purchase secondhand motorbikes and tuk-tuks.

In fact, it appeared that in the new decade people were extracting not less but more. Several people had been picking up their water pumps again. Planetary crises of health and finance had been amenable to the local gold economy. Before reaching Colombia, the COVID-19 virus had been prophesied as a catastrophe in the making by chocoanos, whose towns and villages, after all, were ruthlessly lacking in medical infrastructure. Once the pandemic materialized, though, it held much less sway in Chocó than in the urbanized regions of the Colombian Andes. Yet needless to say, especially in the pandemic's heyday, the virus did inspire much fear as a harbinger of collective illness, and was therefore regulated through stringent mobility restrictions, including the closure of stores, schools, and public buildings. In this context of economic inertia, so I was told afterward, one of the few possibilities for finding money was by secretly roaming the anonymous forest for gold.

A second stimulus of the seemingly increased popularity of the mines was equally planetary in scale—and not completely divorced from COVID-19. Pandemic-mediated instability on financial markets had once more catapulted the global price for gold. In 2023, the price per castellano of chocoano gold was more than twice as high as it was in 2017, boosting the economic incentive to try one's luck in the mines.

Accordingly, the "disappearance" of Chocó, as feared by Lucho, had not yet taken off, nor did it seem likely to take off in the short run. While over the years a few people had indeed left for Medellín and other cities, the majority of research collaborators had stayed put. While many of them continued to think little of the economic future of Chocó, this was still their future. They knew all about the pitfalls of emigration; about how aspirations of a well-off city life—once pronounced by their families, friends, and themselves—had one after the other collapsed into the urban realities of living from paycheck to paycheck, of hopping from one underpaid job to the next, of being laid off in a time of a global health crisis—with no nearby mine providing an economic safety net to catch the fall. They stressed the high rents and public transportation fares in metropoles like Medellín and Bogotá. They noticed that city labor had become increasingly scarce with the arrival of new Venezuelan refugees, who allegedly accepted work for half the minimum wage. But it was not just these economic "facts" that kept Chocó from disappearing. In explaining their nonmigration, people contrasted the reciprocity of the countryside with the individualism of the city; the freedom of their extraction with the strict schedules and racist supervisors that came along with urban work. Gold-mining villages generated a sense of independence, and they would do so in the foreseeable future.

A Postscript on the "Post-Conflict": Armed Actors, Activism, Achiote, Australians

Beyond the pandemic, there were other humanitarian crises sweeping across Colombia after my 2017 fieldwork. If this was a time of "post-conflict," it was a horrifically violent one. Community and environmental leaders were threatened and killed for speaking out against armed actors, corrupt politicians, illicit economies, and industries of extraction, agribusiness, and infrastructure.[4] Much of the violence was connected to the new military landscape. In Chocó and elsewhere, paramilitaries, guerrillas, and other groups moved into the former strongholds of the FARC, leading to new acts of displacement, kidnapping, and murder. For example, both the village of San Miguel (Chapter 2) and the Bebará riverbanks (Chapter 4) have in recent years been subject to heavy fighting between AGC paramilitaries and ELN guerrillas, which in the case of San Miguel resulted in one more wave of massive displacement in August 2021 (*El Universal* 2021).

Chocó's attraction for armed groups was not much different than before, the region remaining a strategic corridor for drug trafficking, being situated along the Pacific Ocean and the inaccessible, rainforest-covered border with Panama.[5] Gold also remained an important driver. Even though most excavator miners had left, the Quito River still hosted a large number of dredges in early 2023, which apparently produced enough gold to compensate for the destruction operations by state troops, and for the bribes paid to the latter to be spared in these operations.

The plan of the Duque government (2018–2022) to combat rural violence mostly consisted of the same strategies that were tested and honed in previous decades: eradication campaigns for the coca crops, dynamite for the gold mines, and televised military operations for the criminals taxing the illegal economies. Yet with national employment, household incomes, and economic stability all plummeting due to COVID-19 (World Bank 2021), such *mano dura* policy was anything but a rewarding path to rural peace and well-being. Coca farmers and gold miners continued to lack attractive subsistence alternatives. What's more, they continued to lack meaningful means to legalize their activities.

The ongoing violence of the countryside would not be the only stain on Duque's troubling legacy. In April 2021, Colombians in Cali, Bogotá, Medellín, Quibdó, and many other cities organized popular protests. Although the catalyst was a controversial tax spike, the nationwide mobilization soon coagulated an array of grievances from different social groups: unemployment, inequality, corruption, poor health care, the scot-free killing of environmental activists, anti-Indigenous and anti-Black institutional racism. The government's reaction to the calls for change was to scale up the repression. State agents killed dozens of activists in two months of protest. Hundreds more were disappeared, beaten, and sexually assaulted.

But the message of a new kind of Colombia could not be wiped out. If the popular activism had demonstrated one thing, it was that a large part of the population was yearning for a new type of state: one less unequal, less neoliberal, less racist. In the succeeding presidential elections of mid-2022, left-wing opposition leader Gustavo Petro seized the political momentum and won the presidency on a ticket of peace, economic equality, and social and environmental justice. His running mate was Francia Márquez, an Afro-Colombian environmental activist and herself a victim of displacement and death threats due to her steadfast resistance to illegal gold mining around her village of La Toma.[6]

Chocó was part and parcel of the presidential success story: 82 percent of local votes went to the Petro-Márquez ticket. Yet when I visited the department's mining areas in January 2023, I encountered not only hope and pride about the electoral victory, but also uncertainty and skepticism. During his campaign, Petro had solidified his image as a man of the people by staying the night in what television journalists described as a *"vivienda humilde"* [humble dwelling] in Quibdó. But now, half a year into the presidency, rural chocoanos noticed that the projects required to upgrade their nontelevised houses, roads, and health centers had yet to arrive. Change had been promised. Chocó had not forgotten.

The jury was also still out on Petro's mining politics. The tides had turned, but in which direction was unclear. Miners and community leaders knew Petro to be an advocate for the poor. But he was also a staunch environmentalist. What would this mean for their not-so-environmentalist livelihoods? What were they to make of his pledge to assuage the country's dependence on minerals and hydrocarbons? Leaders of mining associations I spoke to, from Chocó and other places, were generally more positive. They were in negotiations with the new government over a future small-scale mining agenda. Apparently "Gustavo," as some referred to the president, was a critic of the theretofore preferential treatment that mining multinationals had enjoyed. His election was held as good news for formalization and the cessation of police missions.

However, about a month after these upbeat conversations, several of them were making critical public comments again on social media and news websites about the political exclusion of miners. Five river-polluting dredges had been blown up in the Bajo Cauca in Antioquia, resulting in one more miner strike that blocked the importation of food to several municipalities. Responding to the unrest, president Petro criticized paramilitaries for organizing the local strike and explained that his government would at once promote the titling of "families of small-scale miners" and "destroy the big machines that are used in Colombian rivers for illegal mining" (Valora Analitik 2023). It remained to be seen where he would draw the line between the "small-scale" and the "illegal," and how far it would move away from the lines of Santos and Duque.

All this is not to suggest that in recent years no developments in mining formalization have occurred in Chocó. They have, yet many were driven by actors other than national policymakers. In the past decade, in and beyond

Colombia, growing concerns about gold's relationship with violence, child labor, mercury, and deforestation have spawned small-scale mining development projects, stimulating "alternative economies" and less degrading extraction (remember the Medio Atrato pilot program in Chapter 7). As a region that is scarred by all the aforementioned perils, Chocó has become a popular target for these interventions. In 2019, the Better Gold Initiative, a Swiss public-private partnership, initiated a project in the municipality of Istmina with the goal of creating a transparent gold supply chain. A local buyer pays miners a premium for their gold (0.70 USD per gram) on top of the market price, providing that it is mined in a "responsible" and nonmechanized way.[7] The gold is then transported to Medellín, from where an international buyer exports it to a Swiss refiner.

Another recent development initiative was Oro Legal, a five-year-long, USAID-funded project that was completed in September 2021. Oro Legal encouraged chocoano miners to replace their extractive activities with the cultivation of achiote shrubs,[8] while also offering them legal, technical, and financial assistance with formalization. Such assistance meant that mining communities in the municipalities of Tadó and Unión Panamericana saw their traditional mining reserves (AREs) convert into actual mining titles, a not insignificant achievement (see Chapter 7).

It might still be early to discuss the success of both projects (and doing so is beyond the scope of this ethnography). But as more of these projects are on the horizon in Colombia, one is inclined to mull over a few practical questions. What do miners in projects such as Better Gold make of the obligation to work in worn-out landscapes with hand tools? How do "responsible mining" projects prevent them from using mechanical equipment in isolated mines? Also, to whom and for which prices will miners from the infrastructural margins of Colombia sell agricultural products such as achiote in the short and the long run?[9] Will these "alternative economies" be sufficiently rewarding to entice miners to reduce their gold extraction?[10] And what happens after mining formalization? How will the title beneficiaries exploit the communal titles?

One possible answer to the last question is teaming up with deep-pocketed outsiders. As mentioned in Chapter 7, Colombian legislation has promoted subcontracting arrangements as a way to let small miners work, and become formalized, in the titles of mining corporations. In Chocó, however, subcontracting has begun to be inversely deployed, as mining firms and investors—confronted with prior consultation legislation protecting collective land rights—are now sponsoring the titling requests of Afro-Colombian community councils. That is, in return for being subcontracted by the community and receiving a carte blanche for extraction, mining entrepreneurs have started to cover the high administrative fees and expensive studies that accompany the application for a concession contract. A result of these "joint ventures" is that several communities in and outside Chocó have actually managed to obtain concession contracts for high-tech exploitation.

Most miners and community leaders I spoke to were wary of these ventures. The "multinationals" and other investors, I heard people say, were infamous for predatory contracts, letting them hold on to most gold in the event of a lucky strike, as well as other metals whose presumed existence was unbeknownst to local communities. The outside backers, I also heard, presented to their own countries as "community consent" what was actually the approval of a few paid-off junta leaders. The more shady companies, I heard, used mining titles to launder illegal gold. And what I heard most often was that the mining businesses didn't generate the employment they promised: They required few personnel and refused the entry of barequeros.

These woes conjoined in stories people told about Condoto Platinum, an Australia-based firm that had gotten a foot inside the door of the community council of Nóvita. Having been repeatedly warned about the deceit of this company, I eventually contacted Nóvita's junta directiva. Its representatives told me that some years earlier, the company had bought their community council elections to set in place a "puppet junta" (a former junta, not the one I was talking to), with which it had subsequently signed a contract behind closed doors, giving the Australians the sole right to mine within 105,000 hectares of the collective territory.

I was in no position to distinguish between fact and fiction in these accusations. In another community council, however, I experienced firsthand the dubious logic of externally financed titling. Here, a junior mining firm had paid junta leaders for their work of community consultation. This implied convoking meetings in which community members heard and voted about the company's request to prospect the collective land. I attended one such meeting and was surprised to find the junta leaders giving a speech that sounded a lot like a sales pitch. Standing next to two company representatives (also chocoanos), the leaders stressed that the community approval was for exploration only (and not actual extraction), and praised the firm's technology for being capable of working deep gold deposits. They further noted that the company's geological studies would serve traditional miners by determining the exact whereabouts of smaller deposits, which were of no interest to the corporate geologists.

In conversations with me, people who had attended these consultations expressed their suspicions that the junta members had personal stakes in the project. They also feared that the company did not allow bareque and offered lower profit shares than Colombian retreros. Nevertheless, these conversations also revealed that in almost all the consultation meetings, landholders had voted in favor of the company's arrival—with some votes coming from the same people who had been doubtful when talking to me about the matter. This simultaneous rejection/approval of the project was indicative of the region-wide normative ambivalence that mining firms enjoyed in Chocó. The future, many interlocutors feared, would exclude most of the Colombian retreros. They had been leaving in droves and would not stop leaving in the short haul. Preferably, it would also not include pans and pumps, for they were no match for the depleted upper layers of the underground. And "multinationals"? A future of Australians and Canadians and South Africans? In the resource frontier of steadfast pragmatism—where it was not always easy to distinguish between threats and opportunities—even the sly businesses provoked ambiguous moral evaluations. Whereas interlocutors denounced the firms for their possible thievery and gold laundering, many among them (including the most skeptical) also admitted to some corporate advantages. At least the big players had the economic muscle to pay for formalization. More so, they were the only ones able to get beneath the exhausted surface. Rumor had it that industrial mines could reach several hundred, if not thousand, meters deep. And who knew what was still lying underneath, in the lower subterranea of the forests of afterward?

His damning vision of the future notwithstanding, Lucho was among those who fostered good hopes for foreign intervention:

> Our situation being as chaotic as it is now, God willing some company may come here. I'm in favor of the multinationals, oh yes, I'm in favor. Because there's still a lot of gold here. What you find here in the stream goes a long way down. And where the multinationals work, no small miner will go. They work seventy meters into the earth, at least. The small miner does not go there. But they should at least reach some agreement saying the barequero can enter. Because the owners of the land might earn something, but what about the hundred or more barequeros who go to the mines?

And so, though the wildcat excavator mines might have been coming to an end, the story of extraction was not over yet. The secretive potentiality of gold continued to enflame desires to dig deeper and fears of missing out and being deceived. These desires and fears were nothing new and would not cease anytime soon. "A long way down," Lucho and others knew, grains of gold still scattered in abundance, waiting to be found by someone, someday. This enduring presence of gold seemed to be one of the few points of agreement about an uncertain future that was likely to be messy.

GLOSSARY

agua de panela—Sugarcane water; popular Colombian drink.
aventureros—Unauthorized gold buyers; pay less than authorized buyers.
bajocaucanos—People from the Bajo Cauca.
bareque—Mining method whereby artisanal operators use hand tools to dig out the mud walls of an excavator-mining pit.
barequero—Person who conducts bareque; can also refer to gold panners in general, including those working in streambeds without the assistance of excavators (see *mazamorreo*).
barretón—Four-edged metal bar, used in manual-based mining.
batea—Wooden gold-washing pan.
bebareño—Person from the Bebará River.
betadora—Wooden gold-washing pan, smaller than a *batea* and used for more refined washing.
bogotanos—People from Bogotá.
castellano—Colonial weight measurement for gold; continues to be employed in Chocó.
chocoano—Person from Chocó; can also be used as adjective, as in: pertaining to Chocó.
chorristas—Workers at excavator mines who are in charge of hosing down earth on a classifier (*clasificadora*).
clasificadora—Three-story trough, used to extract gold from sediment.
colono—Term that has been historically used to describe frontier settlers.
condueño—Literally, "co-owner"; a person who is part of an extended family that per customary law owns a piece of land within a collective land.
consejo comunitario—The ensemble of families that owns a collective land in accordance with Afro-Colombian legislation; often, the consejo comunitario is a *consejo comunitario mayor* ("upper community council") that encompasses several local communities, or *consejos comunitarios menores* ("lower community councils").
Constancia de la Alcaldía—Mayor's Certificate; a paper that legally sanctions a person's status as a subsistence miner, which is required to sell gold.
cuadrilla—During colonialism, a working group of enslaved miners.
departamento—"Department," a national subdivision similar to a province.
dragón—Two-story mining dredge; can mean either "dragon" or "large dredge."
draguero—Owner/worker of a *dragón*.
dueño—Owner of an excavator mine.
elevadora—Literally, "elevator"; artisanal mining technique that uses rubber hoses to suck up water from a lower-lying terrain, and subsequently uses that water to spray down higher-up gold-bearing earth.
guagua—Paca, a large rodent.
grupo de trabajo—Entourage of a political candidate during their electoral campaign.
guache—A wooden tunnel used in artisanal mining.
guacheros—People who work in a guache mine.

hermano—Literally, "brother"; also used amicably among friends.

jagua—Black pay dirt, economically worthless for chocoano miners.

junta directiva—The administrative leadership of a consejo comunitario; can be a *junta directiva mayor* or a *junta directiva menor*, depending on the consejo's organizational scale (see *consejo comunitario*).

libres—Free Black people.

líderes de bareque—In Bebará: a person tasked with maintaining order during *bareque* mining.

matraca—Small sluice box.

mazamorreo—Term used in Chocó to describe river panning.

mesa minera—Discussion platform in which state representatives and small-scale mining leaders discuss formalization, on either the national or departmental level.

minería bien hecha—Literally, "well-done mining" (or "mining done well"); catchphrase employed by government officials to designate legal mining.

minidraga—"Mini-dredge"; unlike the bigger *dragón*, a minidraga relies on a human diver.

minidraguero—Operator/diver at a *minidraga*.

mochila—In an excavator-mining cut: a pile of earth from which gold can be extracted.

oficios varios—Term that refers to (lesser-paid) odd jobs in an excavator mine.

Oro Verde—"Green Gold" development initiative, aimed at stimulating environmentally responsible small-scale mining.

paisa—Person from the department of Antioquia; in Chocó, the term can also connote white people more generally.

palenque—Fortified settlement created by free Black people to defend themselves from white colonial society.

paro cívico—General strike.

plana—Term used to designate the pit of an excavator mine.

Procuraduría—Colombian government agency that investigates and sanctions public functionaries.

quema—Literally, a "burning"; used to describe the explosions of excavator and dredge mines at the hands of public forces.

rebusque—Popular term used to describe unstable income, often through informal activities.

retrero—Owner/worker at excavator mine.

sanmigueleños—People from San Miguel.

socio—Stakeholder in a mine, through labor or financial investment.

sujeto de derechos—Literally, a "subject of rights"; refers to humans and nonhumans (e.g., the Atrato River) who are legal subjects.

tía—Aunt.

Unidad de Víctimas—"Victims Unit," a public institution offering redress to victims of the armed conflict.

vacuna—Extortion tax imposed by nonstate armed groups.

viejos—Literally, "old ones"; an affectionate term used to describe parents or ancestors.

NOTES

Introduction

1. A department is a national subdivision, similar to a province in Canada or a state in Mexico or the United States.

2. Santos had been awarded the Nobel Peace Prize three months earlier on December 10, 2016, in recognition of his achievement of brokering peace with the Revolutionary Armed Forces of Colombia (FARC).

3. For Santos's speech inside the aqueduct facility, see www.youtube.com/watch?v =9ZTpHzHzHcY.

4. Based on data from the Entity of Mining and Energy Planning (UPME 2012:44).

5. The average annual gold price rose from 872 USD per ounce in 2008 to 1,669 USD per ounce in 2012 (UMPE 2012:55). This was largely the result of the financial credit crisis, spurring the demand for value-stable precious metals.

6. Chocó's registered production rose from 3,340 kilograms in 2008 to 27,915 in 2011, only to fall a bit in 2012 to 24,438, losing its position of primary gold producer to the department of Antioquia (UPME 2012:49). One should note, though, that because of widespread royalty fraud, registered production rates deviate strongly from actual production levels (Tubb 2020).

7. My calculation based on official data (UPME 2018:147).

8. The average gold price in 2017 was estimated at 1,257.11 USD per ounce (UPME 2018:159), a decrease of roughly 25 percent compared with the price in 2012.

9. For clear examples of such reporting, see *El Tiempo* (2015), *France 24* (2023), *Miami Herald* (2018), and *Semana* (2015a, 2015c, 2018).

10. Already in 1994, David Nugent (1994:333) identified this "oppositional model of state-society relations." In an effort to challenge the mainstream assumption of states locking horns with recalcitrant local communities, he showed how in Peru projects of state centralization were enabled by the organizational activities of rural populations.

11. In this regard, my analysis takes inspiration from the monographs of Marina Welker (2014) and Alex Golub (2014). Their books have argued in the cases of Indonesia and Papua New Guinea, respectively, that what at first glance appear to be monolithic mining companies are actually complex networked systems, whose distinctness from local bureaucracies and communities is hard to discern on the ground. However, the assemblage on which I focus is not the corporation but the state. Thus, while Welker is interested in how "people enact corporations in multiple ways" (2014:1), and Golub in how the abstractions of "the mine" and "the Ipili" (an ethnic group in Papua New Guinea) come "to appear unproblematically as actors" (2014:3), I am mostly concerned with the "enactment" (Welker 2014) of statehood, and on that basis, with the maintenance and disruption of the symbolic boundaries between state and community.

12. Well-known texts in this literature include the monographs of Jeremy Campbell (2015), Kregg Hetherington (2020), Yael Navaro-Yashin (2002), and Monique Nuijten (2003), as well as

the volumes edited by Veena Das and Deborah Poole (2004) and Thomas Blom Hansen and Finn Stepputat (2001, 2005).

13. For illustrative examples of this argument, see Ferguson and Gupta (2002), Harvey (2005), and Navaro-Yashin (2002).

14. In more dramatic accounts, this has led to extraction zones being designated as ungoverned spaces that are "in some ways comparable to the wild west" (Hoogbergen and Kruijt 2004:3).

15. Writing on Indonesia, Nancy Peluso (2018:400–401) observes that "even scholars sympathetic to small-scale mining . . . rarely analyze the governing effects of small-scale gold mining that miners and their variously situated communities produce through territorialization, that is, making the above- and underground spaces into territories within resource frontiers."

16. In a brilliant monograph, María Clemencia Ramírez (2011) describes how coca growers in the Colombian Amazon feel misrecognized by a government that stigmatizes them as guerrilla collaborators and destroys their crops through aerial fumigation. Rather than sheer victims, the *cocaleros* of Ramírez's book actively contest their political exclusion. In daily conversations, they describe coca as a legit choice in a context of state abandonment. In public statements, they stress their virtues as citizens by listing their economic contributions. And in protest marches, they mobilize for government investments in alternative economies. The political context that Ramírez narrates strikes a cunning resemblance to that of small-scale mining. Indeed, I have been asked numerous times to what extent my story about gold is also the story of coca. The armed groups, the government-led destruction of livelihoods, the rural workers being stereotyped as criminals, the workers' own counternarratives of self-development and abandonment; these are all undeniable points of connection. But particularities matter. Given the greater legal ambiguity of gold vis-à-vis coca, I feel the comparison only stretches so far. This is because miners' political critiques stress not only their own moral status as contributing citizens, but also the (potential) legality of their economy. In particular, their political demands center less on economic alternatives than on the legalization of their mines (Chapter 7). Similarly, their performances of legal symbols in yet-to-be-legalized mines (Chapter 3) are arguably more difficult to imagine for coca labs, where formalization has so far not been possible.

17. For geographical examples, see Bebbington and Bury (2013) and Bakker and Bridge (2006). For anthropological examples, see Anand (2017), Li (2015), Lyons (2016), Ruiz-Serna (2023), and—with a specific focus on the underground—Luning (2022).

18. As for the intersection of the state and the underground, Bebbington and Bury (2013:11) give three reasons why political ecologies of subsoil resources offer a rewarding vantage point to look at state power: "the geographical fixity of minerals and hydrocarbons" in specific state territories; the close association between subterranean resources and ideas about sovereignty and nationhood; and the fact that ownership of the subsoil is almost always vested in the state.

19. For example, see Wade (1999) on Colombia, Gustafson (2002) and Postero (2007) on Bolivia, Richards (2010) on Chile, and Muehlmann (2009) on Mexico.

20. With regard to Afro-Colombian legislation in particular, Marta Isabel Domínguez Mejía (2017:77–121) argues that the understanding of Law 70 as a state instrument for territorial control bypasses the crucial role that community representatives from the Pacific littoral have played in the elaboration of this law.

21. As in the census conducted by the Ministry of Culture (Ministerio de Cultura 2019:4).

22. As calculated by DANE (2022:5). For 2021, only the department of La Guajira (67.4) surpassed Chocó's percentage.

23. On several occasions, I have heard people from outside Chocó compare the department to Africa. The trope echoes an anecdote by Nobel Prize–winning novelist Gabriel García Márquez, who traveled to Quibdó in 1954 while working as a journalist and described the city as resembling "an African capital" (see https://www.comitecivicochoco.org/2020/09/garcia-marquez-mi-visita-al-choco-en.html, accessed August 24, 2023).

24. The San Juan is Chocó's second largest river, which (like the Atrato) rises in the Andes and (unlike the Atrato) winds its way to the southwest, where it flows into the Pacific Ocean. Chocó's third important river is the Baudó, whose spring lies in the Serranía del Baudó coastal mountain range and whose basin has no gold.

25. Colombian historian Claudia Leal (2018:33) writes that while in the early seventeenth century the Indigenous population in the upper parts of the Atrato and San Juan may have been as high as 35,000, it was estimated at only 3,850 people in 1867.

26. Anthropologist Michael Taussig (2004:x) notes that Bogotá's much-revered Gold Museum speaks in no way whatsoever about the Black bodies on which the colonial gold economy was built: "The museum is silent as to the fact that for more than three centuries of Spanish occupation what the colony stood for and depended upon was the labor of slaves from Africa in the gold mines."

27. Leal (2018) suggests that the Colombian Pacific is most likely the only place in the Americas where self-purchase entailed the largest percentage of Black manumissions. She lists several environmental reasons for this: the absence of an open frontier (such as in the Amazon) that could facilitate permanent flight and the creation of maroon communities; the presence of gold that enabled enslaved people to save up for their freedom; and the tropical climate that dissuaded white mine owners from settling in the Pacific, leading to weaker control over the mines and a compromised power position, making them more susceptible to grant the option of self-purchase to enslaved miners.

28. Yet as chocoano historian Sergio Mosquera (2002) reveals, Africans and their descendants protested their subjugation in myriad ways, such as slowing down production, washing gold in secret, and engaging in open acts of individual and collective rebellion.

29. Much of what I know about the Chocó Pacífico is from listening to and reading the insightful stories of historian Ann Farnsworth-Alvear. For excellent accounts on the Chocó Pacífico, see also Leal (2018:129–151) and Varela Corredor (2013).

30. For example, it was not until 1944 that one of the two trails that connected Chocó to the interior could be used for road transportation (Leal 2018:197).

31. At the end of 2018, Colombia had accumulated 7.7 million internally displaced persons, by then the highest number of any country in the world.

32. These numbers are based on information found on July 24, 2023, on the webpage of the Unidad de Víctimas: https://www.unidadvictimas.gov.co/es/registro-unico-de-victimas-ruv /37394. Two of the numerous atrocities that have scarred the department particularly stand out: Operation Genesis in 1997, a military/paramilitary campaign against FARC guerrillas that led to the displacement of more than 15,000 people; and the 2022 Bellavista massacre, when amid an armed confrontation between FARC guerrillas and paramilitaries of the United Self-Defense Forces of Colombia, a FARC gas cylinder bomb destroyed a church, killing approximately 119 people who were sheltering inside it.

33. Also known as the Gulf Clan.

34. This quote was attributed to Alberto Carrasquilla, minister of Finance under the presidencies of Uribe and Duque (see *Telesur* 2018).

35. Thus, in most mines, ethnography took on the sheer form of observing and talking. With larger mines, this decision was not just based on my own corporeal limitations. It took me little time in Chocó to abandon the idea of active participation in excavator mining, due to the physically demanding, technically sophisticated, and, most of all, criminalized nature of this activity.

36. For these publications, see *Las2orillas* (2017, 2018) and *Verdad Abierta* (2018). Another idea that community leaders proposed about my participation in village life had nothing to do with my ethnographic work. In Caliche and La Peña, I taught English courses for high school students, to which the juntas directivas were kind enough to contribute the physical infrastructure (buildings, tables, chairs, whiteboards) and accreditation (diplomas adorned with community council logos and leaders' signatures).

37. For similar motives of spatial camouflage, I do not reveal whether miners, in addition to gold, also mined platinum, since this second metal can only be found in certain mining zones.

38. For instance, this is the case with the village of San Miguel and the river of Bebará. The story of San Miguel's community dredge (Chapter 2) is one of a kind, whereas Bebará's history of FARC-assisted mining organization (Chapters 4 and 7) is only analogous to that of the neighboring Bebaramá River—affording a sample size of two rivers, hardly big enough to be tackled by fictional nomenclature. Seeing as the peculiarities of San Miguel and Bebará are well-known among public institutions, my writing does not expose or incriminate these places. The San Miguel dredge was a Chamber of Commerce–registered mine that, regardless of its failed attempts at formalization (including a visit by two community leaders to the Colombian Congress), was blown up by public forces on June 22, 2017. The organizational practices of Bebará have already been documented by local media (*Radio Macondo* 2016), while the river's community leaders have extensively lobbied their mining economy with central state emissaries and, for the purpose of a formalization pilot, have repeatedly welcomed state and civil society representatives to their mines (CIRDI 2017:74; Ministerio de Ambiente y Desarrollo Sostenible 2017).

Chapter 1

1. Between the early 1990s and the late 2000s, Latin America's share in global mineral investment increased from 12 to 30 percent (Lust 2014:193). In the 1990s alone, mineral investment skyrocketed by 300 percent, turning Latin America into the world's largest recipient of exploration capital (Dougherty 2011:406).

2. While "barequeros" is often used to describe miners active in the bareque, the term can also, especially in other parts of Colombia, refer to artisanal gold panners more broadly, including those who work in streambeds without the assistance of excavators (work that in Chocó is known as *mazamorreo*).

3. On the ambivalent temporality of resource frontiers, see also Anna Tsing (2005:27–54).

4. While cooks and operators received fixed returns on their cooking and driving, the rest of the workforce shared a percentage of the mine's profit (often a collective 8 percent). Paying out in percentages allowed dueños to pass the risks of unproductive mines on to the workers, whereas the percentage agreement favored workers in the case of profitable production. Of course, gold booms have their own system of justice. Workers told me that astute dueños switch to paying fixed sums if a lucky gold spell turns out to be a prolonged one.

5. Human intoxication through fish consumption is largely because of a biochemical process called mercury methylation: Smaller contaminated fish and organisms are eaten by larger ones, and in the process mercury evolves from an inactive to a toxic state.

6. Exceptions exist. A number of anthropological studies have shown that Indigenous and Afro-descendant populations living near extraction projects fail to adhere to their popular portrayal as helpless victims of extraction. These studies make visible that extraction-affected communities find joy and meaning in their lives despite the environmental pathologies of mines and oil wells, and may accept some of the benefits that extraction has for accomplishing their life goals (Cepek 2018; Golub 2014; Jacka 2015; Tubb 2020; Welker 2014).

7. The castellano was a colonial gold measurement that continues to be employed in Chocó.

8. *Guagua* is the chocoano term for a paca (a large rodent).

9. "Viejos" means "old ones." The term has a strong family connotation and commonly refers to parents or older-generation ancestors.

10. A similar observation has been made by anthropologist Peter Wade (1993:139), who contends that the labor-absorbing potential of this mining technique renders it a "collective insurance system run on a kinship basis."

11. Elsewhere (Jonkman 2022), I analyze in more detail the value system of artisanal gold mines, describing them as examples of what Anna Tsing (2015:63) terms "pericapitalist" sites: economic spaces that are "simultaneously inside and outside capitalism," as the noncapitalist value forms that emerge there help create marketable commodities.

12. Parallels can be drawn with other small-scale economies. For example, in her ethnographic analysis of matsutake mushroom pickers in Oregon, Tsing (2015:77) writes that "Matsutake picking is 'searching.' It is looking for your fortune, not doing your job."

Chapter 2

1. State forces dismantle mining equipment by blowing it up with explosives. However, miners often invoked the word "burnings" (*quemas*) to refer to such explosions, while describing the action of destroying machinery as "burning" (*quemando*) machinery. Loyal to their prose, I also use "blowing up" and "burning (down)" interchangeably.

2. For example, María Clemencia Ramírez (2011) historicizes the emergence of a social movement of coca growers in the Colombian Amazon. She maintains that the movement developed in response to a three-pronged marginalization by the Colombian state, consisting of institutional abandonment, the stigmatization of farmers as lawless, and the eradication of their coca crops. In a somewhat different vein, Diana Ojeda (2012) shows how "neoliberal conservation" on Colombia's Caribbean coast contributed to the dispossession of "not-green-enough" subjects. She shows how public and private stakeholders in an ecotourism project legitimized the forced eviction of fishermen, transporters, and peasants by typecasting them as nonsustainable "bodies out of place" (364).

3. Ann Farnsworth-Alvear has made me see that mining dredges come in many different forms. Unlike the contemporary "Brazilian" dredges, which use a large suction crane for extraction, the Chocó Pacífico dredges operated through a bucket-line system that scraped sediment from the river's bedrock.

4. Michael Taussig (2004:159–165) writes more extensively on cement as a metaphor for modernity in the Colombian Pacific. He writes that in the town of Guapi, "cement buildings stand out as signs of the modern and the good" (162).

5. A prison in Bogotá.

6. Smaller miners, who had lower chances of getting "burned" (those working in tunnels or with pumps and small dredges), tended to continue working during the police actions. However, some of these miners did pause their operations as a precautionary measure. In fact, there were several occasions when low-tech mining equipment was seized by local police for being operated without the necessary licenses.

7. That same day, these and other miners discussed a recent visit by two army "bosses," who had shown up in the La Peña woods to take coordinates and photos of excavator mines for a pending eradication mission. Apparently, the retreros had negotiated a bribe with the two soldiers, in order for the latter not to pass on the information about their mines to their superiors tasked with the planning of the destruction operations. While I cannot confirm the veracity of the story, it does provide some context to the skepticism of Édgar and Rubén (and of other miners that day) as to why the army was unlikely to protect them—or at least, to do so free of charge.

Chapter 3

1. Although Nuijten's analysis is about hope, it does deal with fear. She writes: "We could even argue that what gives the machine coherence are the enjoyments and pleasures, *fears* and expectations it produces. It becomes a 'desiring-machine' . . ." (Nuijten 2003:120–121, my emphasis). Fear,

here, seems part of a wider set of "desiring" effects (i.e., enjoyments, pleasures, expectations) caused by bureaucratic impression management, which jointly help explain people's belief in government effectiveness and hope for formal solutions. Nonetheless, Nuijten does not theorize much how people's fears may be linked to *actually* effective (and oppressive) government interventions, nor how these fear-inciting interventions may disparage, rather than generate, hope for the state apparatus.

2. As dictated by Resolution 40103 of 2017.

3. As established in Article 2 of the decree. This requirement came on top of the earlier decreed obligations of miners to be inscribed in the registers of the National Mining Agency and the Colombian tax authority.

4. As established in Article 4.

5. In mentioning the "difference of 50,000" pesos, Breiner referred to the approximate price margin per castellano (4.6 grams) that existed between selling legally and selling to unauthorized aventureros.

6. DIAN (Dirección de Impuestos y Aduanas Nacionales [National Directorate of Taxes and Customs]) is the Colombian tax authority. IVA (Impuesto al Valor Agregado [Tax of Added Value]) is the 19 percent tax Colombians pay on their purchases.

7. Poole (2004) discusses this slippage in her analysis on Peruvian statecraft. She proposes that "fluttering, unread, arbitrary, and shifting forms of paperwork" levy the ambiguous and unstable force of state law on subjects of governance (36). As a means of illustration, she recounts how at the height of the Peruvian civil war in the 1980s, the reading of ID cards at military checkpoints engendered great uncertainties for peasants. Insofar as "a lack of documents was the most common reason for detention and . . . documents were often willfully misread," Poole notices that "a personal identity card was simultaneously a peasant's only guarantee and his source of greatest vulnerability to the arbitrary power of the state" (36).

8. RUT stands for Registro Único Tributario (Unique Tax Registry), which is the Colombian taxpayer identification number.

Chapter 4

1. Overall, there were no notable socioeconomic differences between junta representatives and other community members. A lot of leaders had been born into or were still living in mining households—particularly the ones leading smaller community councils. However, leaders of larger councils—especially those occupying the important positions—were more likely than their fellow villagers to hold higher-education qualifications or to be active in better-paid professions in Quibdó. Their higher social mobility often coincided with their being comparatively well versed in the content of Law 70, well connected to people working in local state entities, and well prepared (professionally speaking) to carry out administrative junta duties. Yet what perhaps stuck out most in the demographic makeup of juntas directivas was gender, as men generally held more positions, and more important positions, than women (irrespective of the size of the community council).

2. Both lower and upper juntas directivas are voted in for a period of three years. Usually, voters must choose one of two competing parties, which will have internally distributed the leadership roles to which they aspire. Nonetheless, in lower junta elections voters might also directly elect individuals to fulfil specific functions. The scale of the community council also affects who is voting. Lower juntas are voted in by the entire constituency, whereas upper juntas are commonly chosen by delegates from the lower juntas.

3. Outside Chocó, another great example of resistance is Francia Márquez, who won the Goldman Environmental Prize in 2018 for standing up against excavator miners invading the ancestral lands of her community (La Toma, located in Colombia's southwestern department of

Cauca). Márquez's activism included leading a ten-day march to Bogotá to demand government intervention, and has led to her receiving death threats and becoming displaced. In August 2022, she became vice-president of Colombia, the first Black woman elected to this position.

4. As established by Decree 2613 of 2013.

5. As established by Article 7 of Law 70.

6. As established by Decree 1745 of 1995.

7. For the sake of clarification: This La Peña on the Bebará River is not the "La Peña" (a pseudonym) that I describe in other parts of this book (most notably Chapter 5).

8. The 2018 elections for the FARC proved disastrous. They obtained only 0.34 percent of votes for the Senate and 0.21 percent for the House of Representatives. However, Israel Zúñiga did enter the Senate, occupying one of the five seats that had been guaranteed to the FARC as part of the Havana accords. This, after FARC heavyweight Iván Márquez had given up his seat and abandoned the peace process. Several opinionmakers criticized the congressional status of Zúñiga because of his past. In 2010, before receiving amnesty through the Havana peace deal, he had been sentenced to thirty-six-and-a-half years in prison for the notorious 2002 massacre of Bellavista caused by the FARC (in Chocó's Bojayá municipality, not too far north from the Bebará River; see also note 32 of the Introduction).

9. The 2001 mining code understands *barequeo* (i.e., bareque) as "the washing of sediments in a manual way without the help of machinery or mechanical means" (Congreso de Colombia 2001: Art. 155). Bebareño barequeros do not fit this description, since their manual labor rests on mechanical excavators moving tons of earth.

Chapter 5

1. The leaders also emphasized this message of transparency to non–community members such as excavator miners and myself, both of whom were invited to larger meetings. In fact, during my first get-together with the La Peña junta, they underlined their politics of "no secrets" when explaining that I was welcome to participate in many community council activities.

2. In Caliche, this relinquishment of environmental administration took a similar form. I once discussed with the junta directiva's legal representative the environmental havoc wreaked by a particular retrero. As the latter completely disregarded the territorial rules of the community council, I asked the legal representative why the miner did not face any penal repercussion. "*Jesser*, what do you want me to do?" he replied. "Here we have a secretary whom we have to pay 300,000 [pesos per month] and we don't have a single source of income. We need those excavators."

Chapter 6

1. In Colombia, "rebusque" refers to unstable income often derived from informal activities. For a discussion on rebusque in regard to mining in Chocó, see Daniel Tubb (2020).

2. For more detailed analyses on the relationship between decentralization and pacification, see Ballvé (2012) and Eaton (2006). Apart from the pacification rationale, other factors that explain Colombian decentralization include desires of technocrats to increase government efficiency (Eaton 2006:541); pressures from multilateral agencies to adopt decentralization reforms; civil society demands for improved public services; and previous changes in the political system that had strengthened the power position of local actors vis-à-vis the central government (Gutiérrez Sanín 2010:17–25).

3. An exception is Teo Ballvé's (2012) analysis of decentralization in Urabá, which criticizes the proposition of state failure and has influenced the argument I present here.

4. María Clemencia Ramírez and Victoria Sanford have expressed like-minded concerns. Ramírez (2015) highlights that nowhere in Colombia does one find the idealized impartial state that is claimed to be absent from the periphery. The narrative "is shown to be a projection that seeks to naturalize a particular national project of rule," cementing the hegemonic belief that sovereignty must be reestablished within certain regions (36). Similarly, Sanford (2004) notices that in areas over which the Colombian state claims to have little control, it exercises "its centralized power through the use of violence and surveillance" (256), often by means of proxy paramilitary forces.

5. Jacobo Grajales (2013) makes a similar argument. Describing roughly the same region and the same problematics as Ballvé, Grajales maintains that "crime and violence are constitutive of political competition, accumulation and economic development" (212). He sustains this argument by showing how "agribusiness-related lands grabs in the Lower Atrato Valley" (211) became legally ratified through statutory categories, namely title deeds and usufruct contracts.

6. One result of this job-for-vote exchange was that most municipal positions were filled by people who elected the winning party. However, voters were many and vacant offices were few. Consequently, during the four-year administrative term, workers rotated positions with fellow supporters of the mayor. The most likely to get in were those who had partaken in the *grupo de trabajo* ("working group"), which is the entourage of a mayoral candidate that goes from village to village, and door to door, to collect votes.

7. Given such risk-taking, candidates resorted to different strategies to ensure that voters complied with their voting promise on Election Day—especially if they were "pre-paid" voters who had less to gain from the election and were more susceptible to receiving benefits from various candidates. One aspiring mayor outlined two surveillance mechanisms: obliging voters to cast their ballot in the presence of an escort assigned by the candidate; and buying off the electoral witness (the person in charge of verifying that no voting irregularities occur). Regarding the latter, he said: "We vote in cubicles. So, we have to vote in a cubicle where the electoral witness can see who you're voting for. If you vote in secret [in a cubicle where the electoral witness cannot see your ticket], it's like you haven't voted."

8. Therefore, what is registered as gold sourced from manual and licensed mines may well be mixed up with metal of more dubious provenance. A recent calculation of the Colombian comptroller's office suggests that 85 percent of Colombian exported gold has illegal provenance (Contraloría 2022). However, it's not just the governing practices of state bureaucrats that must confront the underground's illegibility. As Chapter 5 set out, the elusiveness of subterranean gold also allows miners to downplay their production to community leaders.

9. Such fraud has occurred in the construction of roads (*El Espectador* 2017; *La Silla Vacía* 2017), health infrastructure (*El Colombiano* 2018; *Semana* 2015b), and sporting facilities (*Las2orillas* 2016). Mayors, in particular, have been targeted by the Colombian Treasury Inspector for public mismanagement, resulting in several cases in detention (for examples, see *Blu Radio* 2016, Contraloría 2018, Fiscalía 2018, *RCN* 2018).

10. Although the conflict was about a tax for "environmental compensation," the fate of the forest was secondary in the conflict. After Camilo's departure from Santa Teresa, Amed and I visited his former mine. We witnessed giant pools of water, creeks blocked by timber, and not a single planted tree. The devastation, however, did not give way to any sort of punishment for Camilo from the municipal administration.

11. Most notably, in 2017, the comptroller's office issued a critical report about CODECHOCO and its failure to curtail the proliferation of illegal mining (Contraloría 2017).

12. In 2019, the Colombian public attorney's office ordered the capture of Isaías Chala, Quibdó's mayor, for alleged fraud in the construction of a medical facility (*La Silla Vacía* 2019).

13. During later fieldwork trips in 2022 and 2023, a mining engineer who had worked for various government agencies mentioned several other canalization dredges that according to him were cover-ups for mining. Also, in these same fieldwork visits, interviewees who were

(previously) active as public servants explained that such canalization fraud had historical prece-dent. During the mining boom, around 2010, CODECHOCO had apparently confiscated illegal mining machinery, which they then donated to acquainted mayors or juntas directivas (here in-terviewees disagreed) for the legit purpose of environmental management. However, according to the interviewees, the real motive behind the seizure was to use the machinery for mining.

Chapter 7

1. The Ministry of Mines and Energy has, besides its minister, two auxiliary vice-ministers, one of Mines and one of Energy.

2. As taken from a speech by former president Santos (*El Espectador* 2012).

3. Ministry of Defense employee Rodrigo was not the only interviewee making this assess-ment. For example, the director of UNIMIL—the police unit tasked with destroying mines—commented in an interview: "That it [mining] is illicit is less important. It's how they do it! It's the way they contaminate, while talking about their famous formalization, that they don't know anything else and that the state does not give them anything. That doesn't justify the damage they inflict on humanity! Not just on Colombia, on humanity!"

4. As quoted from a newspaper column by Silvana Habib, president of the National Mining Agency from 2015 until 2020 (*El Espectador* 2016).

5. On the multiplier effects of small-scale gold mining, see also MacMillan (1995:162–163) and Siegel and Veiga (2009).

6. For example, in 2015, the Ministry of Mines and Energy decreed that small-scale miners could request the consultancy of the National Mining Agency, which would advise them on de-forestation, accounting, social security, and contracted labor. The decree, however, was explic-itly targeted at titled miners. In 2016, the same ministry entered into an agreement with the Agrarian Bank of Colombia with the purpose of offering low-interest loans to miners hoping to modernize their equipment. The beneficiaries were titled miners.

7. At several moments, mining firms publicly urged the Colombian government to raise its game in expelling "illegal miners" (e.g., *Reuters* 2021), with one company even going so far as to file a free-trade lawsuit of 700 million USD against Colombia for the failure to combat illegal ex-traction (*Financial Post* 2017).

8. By this same token, CIRDI representatives, who had entered the project at a later date, explained in a community meeting that they had joined the pilot program because of the "ex-ceptional organizational capacities" of the local community councils.

9. Each of the community leaderships of Bebará and Bebaramá had applied at the National Mining Agency for "traditional mining" reserves, which would help them to request mining ti-tles. Although two such reserves were indeed allocated on the Bebará shore, the bebareños re-mained—at least until my last visit to Chocó in January 2023—unsuccessful in transforming these into mining titles (on the difficulties of "traditional" miners in acquiring titles, see also this chap-ter's section "Permitted Miners").

10. Subcontracting arrangements could take two forms: *contratos de operación* ["operation contracts"] and *subcontratos de formalización* ["formalization subcontracts"]. The former did not require the mediation of the National Mining Agency; the latter did. With contratos de oper-ación, the titleholder (i.e., mining company) remained in charge of getting licenses, as well as the processing and commercialization of the produced bullion. With subcontratos de formal-ización, on the other hand, small-scale miners themselves were juridically responsible for com-plying with formal protocols, and had more freedom to commercialize their gold as a consequence. This freedom wasn't cheap. Mining leaders told me that in the second scenario, companies still retained a percentage of the extracted gold, which could be as a high as 60 percent.

11. Elevadora literally means "elevator" and refers to pump-mining techniques like Ignacio's, whereby sediments from a pit are suctioned up through rubber tubes and washed with a water hose in higher-up ("elevated") spots.

12. See Álvarez (2016), Pardo Becerra (2013), and Siegel (2013) for this type of analysis for Colombia; see Banchirigah (2007), Damonte (2016), and Hilson and Maconachie (2020) on cases outside Colombia.

13. Data collected from https://www.anm.gov.co/?q=content/%C3%A1reas-de-reserva -especial-declaradas-y-delimitadas-0 (accessed March 2, 2022).

14. For example, see the definition of "traditional mining" in Resolution 40599 of 2015 of the Ministry of Mines and Energy. While describing traditional mining as something that "has been carried out since before the validity of Law 685 of 2001 [the mining code]," and as being conducted by people with "socioeconomic characteristics," the resolution does not elaborate on working techniques (Ministerio de Minas y Energía 2015).

15. This reading was reiterated to me by the agency's Development Coordinator in 2019. Yet as Colombian mining leaders pointed out to me in interviews, this second (nonmechanized) defi-nition of traditional mining renders the ARE's "exploitation prerogative" a somewhat paper benefit, because hand-based techniques were already condoned in Colombia before the ARE be-came regulated.

16. While the ARE's institutionalization happened in the aftermath of the miners' strike, the mining reserve had already been mentioned by the 2001 mining code (Congreso de Colombia 2001: Art. 248, 249).

17. Regarding Colombia, ethnographic studies have specifically scrutinized the perverse sym-biosis that exists between neoliberal restructuring and the armed conflict. While discerning "a larger project of militaristic neoliberalism" (Meger and Sachseder 2020), a development model of "securitisation by dispossession" (Rojas 2009), or an alliance between "paramilitarism and neo-liberalism" (Hristov 2014), much of such scholarship observes that violence by paramilitary and state forces paves the way for extractive and agribusiness industries.

18. This prohibition came from the code's Article 160 (Congreso de Colombia 2001). I know one miner who was indeed detained while working with their mechanical pump within an ARE.

19. The National Mining Agency did provide an exploration study, but, as a former Develop-ment Coordinator of the agency himself admitted to me, this study only provided miners with a "conceptual study" and not with the detailed geological examination needed for a PTO.

20. Effectively, Oro Legal staff argued in a final project report that obtaining an environ-mental license would be an arduous process without their assistance: "It is difficult to imagine how most small miners could undertake this process alone, which is probably the single, most significant barrier to expanding ASGM [artisanal and small-scale gold mining] legalization/ formalization" (USAID 2021:17).

21. This shows that the politics of permittance reached back a long way. Already in 2001, the mining code's Article 155 dictated that manual mining "shall be permitted" (Congreso de Co-lombia 2001). Corporate subcontracts, promoted since the early 2010s, were another clear exam-ple. In fostering community–corporate alliances, subcontracting endorsed the formalization of traditional miners, while at the same time enabling mining companies to retain control over most minerals. As former vice-minister of Mines Henry Medina explained: "This model makes sure that traditional miners can trust the company who has the title and that the companies hand over a little bit of yields in order to work with local communities. It's a win–win strategy for both" (La Silla Vacía 2012).

22. Such assistance brings to mind what Eric Hirsch (2022) calls "extractive care," by which he alludes to the furthering of extractive capitalism through biopolitical interventions that are presented as caring and nurturing.

23. In one interview outside Chocó, a mining leader cum former gold buyer from Antioquia specifically called out this discourse of subsistence. "Those AREs are good for nothing. They are created for whom they call 'subsistence miners.' We are against this discourse. It implies that you have to continue the way you are for the rest of your life, that you cannot progress economically, cannot have your own company, cannot send your children to the university, cannot leave poverty."

24. The appraisal of small-scale mining as a noncapitalized activity is not restricted to bureaucrats. In their analysis on "fair-trade and fair-mined" gold, Sabine Luning and Marjo de Theije (2014) bring up the case of Oro Verde, a development initiative that started in 1999 and promoted responsible mining practices in Chocó. Luning and de Theije note that the website of Solidaridad, a Dutch NGO linked to Oro Verde, presents eye-pleasing images of a small artisanal mine and omits the social context in which this mine is embedded. The authors caution that the website's "one-dimensional message" of "small is beautiful" (66) risks "confining [artisanal operators] to scales of operation and techniques that may be good for the environment, but bad in terms of the arduous working practices and limited revenues endured by the miners" (69).

25. For similar comments of praise by private sector representatives, see https://anglogoldashanticolombia.com/anglogold-ashanti-reitera-su-compromiso-con-proceso-de-formalizacion-en-san-roque/2079/ (May 23, 2019); https://acmineria.com.co/formalizacion-la-veta-del-progreso-para-miles-de-familias-mineras/ (June 18, 2019).

Conclusion

1. But see also Campbell (2015), Ferguson (2009), Nugent (1994), and Nuijten (2003) for eloquent rebuttals of this narrative.

2. Elsewhere, I delve deeper into the ontological frictions between formal legal frameworks and miners, especially in relation to epistemes of nature (Jonkman forthcoming).

3. My approach derives inspiration from anthropologists who have argued that ethnographic practice and writing should reflect the messiness of the social world that it claims to portray (Hetherington 2020; Law 2004).

4. The NGO Frontline Defenders (2023:9) registered that 186 Colombian human rights defenders were killed in 2022 alone, comprising 46 percent of the total number of assassinations worldwide.

5. Located far away from most of Chocó's mines, the Colombian-Panamanian border region is also known as the Darién Gap. In recent years, increasing numbers of Latin Americans, Caribbeans, Africans, and others have risked their lives trekking through this strip of rainforest in their efforts to escape poverty and conflict. In 2023, roughly 520,085 people undertook the perilous journey, a steep increase from the estimated 22,102 and 6,465 people who crossed the region in respectively 2019 and 2020 (*New Humanitarian* 2024). Besides being subjected to dangerous ecological conditions—the Darién Gap is an isolated jungle region—refugees are highly vulnerable to the violence of armed gangs, especially sexual assault (*Guardian* 2024).

6. For more on Francia Márquez, see also note 3 of Chapter 4.

7. The Oro Verde initiative mentioned in note 24 of Chapter 7 worked according to a similar scheme, offering artisanal miners from the municipalities of Tadó and Condoto a premium for their gold.

8. Achiote is a red-orange seed used as a condiment and colorant in food.

9. In the final project report, Oro Legal staff was quite frank about the challenges of establishing a sustainable value chain of achiote. The report raised concerns about, among other things, remote production locations, Chocó's apparent lack of "good governance," the COVID-19

pandemic, and the overall high failure risk of projects of value chain development (USAID 2021:49–50). The concerns were valid in retrospect. Speaking to a former Oro Legal representative in 2023, I learned that the achiote value chain had failed. Supply outgrew demand, and gold pulled people back to the mines: "Many [achiote gardens] are no longer in production. It took too long to find a market and in the meantime the price of gold went up, so people spent all their time mining."

10. A development practitioner who worked in another "alternative economies" project answered this question in the negative. His reason, though, had less to do with market access than with an essentialist notion of culture. "I say that these projects of 'alternative economies' will always fail. There was this project of cacao in Chocó. People would grow cacao instead of mining. It didn't work. . . . It's the culture of the people. They're extractivists."

BIBLIOGRAPHY

Abrams, Philip. 1988[1977]. "Notes on the Difficulty of Studying the State." *Journal of Historical Sociology* 1 (1):58–89.

Agencia Nacional de Minería. 2018. *Areas de Reserva Especial: ARE.* Electronic document. Accessed August 22, 2023. www.anm.gov.co/sites/default/files/DocumentosAnm/ares.pdf.

Álvarez, Juan Diego. 2016. "Governing Mining Resources in the History of Colombia: Between Official Institutions and Resistance." *Law and Development Review* 9 (1):29–67.

Anand, Nikhil. 2017. *Hydraulic City: Water and the Infrastructures of Citizenship in Mumbai.* Durham: Duke University Press.

Anthias, Penelope. 2014. *The Elusive Promise of Territory: An Ethnographic Case Study of Indigenous Land Titling in the Bolivian Chaco.* PhD dissertation. University of Cambridge.

Anthias, Penelope, and Sara A. Radcliffe. 2015. "The Ethno-Environmental Fix and Its Limits: Indigenous Land Titling and the Production of Not-Quite-Neoliberal Natures in Bolivia." *Geoforum* 64:257–269.

Appel, Hannah. 2019. *The Licit Life of Capitalism: US Oil in Equatorial Guinea.* Durham: Duke University Press.

Appelbaum, Nancy P. 2003. *Muddied Waters: Race, Region, and Local History in Colombia, 1846–1948.* Durham: Duke University Press.

Arboleda, Martín. 2020. *Planetary Mine: Territories of Extraction Under Late Capitalism.* London: Verso.

Arias, Enrique Desmond, and Daniel M. Goldstein. 2010. "Violent Pluralism: Understanding the New Democracies of Latin America." In *Violent Democracies in Latin America*, edited by Enrique Desmond Arias and Daniel M. Goldstein, 1–34. Durham: Duke University Press.

Asher, Kiran, and Diana Ojeda. 2009. "Producing Nature and Making the State: Ordenamiento Territorial in the Pacific Lowlands of Colombia." *Geoforum* 40:292–302.

Babidge, Sally. 2018. "Sustaining Ignorance: The Uncertainties of Groundwater and Its Extraction in the Salar de Atacama, Northern Chile." *Journal of the Royal Anthropological Institute* 25:83–102.

Bainton, Nicholas, and Emilia E. Skrzypek (eds.). 2021. *The Absent Presence of the State in Large-Scale Resource Extraction Projects.* Acton: Australia National University Press.

Bakker, Karen, and Gavin Bridge. 2006. "Material Worlds? Resource Geographies and the 'Matter of Nature.'" *Progress in Human Geography* 30 (1):5–27.

Ballvé, Teo. 2012. "Everyday State Formation: Territory, Decentralization, and the Narco Landgrab in Colombia." *Environment and Planning D: Society and Space* 30:603–622.

Banchirigah, Sadia Mohammed. 2007. "How Have Reforms Fueled the Expansion of Artisanal Mining? Evidence from Sub-Saharan Africa." *Resources Policy* 31:165–171.

Bebbington, Anthony, Denise Humphreys Bebbington, Leonith Hinojosa, María-Luisa Burneo, and Jeffrey Bury. 2013. "Anatomies of Conflict: Social Mobilization and New Political Ecologies." In *Subterranean Struggles: New Dynamics of Mining, Oil, and Gas in Latin*

America, edited by Anthony Bebbington and Jeffrey Bury, 241–266. Austin: University of Texas Press.

Bebbington, Anthony, and Jeffrey Bury. 2013. "Political Ecologies of the Subsoil." In *Subterranean Struggles: New Dynamics of Mining, Oil, and Gas in Latin America*, edited by Anthony Bebbington and Jeffrey Bury, 1–25. Austin: University of Texas Press.

Biehl, João. 2005. *Vita: Life in a Zone of Social Abandonment*. Berkeley: University of California Press.

Blu Radio. 2016. *Capturan a la alcaldesa de Bagadó, Chocó*. April 16. Accessed August 18, 2023. https://www.bluradio.com/129220/capturan-la-alcaldesa-de-bagado-choco.

Bocarejo, Diana. 2018. "Thinking with (Il)legality: The Ethics of Living with Bonanzas." *Current Anthropology* 59:S48–S59.

Brysk, Alison, and Carol Wise. 1997. "Liberalization and Ethnic Conflict in Latin America." *Studies in Comparative International Development* 32 (2):76–104.

Burchell, Graham. 1993. "Liberal Government and Techniques of the Self." *Economy and Society* 22 (3):267–283.

Campbell, Jeremy M. 2015. *Conjuring Property: Speculation and Environmental Futures in the Brazilian Amazon*. Seattle: University of Washington Press.

Cárdenas, Roosbelinda. 2012. "Green Multiculturalism: Articulations of Ethnic and Environmental Politics in a Colombian 'Black Community.'" *Journal of Peasant Studies* 39 (2):309–333.

Cepek, Michael L. 2018. *Life in Oil: Cofán Survival in the Petroleum Fields of Amazonia*. Austin: University of Texas Press.

CIRDI. 2017. *Mid-Year Report: For the Period: April 1, 2017–September 30, 2017*. Electronic document. Accessed March 15, 2019. https://cirdi.ca/wp-content/uploads/2017/10/GAC_Mid_Year_RPT_FY2017-18_Rev2_ONLINE.pdf.

Civico, Aldo. 2012. "'We Are Illegal, but Not Illegitimate': Modes of Policing in Medellín, Colombia." *Political and Legal Anthropology Review* 35 (1):77–93.

Cohen, Roseann. 2014. "Extractive Desires: The Moral Control of Female Sexuality at Colombia's Gold Mining Frontier." *Journal of Latin American and Caribbean Anthropology* 19 (2):260–279.

Colloredo-Mansfeld, Rudi. 2007. "The Power of Ecuador's Indigenous Communities in an Era of Cultural Pluralism." *Social Analysis* 51 (2):81–106.

Congreso de Colombia. 1993. *Ley 70 de 1993*. Electronic document. Accessed August 18, 2023. https://www.funcionpublica.gov.co/eva/gestornormativo/norma_pdf.php?i=7388.

———. 2001. *Ley 685 de 2001*. Electronic document. Accessed August 18, 2023. https://www.anm.gov.co/sites/default/files/ley_685_2001_0.pdf.

Contraloría. 2017. *Respuesta de trámite derecho de petición: Denuncia 2017-121717-80274*. Electronic document. Accessed December 21, 2018. https://www.contraloria.gov.co/documents/20181/759938/2017EE0093060+Respuesta+de+tramite+DP+2017-121717-80274-D+CODE CHOCO+.PDF/bc98ae4c-1230-4e40-ac25-37fa95008f2e.

———. 2018. *Capturan al alcalde de Juradó*. July 12. Accessed December 21, 2018. http://contraloria-choco.gov.co/capturan-al-alcalde-de-jurado/.

———. 2022. Un 85 por ciento del oro que exporta Colombia es producto de la minería ilegal, alerta la Contraloría al rendir cuentas del control fiscal sobre medio ambiente. July 28. Accessed August 24, 2023. https://www.contraloria.gov.co/es/w/un-85-por-ciento-del-oro-que-exporta-colombia-es-producto-de-la-miner%C3%ADa-ilegal-alerta-la-contralor%C3%ADa-al-rendir-cuentas-del-control-fiscal-sobre-medio-ambiente.

Cordy, Paul, Marcello M. Veiga, Ibrahim Salih, Sari Al-Saadi, Stephanie Console, Oseas García, Luis Alberto Mesa, Patricio C. Velásquez-López, and Monika Roeser. 2011. "Mercury Contamination from Artisanal Gold Mining in Antioquia, Colombia: The World's Highest per Capita Mercury Pollution." *Science of the Total Environment* 410–411:154–160.

Côte, Muriel, and Benedikt Korf. 2018. "Making Concessions: Extractive Enclaves, Entangled Capitalism and Regulative Pluralism at the Gold Mining Frontier in Burkina Faso." *World Development* 101:466–476.

Coyle Rosen, Lauren. 2020. *Fires of Gold: Law, Spirit, and Sacrificial Labor in Ghana*. Oakland: University of California Press.

d'Avignon, Robyn. 2022. *A Ritual Geology: Gold and Subterranean Knowledge in Savanna West Africa*. Durham: Duke University Press.

Dagnino, Evelina. 2003. "Citizenship in Latin America: An Introduction." *Latin American Perspectives* 30 (2):3–17.

Damonte, Gerardo H. 2016. "The 'Blind' State: Government Quest for Formalization and Conflict with Small-Scale Miners in the Peruvian Amazon." *Antipode* 48 (4):956–976.

DANE. 2022. *Comunicado de prensa: pobreza monetaria año 2021*. April 26. August 24, 2023. https://www.dane.gov.co/files/investigaciones/condiciones_vida/pobreza/2021 /Comunicado-pobreza-monetaria_2021.pdf.

Das, Veena. 2004. "The Signature of the State: The Paradox of Illegibility." In *Anthropology in the Margins*, edited by Veena Das and Deborah Poole, 225–252. Santa Fe: SAR Press.

———. 2011. "State, Citizenship, and the Urban Poor." *Citizenship Studies* 15 (3–4):319–333.

Das, Veena, and Deborah Poole. 2004. "State and Its Margins: Comparative Analyses." In *Anthropology in the Margins*, edited by Veena Das and Deborah Poole, 3–33. Santa Fe: SAR Press.

Davidov, Veronica. 2014. "Land, Copper, Flora: Dominant Materialities and the Making of Ecuadorian Resource Environments." *Anthropological Quarterly* 87 (1):31–58.

de la Cadena, Marisol. 2010. "Indigenous Cosmopolitics in the Andes: Conceptual Reflections Beyond 'Politics.'" *Cultural Anthropology* 25 (2):334–370.

de Theije, Marjo, Judith Kolen, Marieke Heemskerk, Celine Duijves, Mariana Sarmiento, Alexandra Urán, Ingrid Lozada, Helcías Ayala, Jorge Perea, and Armin Mathis. 2014. "Engaging Legal Systems in Small-Scale Gold Mining Conflicts in Three South American Countries." In *Conflicts over Natural Resources in the Global South: Conceptual Approaches*, edited by Maarten Bavinck, Lorenzo Pellegrini, and Erik Mostert, 129–146. London: CRC Press, Taylor & Francis Group.

Doane, Molly. 2012. *Stealing Shining Rivers: Agrarian Conflict, Market Logic, and Conservation in a Mexican Forest*. Tucson: University of Arizona Press.

Domínguez Mejía, Marta Isabel. 2017. *Territorios colectivos: proceso de formación del Estado en el Pacífico colombiano (1993–2009)*. Medellín: Universidad de Antioquia.

Dougherty, Michael L. 2011. "The Global Gold Mining Industry, Junior Firms, and Civil Society Resistance in Guatemala." *Bulletin of Latin American Research* 30 (4):403–418.

Downey, Greg, Monica Dalidowicz, and Paul H. Mason. 2015. "Apprenticeship as Method: Embodied Learning in Ethnographic Practice." *Qualitative Research* 15 (2):183–200.

Eaton, Kent. 2006. "The Downside of Decentralization: Armed Clientelism in Colombia." *Security Studies* 15 (4):533–562.

El Colombiano. 2018. *Investigan exalcaldesa de Quibdó por cargos de corrupción en un hospital*. November 20. Accessed August 18, 2023. http://www.elcolombiano.com/colombia/investigan -exalcaldesa-de-quibdo-por-cargos-de-corrupcion-en-un-hospital-LI9684085.

El Espectador. 2012. *La minería ilegal es "un cáncer que debemos extirpar": Santos*. February 23. Accessed August 18, 2023. https://www.elespectador.com/economia/la-mineria-ilegal-es-un -cancer-que-debemos-extirpar-santos-article-328344/.

———. 2015. *¡Que alguien salve el Atrato!* February 8. Accessed August 18, 2023. https://www .elespectador.com/noticias/medio-ambiente/alguien-salve-el-atrato-articulo-542827.

———. 2016. *Pongámonos el casco por la minería bien hecha*. December 14. Accessed August 18, 2023. https://www.elespectador.com/noticias/medio-ambiente/pongamonos-el-casco-mineria -bien-hecha-articulo-670429.

———. 2017. *Capturan a funcionarios de la Gobernación del Chocó por actos de corrupción.* March 3. Accessed March 11, 2022. https://www.elespectador.com/noticias/judicial/capturan -funcionarios-de-la-gobernacion-del-choco-por-actos-de-corrupcion-articulo-682743.

El Tiempo. 2015. *Nuevos desiertos avanzan detrás de la fiebre del oro.* December 16. Accessed August 18, 2023. https://www.eltiempo.com/archivo/documento/CMS-16460299.

———. 2016. *Gobierno intervendrá mercado del oro para frenar minería ilegal.* July 9. Accessed August 18, 2023. http://www.eltiempo.com/archivo/documento/CMS-16640845.

El Universal. 2021. *Denuncian desplazamiento de 1.227 personas en San Miguel, Chocó.* August 20. Accessed August 18, 2023. https://www.eluniversal.com.co/colombia/denuncian-despla zamiento-de-1227-personas-en-san-miguel-choco-BX5231113.

Escobar, Arturo. 2008. *Territories of Difference: Place, Movements, Life, Redes.* Durham: Duke University Press.

Ferguson, James. 1990. *The Anti-Politics Machine: "Development," Depoliticization, and Bureau-cratic Power in Lesotho.* Cambridge: Cambridge University Press.

———. 2009. "The Uses of Neoliberalism." *Antipode* 41 (1):166–184.

Ferguson, James, and Akhil Gupta. 2002. "Spatializing States: Toward an Ethnography of Neoliberal Governmentality." *American Ethnologist* 29 (4):981–1002.

Financial Post. 2017. *Canada's Gran Colombia Gold Files $700 Million Lawsuit Against Colombia over Marmato Project.* April 10. Accessed August 23, 2023. https://financialpost.com /commodities/mining/canadas-gran-colombia-gold-files-700-million-lawsuit-against -colombia-over-marmato-project?r.

Fiscalía. 2018. *Asegurado alcalde y exsecretario de planeación de San José del Palmar (Chocó).* November 6. Accessed December 21, 2018. www.fiscalia.gov.co/colombia/seccionales /asegurado-alcalde-y-exsecretario-de-planeacion-de-san-jose-del-palmar-choco/.

Fisher, Eleanor. 2008. "Artisanal Gold Mining at the Margins of Mineral Resource Governance: A Case from Tanzania." *Development Southern Africa* 25 (2):199–213.

France 24. 2023. *Colombia's War on Illegal Gold Mines Also Hits Outlaw Armed Groups.* February 3. Accessed August 24, 2023. https://www.france24.com/en/live-news/20230203-colombia -s-war-on-illegal-gold-mines-also-hits-outlaw-armed-groups.

Franco, Isabel B., and Saleem Ali. 2017. "Decentralization, Corporate Community Development, and Resource Governance: A Comparative Analysis of Two Mining Regions in Colombia." *Extractive Industries and Society* 4:111–119.

Frontline Defenders. 2023. *Global Analysis 2022.* Electronic document. Accessed August 24, 2023. https://www.frontlinedefenders.org/sites/default/files/1535_fld_ga23_web.pdf.

García-Villegas, Mauricio, and Javier Eduardo Revelo-Rebolledo. 2010. *Estado alterado: clien-telismo, mafias y debilidad institucional en Colombia.* Bogotá: Ediciones Antropos.

Gill, Lesley. 2007. "'Right There with You': Coca-Cola, Labor Restructuring and Political Vio-lence in Colombia." *Critique of Anthropology* 27 (3):235–260.

Giraldo Ramírez, Jorge. 2013. "El gobierno de oro en el Bajo Cauca: una lectura weberiana sobre la explotación." In *Economía criminal y poder político,* edited by Jorge Giraldo Ramírez, 33–68. Medellín: Universidad EAFIT.

Gledhill, John. 2005. *The New War on the Poor: The Production of Insecurity in Latin America.* London: Zed Books.

Golub, Alex. 2014. *Leviathans at the Gold Mine: Creating Indigenous and Corporate Actors in Papua New Guina.* Durham: Duke University Press.

Grajales, Jacobo. 2013. "State Involvement, Land Grabbing, and Counter-Insurgency in Colom-bia." *Development and Change* 44 (2):211–232.

Greene, Shane. 2007. "Introduction: On Race, Roots/Routes, and Sovereignty in Latin America's Afro-Indigenous Multiculturalisms." *Journal of Latin American and Caribbean Anthropol-ogy* 12 (2):329–355.

Guardian. 2024. "'Deeply Alarming': Sevenfold Increase in Sexual Attacks in Darién Gap, Says MSF." February 5. Accessed February 26, 2024. https://www.theguardian.com/global -development/2024/feb/05/darien-gap-sexual-attacks-panama-colombia-migrants.

Gudynas, Eduardo. 2009. "Diez tesis urgentes sobre el nuevo extractivismo: contextos y demandas bajo el progresismo sudamericano actual." In *Extractivismo, política y sociedad*, 187–225. Quito: CAAP; CLAES.

Güiza, Leonardo, and Juan David Aristizábal. 2013. "Mercury and Gold Mining in Colombia: A Failed State." *Universitas Scientarum* 18 (1):33–49.

Gupta, Akhil. 1995. "Blurred Boundaries: The Discourse of Corruption, the Culture of Politics, and the Imagined State." *American Ethnologist* 22 (2):375–402.

Gustafson, Bret. 2002. "Paradoxes of Liberal Indigenism: Indigenous Movements, State Processes, and Intercultural Reform in Bolivia." In *The Politics of Ethnicity: Indigenous Peoples in Latin American States*, edited by David Maybury-Lewis, 267–306. Cambridge: Harvard University Press.

Gutiérrez Sanín, Francisco. 2010. "Instituciones y territorio: la descentralización en Colombia." In *25 Años de la descentralización en Colombia*, 11–54. Colombia: Konrad Adenauer Stiftung.

Hale, Charles R. 2002. "Does Multiculturalism Menace? Governance, Cultural Rights and the Politics of Identity in Guatemala." *Journal of Latin American Studies* 34 (3):485–524.

———. 2005. "Neoliberal Multiculturalism: The Remaking of Cultural Rights and Racial Dominance in Central America." *Political and Legal Anthropology Review* 28 (1):10–28.

———. 2006. "Activist Research v. Cultural Critique: Indigenous Land Rights and the Contradictions of Politically Engaged Anthropology." *Cultural Anthropology* 21 (1):96–120.

Hansen, Thomas Blom, and Finn Steppatut. 2001. "Introduction: States of Imagination." In *States of Imagination: Ethnographic Explorations of the Postcolonial State*, edited by Thomas Blom Hansen and Finn Steppatut, 1–38. Durham: Duke University Press.

———. 2005. "Introduction: On Empire and Sovereignty." In *Sovereign Bodies: Citizens, Migrants, and States in the Postcolonial World*, edited by Thomas Blom Hansen and Finn Steppatut, 1–36. Princeton: Princeton University Press.

Harvey, Penelope. 2005. "The Materiality of State-Effects: An Ethnography of a Road in the Peruvian Andes." In *State Formation: Anthropological Perspectives*, edited by Christian Krohn-Hansen and Knut G. Nustad. 123–141. London: Pluto Press.

Heemskerk, Marieke. 2004. "Risk Attitudes and Mitigation Among Gold Miners and Others in the Suriname Rainforest." *Natural Resources Forum* 27:1–12.

Heemskerk, Marieke, Celine Duijves, and Mujenca Pinas. 2014. "Interpersonal and Institutional Distrust as Disabling Factors in Natural Resources Management: Small-Scale Gold Miners and the Government in Suriname." *Society & Natural Resources* 28 (2):133–148.

Hetherington, Kregg. 2011. *Guerrilla Auditors: The Politics of Transparency in Neoliberal Paraguay*. Durham: Duke University Press.

———. 2020. *The Government of Beans: Regulating Life in the Age of Monocrops*. Durham: Duke University Press.

High, Mette M. 2017. *Fear and Fortune: Spirit Worlds and Emerging Economies in the Mongolian Gold Rush*. Ithaca: Cornell University Press.

Hilson, Gavin. 2010. "'Once a Miner, Always a Miner': Poverty and Livelihood Diversification in Akwatia, Ghana." *Journal of Rural Studies* 26:296–307.

Hilson, Gavin, Abigail Hilson, Roy Maconachie, James McQuilken, and Halima Goumandakoye. 2017. "Artisanal and Small-Scale Mining (ASM) in Sub-Saharan Africa: Re-Conceptualizing Formalization and 'Illegal' Activity." *Geoforum* 83:80–90.

Hilson, Gavin, and Roy Maconachie. 2020. "For the Environment: An Assessment of Recent Military Intervention in Informal Gold Mining Communities in Ghana." *Land Use Policy* 96:104706.

Hirsch, Eric. 2022. *Acts of Growth: Development and the Politics of Abundance in Peru.* Stanford: Stanford University Press.

Holston, James. 2008. *Insurgent Citizenship: Disjunctions of Democracy and Modernity in Brazil.* Princeton: Princeton University Press.

———. 2011. "Contesting Privilege with Right: The Transformation of Differentiated Citizenship in Brazil." *Citizenship Studies* 15 (3–4):335–352.

Hoogbergen, Wim, and Dirk Kruijt. 2004. "Gold, 'Garimpeiros' and Maroons: Brazilian Migrants and Ethnic Relationships in Post-War Suriname." *Caribbean Studies* 32 (2):3–44.

Hristov, Jasmin. 2014. *Paramilitarism and Neoliberalism: Violent Systems of Capital Accumulation in Colombia and Beyond.* London: Pluto.

Idrobo, Nicolás, Daniel Mejía, and Ana María Tribin. 2013. "Illegal Gold Mining and Violence in Colombia." *Peace Economics, Peace Science and Public Policy* 20 (1):83–111.

InSight Crime. 2013. *Colombia's Wild West: Gold, Prostitutes and Urabeños.* November 19. Accessed August 18, 2023. https://www.insightcrime.org/news/analysis/the-illegal-gold-rush -and-colombias-new-wild-west/.

Jacka, Jerry K. 2015. *Alchemy in the Rain Forest: Politics, Ecology, and Resilience in a New Guinea Mining Area.* Durham: Duke University Press.

Jaffe, Rivke. 2013. "The Hybrid State: Crime and Citizenship in Urban Jamaica." *American Ethnologist* 40 (4):737–748.

Jaramillo, Pablo. 2020. "Mining Leftovers: Making Futures on the Margins of Capitalism." *Cultural Anthropology* 35 (1):48–73.

Jonkman, Jesse. 2022. "Extracting Empirically: A Ground's-Eye View of Small-Scale Mining in Colombia." *Anthropological Quarterly* 95 (3):649–680.

———. Forthcoming. "The Artisanal Underground: Gold, Subsistence, and Subsurface Materiality in Colombia." *Journal of the Royal Anthropological Institute.*

Jonkman, Jesse, and Marjo de Theije. 2022. "Amalgamation: Social, Technological, and Legal Entanglements in Small-Scale Gold-Mining Regions in Colombia and Suriname." *Geoforum* 128:202–212.

Kaufmann, Christoph, and Muriel Côte. 2021. "Frames of Extractivism: Small-Scale Goldmining Formalization and State Violence in Colombia." *Political Geography* 91:102496.

Kirsch, Stuart. 2014. *Mining Capitalism: The Relationship Between Corporations and Their Critics.* Oakland: University of California Press.

La Silla Vacía. 2012. *Las multinacionales, a montar a los pequeños mineros en la locomotora.* December 19. Accessed August 22, 2023. https://lasillavacia.com/historia/las-multinacionales -montar-los-pequenos-mineros-en-la-locomotora-40694.

———. 2017. *El poderoso contratista de la obra que enreda funcionarios de Chocó.* March 3. Accessed August 22, 2023. https://lasillavacia.com/historia/el-poderoso-contratista-de-la-obra -que-enreda-funcionarios-de-choco-60009.

———. 2019. *La captura del alcalde Chalá golpea la campaña de Quibdó.* August 23. Accessed August 22, 2023. https://lasillavacia.com/silla-pacifico/captura-del-alcalde-chala-golpea -campana-quibdo-73104.

Las2orillas. 2016. *Los elefantes blancos que arruinaron al Chocó.* July 5. Accessed August 22, 2023. https://www.las2orillas.co/el-dossier-de-las-obras-fantasmas-de-un-millonario-desfalco/.

———. 2017. *"Dónde está Santos?, Santos no está aquí," la gente en el Chocó le pide al Presidente aparacerse.* May 30. Accessed August 22, 2023. https://www.las2orillas.co/donde-esta-santos -santos-no-esta-aqui-la-gente-choco-le-pide-al-presidente-aparecerse/.

———. 2018. *Después de la guerrilla y antes de la formalidad: el limbo político de los mineros de Bebará, Chocó.* January 18. Accessed August 22, 2023. https://www.las2orillas.co/un-pueblo -en-el-choco-donde-la-mineria-salva-vidas/.

Law, John. 2004. *After Method: Mess in Social Science Research.* London: Routledge.

Leal, Claudia. 2018. *Landscapes of Freedom: Building a Postemancipation Society in the Rainforests of Western Colombia*. Tucson: University of Arizona Press.

Li, Fabiana. 2015. *Unearthing Conflict: Corporate Mining, Activism, and Expertise in Peru*. Durham: Duke University Press.

Li, Tania Murray. 1999. "Compromising Power: Development, Culture, and Rule in Indonesia." *Cultural Anthropology* 14 (3):295–322.

———. 2007. *The Will to Improve: Governmentality, Development, and the Practice of Politics*. Durham: Duke University Press.

———. 2009. "To Make Live or Let Die? Rural Dispossession and the Protection of Surplus Populations." *Antipode* 41 (1):66–93.

———. 2014. *Land's End: Capitalist Relations on an Indigenous Frontier*. Durham: Duke University Press.

Lund, Christian. 2006. "Twilight Institutions: Public Authority and Local Politics in Africa." *Development and Change* 37 (4):685–705.

———. 2011. "Property and Citizenship: Conceptually Connecting Land Rights and Belonging in Africa." *Africa Spectrum* 46 (3):71–75.

Luning, Sabine. 2014. "The Future of Artisanal Miners from a Large-scale Perspective: From Valued Pathfinders to Disposable Illegals?" *Futures* 62:67–74.

———. 2022. "Underground." In *The Anthropology of Resource Extraction*, edited by Lorenzo D'Angelo and Robert Jan Pijpers, 185–201. New York: Routledge.

Luning, Sabine, and Marjo de Theije. 2014. "Global Gold Connections: Ethical Consumption and the Beauty of Bonding Artisans." In *Green Consumption: The Global Rise of Eco-Chic*, edited by Bart Barendregt and Rivke Jaffe, 56–70. London: Bloomsbury.

Luning, Sabine, and Robert J. Pijpers. 2017. "Governing Access to Gold in Ghana: In-Depth Geopolitics on Mining Concessions." *Africa* 87 (4):758–779.

Lust, Jan. 2014. "Peru: Mining Capital and Social Resistance." In *The New Extractivism: A Post-Neoliberal Development Model or Imperialism of the Twenty-First Century?*, edited by Henry Veltmeyer and James Petras, 192–221. London: Zed Books.

Lyons, Kristina. 2016. "Decomposition as Life Politics: Soils, *Selva*, and Small Farmers Under the Gun of the U.S.-Colombian War on Drugs." *Cultural Anthropology* 31 (1):56–81.

MacMillan, Gordon. 1995. *At the End of the Rainbow? Gold, Land, and People in the Brazilian Amazon*. London: Earthscan.

Martinez-Alier, Joan. 2002. *The Environmentalism of the Poor: A Study of Ecological Conflicts and Valuation*. Cheltenham: Edward Elgar.

Martínez Basallo, Sandra Patricia. 2013. "Hacia una etnografía del Estado: reflexiones a partir del proceso de titulación colectiva a las comunidades negras del Pacífico colombiano." *Universitas Humanística* 75:157–187.

Meger, Sara, and Julia Sachseder. 2020. "Militarized Peace: Understanding Post-Conflict Violence in the Wake of the Peace Deal in Colombia." *Globalizations* 17 (6):953–973.

Miami Herald. 2018. *Dirty Gold Is the New Cocaine in Colombia—and It's Just as Bloody*. January 16. Accessed August 22, 2023. https://www.miamiherald.com/news/nation-world/world/americas/colombia/article194188034.html.

Ministerio de Ambiente y Desarrollo Sostenible. 2017. *Estamos trabajando por un Chocó libre de mercurio: Minambiente*. July 27. Accessed August 22, 2023. https://archivo.minambiente.gov.co/index.php/noticias-minambiente/3087-estamos-trabajando-por-un-choco-libre-de-mercurio-minambiente.

Ministerio de Cultura. 2019. *Afrocolombianos, población con huellas de africanía*. Electronic document. Accessed August 22, 2023. https://www.mincultura.gov.co/areas/poblaciones/comunidades-negras-afrocolombianas-raizales-y-palenqueras/Documents/Caracterizaci%C3%B3n%20comunidades%20negras%20y%20afrocolombianas.pdf.

Ministerio de Minas y Energía. 2015. *Resolución 40599*. Electronic document. Accessed August 22, 2023. https://www.anm.gov.co/sites/default/files/res_40599_15_glosario_tecnico_minero.pdf.

———. 2017. *Relación de contratos del mes de marzo de 2017*. Electronic document. Accessed November 7, 2018. www.minminas.gov.co/documents/10180/23856220/ MARZO+2017. pdf/3f7bab29-67fd-4dad-bc06-75673098908f.

Mitchell, Timothy. 2006. "Society, Economy, and the State Effect." In *The Anthropology of the State: A Reader*, edited by Aradhana Sharma and Akhil Gupta, 169–186. Malden: Blackwell.

Mosquera, Sergio. 2002. "Los procesos de manumisión en las provincias del Chocó." In *Afrodescendientes en las Américas: trayectorias sociales e identitarias*, edited by Claudia Mosquera, Mauricio Pardo, and Odile Hoffmann, 99–119. Bogotá: Universidad Nacional de Colombia.

Muehlmann, Shaylih. 2009. "How Do Real Indians Fish? Neoliberal Multiculturalism and Contested Indigeneities in the Colorado Delta." *American Anthropologist* 111 (4):468–479.

———. 2015. *When I Wear My Alligator Boots: Narco-Culture in the U.S.-Mexico Borderlands*. Berkeley: University of California Press.

Nash, June. 1979. *We Eat the Mines and the Mines Eat Us: Dependency and Exploitation in Bolivian Tin Mines*. New York: Columbia University Press.

Navaro-Yashin, Yael. 2002. *Faces of the State: Secularism and Public Life in Turkey*. Princeton: Princeton University Press.

———. 2007. "Make-Believe Papers, Legal Forms, and the Counterfeit: Affective Interactions Between Documents and People in Britain and Cyprus." *Anthropological Theory* 7 (1):79–98.

New Humanitarian. 2024. "The Darién Gap Migration Crisis in Six Graphs, and One Map." January 15. Accessed February 26, 2024. https://www.thenewhumanitarian.org/maps-and -graphics/2024/01/15/darien-gap-migration-crisis-six-graphs-and-one-map#:~:text=A%20 record%20520%2C000%20migrants%20crossed,surge%20is%20expected%20in%202024.

Newsweek. 2016. *Illegal Gold Mining in Colombia Is Destroying the Rainforest*. November 16. Accessed August 22, 2023. http://www.newsweek.com/2016/11/25/colombia-illegal-gold-mining -521717.html.

Ng'weno, Bettina. 2007. *Turf Wars: Territory and Citizenship in the Contemporary State*. Stanford: Stanford University Press.

Nordstrom, Carolyn. 2000. "Shadows and Sovereigns." *Theory, Culture & Society* 17 (4):35–54.

———. 2007. *Global Outlaws: Crime, Money, and Power in the Contemporary World*. Berkeley: University of California Press.

Nugent, David. 1994. "Building the State, Making the Nation: The Bases and Limits of State Centralization in 'Modern' Peru." *American Anthropologist* 96 (2):333–369.

Nuijten, Monique. 2003. *Power, Community, and the State: The Political Anthropology of Organization in Mexico*. London: Pluto Press.

Ojeda, Diana. 2012. "Green Pretexts: Ecotourism, Neoliberal Conservation, and Land Grabbing in Tayrona National Natural Park, Colombia." *Journal of Peasant Studies* 39 (2):357–375.

Ong, Aihwa. 2007. "Neoliberalism as a Mobile Technology." *Transactions of the Institute of British Geographers, New Series* 32 (1):3–8.

Orjuela Escobar, Luis Javier. 2001. "La debilidad del Estado colombiano en tiempos del neoliberalismo y el conflicto armado." *Colombia Internacional* 49–50:103–116.

Pardo Becerra, Luis Álvaro. 2013. "Propuestas para recuperar la gobernanza del sector minero colombiano." In *Minería en Colombia: fundamentos para superar el modelo extractivista*, 175–209. Bogotá: Contraloría General de la República.

Paschel, Tianna S. 2016. *Becoming Black Political Subjects: Movements and Ethno-Racial Rights in Colombia and Brazil*. Princeton: Princeton University Press.

PBI. 2011. *Mining in Colombia: At What Cost?* Bogotá: Editorial CODICE.

Pécaut, Daniel. 2004. "Conflictos armados, guerras civiles y política: relación entre el conflicto armado colombiano y otras guerras internas contemporáneas." In *Colombia a comienzos del nuevo milenio: VIII Coloquio Nacional de Sociología*, edited by Luis Carlos Castillo, 23–48. Cali: Universidad del Valle.

Peluso, Nancy Lee. 2018. "Entangled Territories in Small-Scale Gold Mining Frontiers: Labor Practices, Property, and Secrets in Indonesian Gold Country." *World Development* 101:400–416.

Perreault, Tom. 2013. "Dispossession by Accumulation: Mining, Water and the Nature of Enclosure on the Bolivian Altiplano." *Antipode* 45 (5):1050–1069.

PND. 2011. *Plan Nacional de Desarrollo: "Prosperidad para todos" (resumen ejecutivo)*. Colombia: Presidencia de la República. Electronic document. Accessed August 22, 2023. https://colaboracion.dnp.gov.co/CDT/PND/Resumen%20Ejecutivo%20Ultima%20Version.pdf.

Pommier de Santi, Vincent, Aissata Dia, Antoine Adde, Georges Hyvert, Julien Galant, Michel Mazevet, Christophe Nguyen, Samuel B. Vezenegho, Isabelle Dusfour, Romain Girod, and Sébastien Briolan. 2016. "Malaria in French Guiana Linked to Illegal Gold Mining." *Emerging Infectious Diseases* 22 (2):344–346.

Poole, Deborah. 2004. "Between Threat and Guarantee: Justice and Community in the Margins of the Peruvian State." In *Anthropology in the Margins*, edited by Veena Das and Deborah Poole, 35–65. Santa Fe: SAR Press.

Portafolio. 2016. *El 88% de la producción de oro en Colombia es ilegal: ACM*. August 2. Accessed August 22, 2023. https://www.portafolio.co/economia/el-88-de-la-produccion-de-oro-en-colombia-es-ilegal-499274.

Postero, Nancy Grey. 2007. *Now We Are Citizens: Indigenous Politics in Postmulticultural Bolivia*. Stanford: Stanford University Press.

Potter, Cuz, and Alexander Costantine Lupilya. 2016. "'You Have Hands, Make Use of Them!': Child Labour in Artisanal and Small-Scale Mining in Tanzania." *Journal of International Development* 28:1013–1028.

Povinelli, Elizabeth A. 2011. *Economies of Abandonment: Social Belonging and Endurance in Late Liberalism*. Durham: Duke University Press.

Presidencia de la República. 2015a. *Gobierno le declara la guerra a la minería criminal*. July 30. Accessed October 1, 2018. wp.presidencia.gov.co/Noticias/2015/Julio/Paginas/20150730_02-Gobierno-declara-objetivo-prioritario-de-alto-valor-la-mineria-criminal.aspx.

———. 2015b. *Palabras del presidente Juan Manuel Santos en la clausura del Congreso Nacional de Minería*. April 24. Accessed October 1, 2018. wp.presidencia.gov.co/ Noticias/2015/Abril/Paginas/20150424_08-Palabras-Presidente-Juan-Manuel-Santos-clausura-Congreso-Nacional-Mineria.aspx.

Radio Macondo. 2016. *La minería que el Estado colombiano no quiere que conozcas*. November 22. Accessed August 22, 2023. https://www.radiomacondo.fm/sin-categoria/la-mineria-estado-colombiano-no-quiere-conozcas/.

Rajak, Dinah. 2011. *In Good Company: An Anatomy of Corporate Social Responsibility*. Stanford: Stanford University Press.

Ramírez, María Clemencia. 2011. *Between the Guerrillas and the State: The Cocalero Movement, Citizenship, and Identity in the Colombian Amazon*. Durham: Duke University Press.

———. 2015. "The Idea of the State in Colombia: An Analysis from the Periphery." In *State Theory and Andean Politics: New Approaches to the Study of the Rule*, edited by Christopher Krupa and David Nugent, 33–55. Philadelphia: University of Pennsylvania Press.

Ramos, Acilda Rita. 2010. "A Tale of Gold and Tears: The El Dorado of the Yanomami." *INDIANA* 27:123–139.

Rasch, Elisabet Dueholm. 2012. "Transformations in Citizenship: Local Resistance Against Mining Projects in Huehuetenango (Guatemala)." *Journal of Developing Societies* 28 (2):159–84.

Rasmussen, Mattias Borg. 2015. *Andean Waterways: Resource Politics in Highland Peru*. Seattle: University of Washington Press.

———. 2017. "Tactics of the Governed: Figures of Abandonment in Andean Peru." *Journal of Latin American Studies* 49:327–353.

RCN. 2018. *Pecados capitales: la promesa de un hospital de primer nivel en Quibdó.* November 20. Accessed August 22, 2023. https://noticias.canalrcn.com/nacional-regiones-pacifico/pecados -capitales-promesa-un-hospital-primer-nivel-quibdo.

Restrepo, Eduardo. 2017. "Afrodescendientes y minería: tradicionalidades, conflictos y luchas en el Norte del Cauca, Colombia." *Vibrant* 14 (2):1–15.

Rettberg, Angelika, and Juan Felipe Ortiz-Riomalo. 2016. "Golden Opportunity, or a New Twist on the Resource-Conflict Relationship: Links Between the Drug Trade and Illegal Gold Mining in Colombia." *World Development* 84:82–96.

Reuters. 2021. *Focus: Gold Diggers: Illegal Mining near Colombian Town Hits Zijin Output.* May 18. Accessed August 23, 2023. https://www.reuters.com/world/china/gold-diggers-illegal-mining -near-colombian-town-hits-zijin-output-2021-05-18/.

Ribot, Jesse C., and Nancy Lee Peluso. 2003. "A Theory of Access." *Rural Sociology* 68 (2):153–181.

Richards, Patricia. 2010. "Of Indians and Terrorists: How the State and Local Elites Construct the Mapuche in Neoliberal Multicultural Chile." *Journal of Latin American Studies* 42 (1):59–90.

Roitman, Janet. 2004. "Productivity in the Margins: The Reconstitution of State Power in the Chad Basin." In *Anthropology in the Margins*, edited by Veena Das and Deborah Poole, 191–224. Santa Fe: SAR Press.

Rojas, Cristina. 2009. "Securing the State and Developing Social Insecurities: The Securitisation of Citizenship in Contemporary Colombia." *Third World Quarterly* 30 (1):227–245.

Roldán, Mary. 2003. *A sangre y fuego: La Violencia en Antioquia, Colombia, 1946–1953.* Bogotá: ICANH/Fundación para la Promoción de la Ciencia y la Tecnología.

Rose, Nikolas. 1999. *Powers of Freedom: Reframing Political Thought.* Cambridge: Cambridge University Press.

Rozo, Esteban. 2022. "Mineros e indígenas: gobernanza local, extracción de oro y disputas ambientales en Guainía." *Revista Colombiana de Antropología* 58 (3):34–58.

Ruiz-Serna, Daniel. 2023. *When Forests Run Amok: War and Its Afterlives in Indigenous and Afro-Colombian Territories.* Durham: Duke University Press.

Salman, Ton. 2004. "Apocryphal Citizenship: Anthropologizing the Citizenship Debate in Latin America." *Journal of Urban History* 30 (6):853–873.

Salman, Ton, and Marjo de Theije. 2017. "Analyzing Conflicts Around Small-Scale Gold Mining in the Amazon: The Contribution of a Multi-Temporal Model." *Extractive Industries and Society* 4:586–594.

Salo, Matti, Juha Hiedanpää, Teemu Karlsson, Luciano Cárcamo Ávila, Juha Kotilainen, Pekka Jounela, and Róger Rumrrill García. 2016. "Local Perspectives on the Formalization of Artisanal and Small-Scale Mining in the Madre de Dios Gold Fields, Peru." *Extractive Industries and Society* 3: 1058–1066.

Sanford, Victoria. 2004. "Contesting Displacement in Colombia: Citizenship and State Sovereignty at the Margins." In *Anthropology in the Margins of the State*, edited by Veena Das and Deborah Poole, 253–278. Santa Fe: SAR Press.

Sarmiento, Mariana, Beatriz Helena Giraldo, Helcías Ayala, Alexandra Urán, Ana Cristiana Soto, and Leyla Martínez. 2013. "Characteristics and Challenges of Small-Scale Gold Mining in Colombia." In *Small-Scale Gold Mining in the Amazon*, edited by Leontien Cremers, Judith Kolen, and Marjo de Theije, 46–67. Amsterdam: CEDLA.

Sawyer, Suzana. 2004. *Crude Chronicles: Indigenous Politics, Multinational Oil, and Neoliberalism in Ecuador.* Durham: Duke University Press.

Scott, James C. 1998. *Seeing Like a State: How Certain Schemes to Improve the Human Condition Have Failed.* New Haven: Yale University Press.

———. 2009. *The Art of Not Being Governed: An Anarchist History of Upland Southeast Asia.* New Haven: Yale University Press.

Semana. 2013. *Chocó, tierra de dragones.* March 29. Accessed August 22, 2023. https://www .semana.com/nacion/articulo/choco-tierra-dragones/338108-3/.

———. 2015a. *El nuevo flagelo que devora a Colombia.* March 30. Accessed August 22, 2023. https://www.semana.com/nacion/multimedia/la-guerra-contra-la-mineria-ilegal-criminal -en-colombia/422834-3/.

———. 2015b. *La trama para intentar esconder un fraude en Chocó.* November 24. Accessed August 22, 2023. https://www.semana.com/fraude-la-salud-en-choco-gobernador-tramo -silenciar-testigo/451095-3/.

———. 2015c. *Minería ilegal: ¿una nueva guerra?* August 1. Accessed August 22, 2023. https:// www.semana.com/nacion/articulo/mineria-ilegal-una-nueva-guerra/437053-3/.

———. 2017a. *El mercurio en los ríos de Quibdó hizo que los pescadores guardaran sus atarrayas.* December 5. Accessed August 22, 2023. https://sostenibilidad.semana.com/impacto/articulo /mercurio-en-choco-la-pesca-desaparecio-porque-las-aguas-estan-contaminadas/39096.

———. 2017b. *"Queremos minería bien hecha y no a cualquier costo": Germán Arce.* December 15. Accessed August 22, 2023. https://www.semana.com/contenidos-editoriales/atrato-el-rio -tiene-la-palabra/articulo/queremos-mineria-bien-hecha-y-no-a-cualquier-costo-german -arce/551270/.

———. 2018. *Tumaco: minería ilegal: el cáncer que mata la tierra.* Accessed March 8, 2022. http:// especiales.semana.com/deforestacion/tumaco.html.

Serje, Margarita. 2005. *El revés de la nación: territorios salvajes, fronteras y tierras de nadie.* Bogotá: Universidad de los Andes.

———. 2013. "El mito de la ausencia del Estado: la incorporación económica de las 'zonas de frontera' en Colombia." *Cahiers des Amériques Latines* 71:95–117.

Sharp, William F. 1975. "The Profitability of Slavery in the Colombian Chocó, 1680–1810." *Hispanic American Historical Review* 55 (3):468–495.

Siegel, Shefa. 2013. "Community Without Solidarity: Mercury Pollution from Small-Scale Mining and Colombia's Crisis of Authority." *Community Development Journal* 48 (3):1–15.

Siegel, Shefa, and Marcello M. Veiga. 2009. "Artisanal and Small-Scale Mining as an Extralegal Economy: De Soto and the Redefinition of 'Formalization.'" *Resources Policy* 34:51–56.

Snyder, Richard. 2006. "Does Lootable Wealth Breed Disorder? A Political Economy of Extraction Framework." *Comparative Political Studies* 39 (8):943–968.

Stoller, Paul. 2005. "The Presence of the Ethnographic Present: Some Brief Comments on Loïc Wacquant's *Body and Soul*." *Qualitative Sociology* 28 (2):197–199.

Stoller, Paul, and Cheryl Olkes. 1987. *In Sorcery's Shadow: A Memoir of Apprenticeship Among the Songhay of Niger.* Chicago: University of Chicago Press.

Svampa, Maristella. 2015. "Commodities Concensus: Neoextractivism and Enclosure of the Commons in Latin America." *South Atlantic Quarterly* 114 (1):65–82.

Swenson, Jennifer J., Catherine E. Carter, Jean-Christophe Domec, and Cesar I. Delgado. 2011. "Gold Mining in the Peruvian Amazon: Global Prices, Deforestation, and Mercury Imports." *PLoS ONE* 6 (4):1–7.

Taussig, Michael. 1980. *The Devil and Commodity Fetishism in South America.* Chapel Hill: University of North Carolina Press.

———. 2004. *My Gold Museum.* Chicago: University of Chicago Press.

Telesur. 2018. *Ministro de Hacienda de Uribe repetirá cargo con Duque.* July 11. Accessed August 22, 2023. https://www.telesurtv.net/ news/duque-uribe-alberto-carrasquilla-colombia-panama -papers-20180711-0044.html.

Trouillot, Michel-Rolph. 2001. "The Anthropology of the State in the Age of Globalization: Close Encounters of the Deceptive Kind." *Current Anthropology* 42 (1):125–138.

Tschakert, Petra. 2009. "Digging Deep for Justice: A Radical Re-Imagination of the Artisanal Gold Mining Sector in Ghana." *Antipode* 41 (4):706–40.

Tsing, Anna L. 1993. *In the Realm of the Diamond Queen: Marginality in an Out-of-the-Way Place*. Princeton: Princeton University Press.

———. 2005. *Friction: An Ethnography of Global Connection*. Princeton: Princeton University Press.

———. 2015. *The Mushroom at the End of the World: On the Possibility of Life in Capitalist Ruins*. Princeton: Princeton University Press.

Tubb, Daniel. 2014. *Gold in the Chocó, Colombia*. PhD dissertation. Carleton University.

———. 2015. "Muddy Decisions: Gold in the Chocó, Colombia." *Extractive Industries and Society* 2: 722–733.

———. 2020. *Shifting Livelihoods: Gold Mining and Subsistence in the Chocó, Colombia*. Seattle: University of Washington Press.

UPME. 2012. *Boletín estadístico de minas y energía 2008–2012*. Electronic document. Accessed March 14, 2019. http://www1.upme.gov.co/PromocionSector/SeccionesInteres/Documents /Boletines/Boletin_estadistico_2008-2012.pdf.

———. 2018. *Boletín estadístico de minas y energía 2018*. Electronic document. Accessed March 14, 2019. http://www1.upme.gov.co/PromocionSector/SeccionesInteres/Documents /Boletines/Boletin_Estadistico_2018.pdf.

Uribe, Simón. 2017. *Frontier Road: Power, History, and the Everyday State in the Colombian Amazon*. Oxford: Wiley-Blackwell.

USAID 2021. *Final Report: Artisanal Gold Mining—Environmental Impact Reduction Activity (Oro Legal)*. Electronic document. Accessed August 22, 2023. www.planetgold.org/sites/default /files/USAID-Colombia_Oro%20Legal_Final%20Report.pdf.

Valora Analitik. 2023. *Petro anuncia control a maquinaria minera; reabren algunas vías en paro minero*. March 12. Accessed August 24, 2023. https://www.valoraanalitik.com/2023/03/12 /paro-minero-petro-dice-que-habra-control-a-maquinaria-amarilla/.

Van Cott, Donna Lee. 2000. *The Friendly Liquidation of the Past*. Pittsburgh: University of Pittsburgh Press.

———. 2006. "Multiculturalism versus Neoliberalism in Latin America." In *Multiculturalism and the Welfare State: Recognition and Redistribution in Contemporary Democracies*, edited by Keith Banting and Will Kymlycka, 272–291. Oxford: Oxford University Press.

Varela Corredor, Daniel. 2013. *Los saberes del monte: desindustrialización, crisis y reinvención campesina en Andagoya, Chocó (1974–1991)*. Master's thesis. Universidad Nacional de Colombia.

Vélez-Torres, Irene. 2014. "Governmental Extractivism in Colombia: Legislation, Securitization and the Local Settings of Mining Control." *Political Geography* 38:68–78.

———. 2016. "Disputes over Gold Mining and Dispossession of Local Afro-Descendant Communities from the Alto Cauca, Colombia." *Third World Thematics* 1 (2):235–248.

Verbrugge, Boris. 2015. "The Economic Logic of Persistent Informality: Artisanal and Small-Scale Mining in the Southern Philippines." *Development and Change* 46 (5):1023–1046.

Verdad Abierta. 2018. A los mineros de San Miguel les quemaron un "dragón" amigable. February 19. Accessed August 22, 2023. https://verdadabierta.com/los-mineros-san-miguel-les -quemaron-dragon-amigable/.

Vila Benites, Gisselle. 2023. "Natures of Concern: The Criminalization of Artisanal and Small-Scale Mining in Colombia and Peru." *Extractive Industries and Society* 13:101105.

Wacquant, Loïc. 2005. "Carnal Connections: On Embodiment, Apprenticeship, and Membership." *Qualitative Sociology* 28 (4):445–474.

———. 2009. *Punishing the Poor: The Neoliberal Government of Social Insecurity*. Durham: Duke University Press.

Wade, Peter. 1993. *Blackness and Race Mixture: The Dynamics of Racial Identity in Colombia*. Baltimore: Johns Hopkins University Press.

———. 1999. "The Guardians of Power: Biodiversity and Multiculturality in Colombia." In *The Anthropology of Power: Empowerment and Disempowerment in Changing Structures*, edited by Angela Cheater, 71–85. London: Routledge.

Weitzner, Viviane. 2017. "'Nosotros Somos Estado': Contested Legalities in Decision-Making About Extractives Affecting Ancestral Territories in Colombia." *Third World Quarterly* 38 (5):1198–1214.

Welker, Marina. 2014. *Enacting the Corporation: An American Mining Firm in Post-Authoritarian Indonesia*. Berkeley: University of California Press.

West, Robert C. 1952a. *Colonial Placer Mining in Colombia*. Baton Rouge: Louisiana State University Press.

———. 1952b. "Folk Mining in Colombia." *Economic Geography* 28 (4):323–330.

World Bank. 1996. *A Mining Strategy for Latin America and the Caribbean. World Bank Technical Paper: No. 345*. Washington: World Bank.

———. 2020. *2020 State of the Artisanal and Small-Scale Mining Sector*. Washington: World Bank.

———. 2021. *Supporting Colombia's COVID-19 Crisis Response*. April 9. Accessed August 22, 2023. https://www.worldbank.org/en/results/2021/04/09/supporting-columbia-s-covid-19 -crisis-response.

World Gold Council. 2022. *Lessons Learned on Managing the Interface Between Large-Scale and Artisanal and Small-Scale Gold Mining*. Electronic document. Accessed August 24, 2023. https://www.gold.org/download/file/17063/ASGM-Report-2022-English.pdf.

Yashar, Deborah J. 1999. "Democracy, Indigenous Movements, and the Postliberal Challenge in Latin America." *World Politics* 52:76–104.

Zeiderman, Austin. 2013. "Living Dangerously: Biopolitics and Urban Citizenship in Bogotá, Colombia." *American Ethnologist* 40 (1):71–87.

———. 2020. "Concrete Peace: Building Security Through Infrastructure in Colombia." *Anthropological Quarterly* 93 (3):487–528.

INDEX

abandonment: by central government authorities, 73–75, 79–81; experiences of, 229; felt by *retreros*, 72–75, 79, 97; political, 73–75, 79, 86; zones of, 73, 88–91

Abrams, Philip, 10–11, 16

Afro-Colombians, Law 70 and, 18–19, 121–22, 124, 127, 248n20

AGC. *See* Gaitanista Self-Defense Forces of Colombia

Agreement 214, 183–84

alternative economies, 240, 248n16, 258n10

Anthropocene, 17

Antinarcotics Unit (Colombia), 80–81

Antioquia Department, 27, 50, 90, 239, 257n23

apprenticeship ethnography, 30

Arce, Germán, 108

Área de Reserva Especial para Comunidades Mineras (ARE), 108, 212–23, 240, 247n23, 256nn15–16

armed conflict (Colombia), 26–27, 111, 129, 237–38, 249nn31–32, 256n17, 257n4

artisanal mining and miners: autonomy of, 61, 64–68, 229–30; *bareque* panning, 46, 54–56, 60, 64, 111–12, 131–34, 134fig., 136–37, 250n2, 253n9; grievances of, 1–5, 58–59, 113, 230; *guaches*, 61–66, 63fig.; *matraca* washing operation, 44–46; *mazamorreo* panning, 47–48, 49; as pericapitalist sites, 251n11; production levels, 68; stereotypes of, 201–2, 233; workforce camaraderie, 64–66

Asociación de Barequeros de Minería Artesanal del Medio Atrato (ASOBAMINARMEA), 131–33, 136, 207–9

Atrato River: description of, 23–24; dredge operations, 190–93; legal personhood of, 7, 126

AUC. *See* United Self-Defense Forces of Colombia

autonomy, 61, 64–68, 229–30

Bajo Cauca Region, 50, 239

Ballvé, Teo, 174, 253n3

bandits, 8, 72, 89–91, 93–96

bareque panning, 46, 60, 64, 111–12, 131–34, 134fig., 136–37, 250n2; mining code definition, 253n9; profits from, 55; risks of, 54–56, 131

Baudó River, 249n24

Bebará River: AGC-ELN fighting, 237–38; ASOBAMINARMEA leadership, 131–33; *bareque* panning, 54–55, 111–12, 131–34, 134fig., 136–37, 253n9; code of conduct, 130–31; community councils, 121–23, 129; description of, 28; FARC governance, 129–33, 137, 250n38; formalization pilot program, 209–12, 255n8; government destruction of equipment, 211; ID cards, 136–37, 207–9; Mayor's Certificate concerns, 111–14; mining governance, 126–27, 131–32, 182; multicultural law performance, 121–23; photo, 130fig.; underground multiculturalism, 123, 135–36, 207

Better Gold Initiative, 240

betting, voting as, 175–78

Black cultural identity, institutionalization of, 18

Caliche (municipality, pseudonym): Agreement 214 enforcement, 183–85; description of, 28; mining governance in, 169–71, 178–85; taxation conflicts, 178–85, 254n10

Campbell, Jeremy, 116, 118

ACKNOWLEDGMENTS

This book has benefited from the support of many. I am wholeheartedly thankful to the people of Chocó, the miners, community leaders, and residents of which provide this book with its spirit. Writing about a contentious topic such as wildcat mining requires a cautious handling regarding the identities of the story's protagonists. For this reason, I cannot mention here the real names of many of the wonderful individuals who made this book possible—and who foray into its pages with invented aliases. I hope they will realize that, in spite of this caveat, my flawed word of gratitude is no less heartfelt, and my debt to them no less massive. *Gracias Chocó. Gracias por abrirme las puertas. Gracias por la amistad, el consejo y la hospitalidad.*

In the same spirit, I am greatly indebted to various organizations that facilitated my field research in Colombia, among which stand out: ASOBAM-INARMEA, CIRDI, COCOMACIA, CODECHOCO, CONALMINERCOL, FEDEMICHOCO, IIAP, OHCHR, Oro Legal, Tierra Digna, UNIDO, and, above all, the consejos comunitarios of "Caliche," "La Peña," and Bebará. For offering me their time, knowledge, and kindness during fieldwork, my warmest thanks to Helcías Ayala, Iván Avellaneda, Edwin Blandón, Natalia Castillo, César Córdoba, Mauricio Gómez, Rubén Darío Gómez, Thomas Hentschel, Yonny Moreno Cuesta, Bernardino Mosquera, Juan Manuel Pinzón, Aurelino Quejada, Ariel Quinto, Luz Estela Ramírez, and Germán Suarez. For providing the university affiliation that allowed me to spend a year doing fieldwork in Colombia, I thank Francisco Gutiérrez Sanín and the Universidad Nacional de Colombia.

The research for this book was realized through the generous financial support of several agencies and institutions. The Latin American Studies Programme (Dutch Research Council) financed my PhD research, while additional funding came from the Dutch Research Council (a Rubicon postdoctoral grant), the Amsterdam Sustainability Institute, the GOMIAM research project, and, at the Vrije Universiteit Amsterdam, the Graduate

School of Social Sciences and the departments of Social & Cultural Anthropology and Organization Sciences.

I was more than lucky with the editorial guidance at Penn Press. Jenny Tan gave brilliant advice on text structure and argumentation and found two anonymous reviewers whose readings significantly improved my analysis. I also appreciate the kind permissions of *Anthropological Quarterly*, *The Extractive Industries and Society*, and the *Journal of Latin American Studies*, which enabled me to reuse here parts of articles that previously appeared in their journals.

Colleagues at the Vrije Universiteit Amsterdam and the University of New Brunswick granted me the perceptive ears, astute tongues, and correcting gazes that are indispensable to any productive writing process. I thank my PhD supervisors: Marjo de Theije for arousing my gold fever and giving me the confidence to follow my ideas; Ton Salman for helping me find my writing voice; and Kees Koonings (CEDLA—University of Amsterdam) for shaking up my ideas about politics. At VU, I thank my colleagues at the Anthropology and Organization Sciences departments for their everyday companionship and lengthy conversations. I especially thank Dimitris Dalakoglou, Aniko Horvath, Yannis Kallianos, Jop Koopman, Luciana Massaro, Eva van Roekel, Luisa Schneider, May Ling Thio, Santiago Vargas Hernández, Michiel Verver, Ioana Vrăbiescu, Sierk Ybema, and Harry Wels for stimulating me to think about political ethnography in new ways. At UNB, I thank Judy Babin, Christine Jean, Noah Pleshet, Faith Timipere Allison, Dallas Tomah, and Daniel Tubb for making Canada a temporary home. I thank Noah, Dallas, and Daniel for countless hours of talking about extractivism, ethnography, infrastructure, ecology, Claude Lévi-Strauss, Belgian fries, inferior Dutch fries, and the political ontology of canned beer. I hope that this small word of appreciation eases some of the annoyance they must have felt whenever I interrupted their workflows to bounce ideas off them.

Outside these two universities, I crossed paths and swapped talks with an array of individuals pursuing similar research agendas, whose viewpoints made an imprint on my own. Thanks, therefore, to Irene Arends, Merel de Buck, Filipe Calvão, Jorge Calvimontes, Wilmar Cano, Gerardo Damonte, Bibiana Duarte, Bram Ebus, Ann Farnsworth-Alvear, Felipe Fernández, Eleanor Fisher, Luis Alberto Galeano, Sara Geenen, Francisco Gutiérrez Sanín, Eric Hirsch, Barbara Hogenboom, Andrew Hook, Pablo Jaramillo, Christoph Kaufmann, Sabine Luning, Diego Melo, Eugenia Robles Mengoa, Dalila Mello, Januaria Mello, Martijn Oosterbaan, Álvaro Pardo, Luciana Quispe,

Jovani Rivera, Axel Rojas, Yohana Ruffiner, Mayra Parra, Rodrigo Peña, Sebastián Rumie Rojo, Steven Schwartz, Whodson Silva, Finn Stepputat, Paul Stoller, Karolien van Teijlingen, Alexandra Urán, Daniel Varela Corredor, Marcello Veiga, Gisselle Vila Benites, Alejandra Villanueva Ubillús, Julienne Weegels, and Nikkie Wiegink.

This research would have never taken off without the support of my family and friends. *Bedankt* and *gracias* to *mam, pap*, Nini, Joris, Tara, Niek, Elba, Ben, Carmen, Miguel, Adriana, Saúl, Emiliano, Daniel, David, Noé, Janny, Luc, Marjolein, Matthias, Nick, Reitze, Rodrigo, Tamara, and Thijs. Me being us means the world to me.

By far my greatest debt is to Rocío, whose love and patience removed all momentary writing blocks; whose intelligence invigorated my thinking, every step—every page—along the way; who listened, advised, and encouraged; who was there, always. Naturally, it is to her that I dedicate the fruits of my work.

Underground Politics

CONTEMPORARY ETHNOGRAPHY

Alma Gottlieb, Series Editor

A complete list of books in the series is available from
the publisher.